ATLA Monograph Series
edited by Dr. Kenneth E. Rowe

1. Ronald L. Grimes. *The Divine Imagination: William Blake's Major Prophetic Visions*. 1972.
2. George D. Kelsey. *Social Ethics Among Southern Baptists, 1917–1969*. 1973.
3. Hilda Adam Kring. *The Harmonists: A Folk-Cultural Approach*. 1973.
4. J. Steven O'Malley. *Pilgrimage of Faith: The Legacy of the Otterbeins*. 1973.
5. Charles Edwin Jones. *Perfectionist Persuasion: The Holiness Movement and American Methodism. 1867–1936*. 1974.
6. Donald E. Byrne, Jr. *No Foot of Land: Folklore of American Methodist Itinerants*. 1975.
7. Milton C. Sernett. *Black Religion and American Evangelicalism: White Protestants, Plantation Missions, and the Flowering of Negro Christianity, 1787–1865*. 1975.
8. Eva Fleischner. *Judaism in German Christian Theology Since 1945: Christianity and Israel Considered in Terms of Mission*. 1975.
9. Walter James Lowe. *Mystery & The Unconscious: A Study in the Thought of Paul Ricoeur*. 1977.
10. Norris Magnuson. *Salvation in the Slums: Evangelical Social Work, 1865–1920*. 1977.
11. William Sherman Minor. *Creativity in Henry Nelson Wieman*. 1977.
12. Thomas Virgil Peterson. *Ham and Japheth: The Mythic World of Whites in the Antebellum South*. 1978.
13. Randall K. Burkett. *Garveyism as a Religious Movement: The Institutionalization of a Black Civil Religion*. 1978.
14. Roger G. Betsworth. *The Radical Movement of the 1960's*. 1980.
15. Alice Cowan Cochran. *Miners, Merchants, and Missionaries: The Roles of Missionaries and Pioneer Churches in the Colorado Gold Rush and Its Aftermath, 1858–1870*. 1980.
16. Irene Lawrence. *Linguistics and Theology: The Significance of Noam Chomsky for Theological Construction*. 1980.
17. Richard E. Williams. *Called and Chosen: The Story of Mother Rebecca Jackson and the Philadelphia Shakers*. 1981.
18. Arthur C. Repp, Sr. *Luther's Catechism Comes to America: Theological Effects on the Issues of the Small Catechism Prepared In or For America Prior to 1850*. 1982.
19. Lewis V. Baldwin. *"Invisible" Strands in African Methodism*. 1983.
20. David W. Gill. *The Word of God in the Ethics of Jacques Ellul*. 1984.
21. Robert Booth Fowler. *Religion and Politics in America*. 1985.
22. Page Putnam Miller. *A Claim to New Roles*. 1985.
23. C. Howard Smith. *Scandinavian Hymnody from the Reformation to the Present*. 1987.
24. Bernard T. Adeney. *Just War, Political Realism, and Faith*. 1988.
25. Paul Wesley Chilcote. *John Wesley and the Women Preachers of Early Methodism*. 1991.
26. Samuel J. Rogal. *A General Introduction of Hymnody and Congregational Song*. 1991.
27. Howard A. Barnes. *Horace Bushnell and the Virtuous Republic*. 1991.
28. Sondra A. O'Neale. *Jupiter Hammon and the Biblical Beginnings of African-American Literature*. 1992.
29. Kathleen P. Deignan. *Christ Spirit: The Eschatology of Shaker Christianity*. 1992.
30. D. Elwood Dunn. *A History of the Episcopal Church in Liberia, 1821–1980*. 1992.

Christ Spirit

The Eschatology of Shaker Christianity

by Kathleen Deignan

ATLA Monograph Series, No. 29

The American Theological Library Association
and
The Scarecrow Press, Inc.
Metuchen, N.J., & London
1992

This book is based on the author's doctoral dissertation, "The Eschatology of Shaker Christianity," Fordham University, 1986.

British Library Cataloguing-in-Publication data available

Library of Congress Cataloging-in-Publication Data

Deignan, Kathleen P., 1947-
    Christ Spirit : the eschatology of Shaker Christianity /
Kathleen P. Deignan.
        p.   cm. — (ATLA monograph series ; no. 29)
    Includes bibliographical references and index.
    ISBN 0-8108-2489-2 (alk. paper)
    1. Shakers — Doctrines — History. 2. Second Advent —
History of doctrines. 3. Holy Spirit — History of doctrines.
4. Eschatology — History of doctrines I. Title II. Series.
BX9778.S4D45 1992
236' .08'8288 — dc20   91-40688

To my Gospel Kindred

Gospel Kindred, how I love thee
tongue nor pen cannot portray
the very feelings of affection
growing stronger day by day.

Bind these sacred ties together
knit with friendship ever true
and show to all that Christ the Savior
is creating things anew.

— *Shaker hymn*

Acknowledgments

This book has been supported and encouraged by many people: my community, the Congrégation de Notre Dame; my family; my colleagues at Iona College; Dr. Rosemary Radford Ruether; and my dear friends at the Benedictine Grange, with whom I have shared the love of the Shaker spirit. My particular thanks are due to Dr. Ron William Walden, for his gracious generosity of time and energy, and for his challenging direction of this project in its dissertation form; to Sister Mary Anne Foley, C.N.D., for her painstaking labors on several occasions, in the clarification of ideas and their expression; to Brother Robert Durning, C.F.C., for his editorial assistance; to Elena Procario-Foley and Cynthia Luden for indexing; to Greta D. Sibley for designing the book; to the Iona secretarial services staff for the manuscript preparation; and to the Shakers themselves, past and present, who inspired this study — particularly the Sabbathday Lake community who welcomed me into their library and into their hearts and who taught me their songs.

Kathleen Deignan, C.N.D.
Associate Professor of Religious Studies
Iona College
New Rochelle, NY

Contents

Editor's Foreword vii

Foreword, *by Rosemary Radford Ruether* ix

Preface xv

Introduction 1

1. The Second Coming and the Holy Spirit:
   A Historical Overview. 6
   The Early Church 6
   Subsequent Christian History 12

2. The Birth of Shaker Eschatology: The Second
   Appearing of Christ in Mother Ann 29
   Ann Lee of History 30
   Mother Ann of Faith 40
   Conclusion 58

3. The Growth of Shaker Eschatology: The Second
   Appearing of Christ as the Millennial Church 65
   Introduction 65
   Meacham's Concise Statement: *The Second Appearing
   of Christ as a People* 67
   Youngs' Testimony: *The Second Appearing of Christ
   as the Church Born of Woman* 89
   Dunlavy's Manifesto: *The Second Appearing of Christ
   as the Union of Believers* 125

Green's Millennial Church: *The Second Appearing
of Christ as the Dawn of the Millennium* 157

Conclusion 186

4. The Maturity of Shaker Eschatology: The Second Appearing
of Christ as the Universality of the Christ Spirit 193

The Context for the Revision of Shaker Eschatology 196

Influences of American Culture on Later Shaker Eschatology...201

The Revision of Shaker Eschatology 216

Conclusion 229

Conclusion 237

Appendix...245

Bibliography 248

Works By the Shakers 248

Works About the Shakers...255

General..262

Index...275

About the Author 296

Editor's Foreword

Since 1972 the American Theological Library Association has undertaken responsibility for a modest dissertation series in religious studies. Our aim in this series is to publish two dissertations of quality each year. Titles are selected from studies in a wide variety of religious and theological disciplines. Readers expert in their fields advise the editor and the ATLA publications section which oversees the series. We are pleased to publish Kathleen Deignan's study of Shaker eschatology as number 29 in our series.

Professor Deignan majored in English during her undergraduate studies at Sacred Heart University (Fairfield, CT). She holds a master's degree in spirituality and a doctorate in historical theology from Fordham University. A popular lecturer on campus and in parishes, Dr. Deignan is the author of several articles and reviews and has recorded several albums of original musical compositions. She currently teaches religious studies at Iona College.

Kenneth E. Rowe
Series Editor
Drew University Library
Madison, NJ 07940

Foreword

The Anglo-American sect, the United Society of Believers in Christ's Second Appearing, better known as the Shakers, remains one of the most mysterious and intriguing of the religious groups that have developed on North American soil. Originating in the 1740s in England and transplanted to America during the ferment of the American Revolution, it reached its largest expansion in the 1840s with 6,000 members in 58 families from New England to Kentucky. After the Civil War its members dwindled to some 1,000 by the end of the century, and today only a handful of elderly Shakers live on in two centers.

The impending extinction of the Shakers has brought forth a rebirth of interest in the significance of this movement: its art, architecture, music, and theology. Kathleen Deignan's study of Shaker eschatology is a major contribution in this new wave of interpretation of the Shaker contribution to theology. Deignan carefully charts the evolution of Shaker theology through the major stages of their history: the period of foundation in the 1770s and 1780s, the period of rapid growth and consolidation from 1795 to the Civil War, and the period of declining numbers in the second half of the nineteenth century. Deignan situates Shaker eschatology in the context of Christian historical theology, beginning with the apostolic era. She hopes through this study to make possible an appropriation of Shaker theological reflection on eschatology as a part of mainstream Christian systematics.

The Shakers, as Deignan makes clear, pick up and renew a pattern of Christian eschatological thought that was deeply rooted in the earliest Christian Church. This perspective on realized eschatology was marginalized by patriarchal and episcopal forms of Christianity that arose in the second century, but it has never entirely vanished. It has been continually rediscovered and renewed among mystical and millennialist countercultural groups throughout the centuries, from the Montanists of the second century, to radical medieval sects, such as the Joachites (followers of Joachim of Fiore) and the Spiritual Franciscans, to the left-wing Puritans, such as the Quakers, in seventeenth-century England.

Like the early Church in the Acts of the Apostles, the Shakers saw themselves as living in the dawn of the millennium or the redemptive age of world history. The dawning of this redemptive era was signaled by the outpouring of the Holy Spirit, expressed in prophetic gifts given to women and men alike. The Shakers renew early Christian eschatological asceticism in their belief that celibacy represents the resurrection mode of being. They also develop an economy based on community of goods. Both of these are seen as key to the life-style of realized eschatology or the new heavenly order where there is neither marriage nor giving in marriage and all things are held in common.

But, unlike most mystical and millennial sects, the Shakers bring to a high level of development the idea of sexual egalitarianism which is only suggested in the Pentecostal story of Acts 2:17. The Shakers claimed Ann Lee, a charismatic woman of working-class background from Manchester, England, not only as their founder, but as the cornerstone of the new Millennial Church, as Jesus had been the cornerstone of the New Covenant. Ann Lee becomes the first embodiment of Christ's Second Appearing, complement and completion of the revelation of the Christ Spirit in Jesus. She is both the first member of this Millennial Church and its "mother" through whose messianic birth pangs the redeemed community is born. She also is seen as the manifestation of the Wisdom, or female aspect, of the divine.

Deignan shows that the basic Shaker belief — that, through Ann Lee, the Millennial Church of Christ's Second Coming has appeared — powerfully unites the traditionally distinct Christian themes of christology, ecclesiology, and pneumatology. Ann Lee as Bride of the Heavenly Christ and cornerstone of the Millennial Church merges into the understanding of the community itself as corporate representative of the Body of the glorified Christ. The redemptive power of Christ, in both its first and second anointings in Jesus and Ann, are finally grounded in Shaker pneumatology. It is the Holy Spirit that grounds the whole creative and redemptive process of world history and whose final outpouring in the last days founds the Millennial Church.

Shaker theology of atonement is exemplarist rather than substitutionary. Each member of the Millennial Church must go through his or her own transformation in the Spirit, enter into the millennial community, and thus become a new Christ. The community corporately is the paradigm or exemplification of what the redemption of humans in community in the perfected state means. Shakers develop a progressive view of redemption, seeing the Spirit at work in progressive disclosure of the divine presence from creation through the fall, the era of the corruption of the Church (which they date from the apostolic era to their own time), and the beginning of the final era of salvation with the birth of their own community. Revelation, for them, remains experimental, a matter of actualized holiness, and not doctrinal.

Deignan's most poignant description of the development of Shaker thought occurs in her chapter on their period of decline in the late nineteenth century. As the Shakers face the possibility of their own extinction, their thought does not become narrow and defensive, but rather breaks its own

sectarian boundaries in expansive universalism. The Shakers of
that era throw off the sectarian separatism that had looked at
Catholic and Protestant forms of Christianity as part of the fallen
and apostate Church. They also overcome the tendency to
withdraw in sectarian perfectionism over against the secular world.
They begin to reach out to the other Christian churches in the
quest for ecumenical unity around key themes and hopes for
redemption. They also look beyond Christianity to the world
religions for confirmation of the presence of the Spirit in all faiths.
Finally they become eager followers and supporters of the great
progressive reform movements of the day — such as abolitionism,
feminism, and world peace — as signs of God's redemptive Spirit
at work in human history among all people everywhere.

Perhaps the ultimate test of the authenticity of the Shaker
quest for the anticipatory realization of the millennium was this
ability to face with equanimity their own demise as a historical
embodiment of this hope. They believed that the Shaker
community, with its renunciation of sexual intercourse and
private property, with its cultivation of celibacy, community of
goods, nonviolence or "practical peace," and gender and racial
equality was the harbinger of how humanity as a whole should
live in the millennial age. But they could come to see
themselves as a sign of this coming world and mode of human
community, rather than its sole vehicle or means of fulfillment.
Like a seed that must fall into the ground and die in order to
bring forth a greater harvest, Shakers see their impending death
as part of a mystery of the work of the Spirit active in history to
bring about the universal ingathering of humanity into the
coming age.

This final Shaker perspective on their own millennial faith
and hope casts out a challenge to other Christians and indeed
all humans who hope for human improvement. Shaker faith
now remains only in the silent witness of their texts and
artifacts. If the faith and hope in a coming age of peace, justice,
and community among expanding groups of people throughout

the world is to be realized, if the destructiveness of human violence is to be averted from its apocalyptic denouement, it is the rest of us who must become the vehicles of this transformative progress. To put it in Shaker terms, we must become the place where the ongoing anointing of the Spirit of Christ's Second Appearing is at work in the world.

Rosemary Radford Ruether
Georgia Harkness Professor of Theology
Garrett-Evangelical Seminary
Evanston, Illinois

Preface

THE TASK

The Shakers speak of the ultimate event of the Christian story, the Second Coming of Christ, in strange and promising ways. This work is an effort to make the Shakers' belief in Christ's Second Appearing available for systematic theology. As a historical project undertaken in theological interests, its fundamental task is to retrieve, interpret, and translate the sources of Shakerism's eschatological tradition which are found in the classic texts of its two-hundred-year tradition.

Shaker studies have clearly emerged as a separate field of inquiry in the last two decades, with numerous books being written on Shakerism from various aspects. The present work contributes to this growing corpus of scholarship by attempting a systematic exposition and interpretation of the specifically theological meaning of Shakerism's understanding of Christ's Second Appearing.

The task, therefore, is twofold: the exposition of the implicit or explicit eschatologies in the most significant Shaker texts spanning the three discernible phases of Shakerism's development, and a theological interpretation of the Believers' understanding of Christ's Second Appearing in each of the phases. Thus, some of the rich, complex, and provocative notions of Christ's Second Appearing are made available to Shaker scholars in particular and contemporary eschatologists in general.

THE METHOD

Shaker eschatology presents a number of methodological problems to the systematic theologian. While some previous studies have addressed various features of the Shaker phenomenon, such as its social arrangements, sexual habits, industry, history, spirituality, folk culture, and art, few have tackled the theological subject as such. Although the complex work of other scholarship — historical, literary, socio-scientific — has been valuable, it has left explicitly theological matters a bit to one side. This study is a preliminary attempt to deal directly with select and significant Shaker theological texts. While it is clear that further studies must be done in the historical-critical reconstruction of the texts through such techniques as form-and-reaction criticism and a variety of analytical methods, what is offered here is the systematic theologian's instinct for explicitly theological meaning: to retrieve the religious myth at the heart of the tradition, to expose it in its own theological context, and to offer a tentative interpretation.[1]

Therefore, throughout these chapters primary sources have been presented extensively in an effort to make both the rhetoric and idiom of Believer's theology available to the reader. The intention, then, is to offer a deliberate explication of those intentionally theological texts in which Shakers offer an expression of their faith to the world. This approach endeavors to draw into relief, against the historical, sociological, psychological, cultural, or even religious interpretations of other scholars, the distinctly theological power of Shakerism's eschatological myth.

The theological method, therefore, is also twofold. The historical inquiry into the development of Shaker eschatology examines select religious texts of different genres from different periods in order to highlight within each the basic theological motifs which disclose Shakerism's understanding of Christ's Second Appearing; the theological inquiry interprets this subject matter in as simple and coherent a way as possible according to the categories of systematic theology, making that interpretation available to contemporary Shaker studies and to Christian theology.

THE FORMAT

The introduction describes the underlying theological concerns of this book, namely how Shakerism's understanding of Christ's Second Appearing relates eschatology and pneumatology in an unusual expression of Christian faith. The first chapter presents the background for such a conjunction of pneumatology and eschatology, particularly in regard to the notion of the Second Coming of Christ, in a brief and general survey of certain relevant traditions from the New Testament to the French Prophets. The work of this investigation proper begins in the second chapter with a study of Shakerism's *Testimonies* tradition. This tradition offers a christological image of Christ's Second Appearing expressed in the metaphor of foundress Ann Lee's messianic motherhood. The third chapter studies a short late-eighteenth-century work by Joseph Meacham and the three major theological books of the early nineteenth century by Benjamin Seth Youngs, John Dunlavy, and Calvin Green. All of these works present various ecclesiological images of Christ's Second Appearing. The fourth chapter brings the study of Shaker eschatology to a close in a presentation of later nineteenth-century writings from the community's journals, which suggest the final pneumatological images for Christ's Second Appearing.

NOTE

1. See David Tracy, *The Analogical Imagination: Christian Theology and the Culture of Pluralism* (New York: Crossroad, 1981).

Introduction

The hope of the Second Coming of Christ, the *parousia,* seems
in our time a detached, discounted, and somewhat distorted
element of faith in the lives of believers. It remains a distant
and sometimes threatening promise, shrouded in fantastic,
otherworldly, and often destructive images. Although for more
than a century biblical scholars and others have taken up an
inquiry and debate concerning the meaning of the Second
Coming,[1] their work in eschatology seems for the most part to
go on without influencing the lives of Christians. While the
confessing Church keeps an awkward silence on the matter of
the Second Advent of Christ and the cluster of issues associated
with it — the last judgment, the resurrection of the dead, the
end of the age or the world, and the realization of the reign of
God — other voices take them up in more secular apocalyptic
ways, cut off from the broader continuity of faith and revelation
in which *parousia* hope alone makes sense and meaning.[2]

The dilemma for Christian faith in general and for theology
in particular is complex and manifold. On one hand, the notion
of the Second Coming, once so integral to Christian belief, no
longer has a vibrant or sustaining mythic context in which to
cohere. Furthermore, the essential futurity of Christ's ultimate
advent renders it a matter for speculation and conjecture rather
than experience. For many Christians throughout history, the
Second Coming was a powerful religious symbol which exerted
its formative influence to the degree that its promise — or
threat — was actively held in imagination. But the notion of

1

the Second Coming, like many other religious realities, has suffered a dislocation in the modern Christian imagination; projected past the farthest horizon of Christian hope, its nature, purpose, and effect are unavailable for reflection and understanding, for inspiration and invigoration. Unlike the more familiar mysteries associated with the historical Jesus — incarnation, passion, and resurrection — the complex symbol of *parousia* has a power largely inaccessible to Christians since, as the Shakers say, "The coming of Christ is a matter unknown to all men, until learned in the event."[3]

It is the claim of the United Society of Believers in Christ's Second Appearing that they have learned, in the actual event, the revelation of the *parousia*, and it has been their mission to bear witness to the faith and work of the Second Coming. As a unique species of Christianity, the Shakers have experientially explored the fulfillment of Christ's promise to come again in glory to inaugurate the new age. In heterodox and unexpected ways, the Shakers fashioned a radically millennial style of Christian life which has lasted for more than two hundred years[4]: long enough for them to engage in serious theological reflection on their experience of faith, long enough for there to be discernible development of understanding regarding Christ's Second Appearing. Their legacy to the larger body of Christians whose faith does not include the experience of Christ's Second Appearing is a rich testimony, both in word and works, of religion focused on the eschatological promises of Christ. Furthermore, they offer the systematic theologian a unique laboratory for exploring the elements and effects of a thoroughgoing and realized eschatological faith.

When the last things are put first in actual Christian living and not just in theological formulation, what are the effects on the believer, the community of the Church, the society? What recessive attributes of Christian faith now come to the fore in this new eschatological situation? What, in consequence, recedes or diminishes? And what is the new configuration of belief and praxis? What new language and symbols of expression appear? Such eschatological questions regarding the Shaker understanding of Christ's Second Appearing yield a pneumatological response: for believers, the *parousia* does not point to the advent of Jesus, but to the advent of the Christ Spirit. Therefore, eschatology in Shakerism is radically pneumatological, and pneumatology radically eschatological.

The significance of this insight becomes apparent in light of the weakness of both eschatology and pneumatology in mainstream systematic theology. Ordinarily, eschatology is a discussion of the last things, or rather things put last; of the end, or perhaps things left for the end. Likewise, pneumatology is a discussion of the last person of the Trinity, or the one considered last; of the final divine procession or mission, or the one finally considered. As the concluding treatise of the classical schema of dogmatic theology, the cluster of issues which comprise eschatology has for centuries suffered a kind of conspicuous neglect, not simply in having its various concerns underdeveloped and unintegrated within the greater understanding of Christian life, but in depriving all of theology of its most radical and comprehensive context: a vision of the ultimate meaning and purpose of life in Christ. As Karl Rahner reminds us, eschatology is the necessary human propensity to look forward and direct our gaze "towards the definitive fulfillment of precisely the human situation which is already an eschatological one."[5]

Similarly, pneumatology comes at the end of the Church's dogmatic reflection on God and Christ, as it does in the third article of the Nicene Creed, where it is simply one of a series of affirmations. In fact there is no coherently developed theology of the Holy Spirit in Christian dogmatics, but rather a doctrine of grace and sacraments in its stead, a perspective which discounts the centrality and import of the Holy Spirit as the ultimate horizon of Christian faith.[6] The Spirit has been called the contact function of the Trinity, "the finger of God's right hand" as hymned in the ancient chant, the meeting place and medium of a double movement: in one direction, of God's self-giving through Christ in history, and conversely, of the world's ingathering through Christ back into the mystery of God. The Spirit then as an economic procession of the Trinity is both the last and the first person in the life of grace. Therefore it can be argued that pneumatology alone provides the basis of meaning for all the issues of Christian theology, whether christology, ecclesiology, or the Trinity.

It is not the specific intention of this investigation to argue for the fundamental theological importance of and relationship between eschatology and pneumatology, but to present the way in which the Shakers perceived this relationship by exploring in their theological writing the symbol of Christ's Second Appearing, with all its constitutive features, as the ultimate revelation of the Christ Spirit.

Therefore, this is a work of historical theology since it traces the development of a particular notion — in this case Christ's Second Appearing — from the beginning of the Shaker theological tradition in the eighteenth century to its end in the twentieth century. However, this inquiry uses the categories, indeed the rubrics, of systematic theology to name the phases of eschatological development in terms of its early christological, its later ecclesiological, and its final pneumatological expressions. By using the categories of systematic theology in this historical study, an ordered depiction of the development of Shaker eschatology discloses the unique pneumatological eschatology at the heart of Shakerism's belief in Christ's Second Appearing.

NOTES

1. The issue of the Second Coming of Christ is part of a larger complex discussion of the apocalyptic nature of early

Christianity. There are several works representative of significant scholarship listed in the bibliography. Of particular interest is John J. Collins, *The Apocalyptic Imagination: An Introduction to the Jewish Matrix of Christianity* (New York: Crossroad, 1984).

2. For a reflection on the contemporary cultural and political preoccupation with apocalyptic themes, see works by Barkun, Koch, Russell, Hans Schwartz, and Zamora listed in the bibliography.

3. John Dunlavy, *The Manifesto, or A Declaration of the Doctrines and Practice of the Church of Christ* (New York: E. O. Jenkins, 1847), p. 105.

4. The Shaker covenant was closed by the Canterbury Ministry in 1958. At present there are fewer than a dozen living Shakers, one of whom lives at Canterbury, New Hampshire, the others at Sabbathday Lake, Maine.

5. *Sacramentum Mundi*, s.v. "Eschatology," by Karl Rahner. This is the consensus of other prominent theologians, such as Käsemann, Pannenberg, and Schillebeeckx. See in particular works by Jürgen Moltmann listed in the bibliography.

6. Pneumatology has become an important area of inquiry in recent years. See works by Congar, Ditmanson, Dunn, Hamilton, Huizing, Kilian, Malatesta, McDonald, Moltmann, Montague, Pannenberg, Regan, Rosato, Schweitzer, and Tillich cited in the bibliography.

1 The Second Coming and the Holy Spirit: A Historical Overview

The Shakers belong to that variety of Christianity which distinguishes itself by the way it focuses on the Second Coming of Christ, bringing together in this notion eschatological and pneumatological themes. This chapter presents some theological and historical context for understanding the insistence of the Millennial Church that Christ's Second Appearing refers to the ultimate gift of the Holy Spirit. What becomes evident is that there has survived, in various Christian movements and traditions from the early Church through the Shakers, an explicitly pneumatological understanding of the Second Coming, envisioned as the ultimate event in which God would pour out the Spirit upon all flesh.

THE EARLY CHURCH

The New Testament
The notion of the Second Coming is a Christian invention, a term which points to the way in which the earliest believers imagined that Jesus, the Risen Christ, would fulfill his eschatological task: to effect the end of the age and to gather the just into the resurrection. It is difficult to locate the origin of the hope for the return of Christ in the Christian tradition; it is simply presumed and widespread in the New Testament, as texts like 2 Thessalonians 2 and Mark 13 suggest. This expectation of

the Risen Christ's imminent return is logically linked to faith in the resurrection of the just, a notion derived from a cluster of themes from Jewish apocalyptic thought which related the concept of the Messiah, the one anointed to deliver the chosen people, to the ultimate victory of God on behalf of the just in the resurrection beyond history.[1] The influence of such an apocalyptic perspective is reflected in this early Pauline text:

> We say to you, as if the Lord himself had said it, that we who live, who survive until his coming, will in no way have an advantage over those who have fallen asleep. No, the Lord himself will come down from heaven at the word of command, at the sound of the archangel's voice and God's trumpet, and those who have died with Christ will rise first. Then we the living, the survivors, will be caught up with them in the clouds to meet the Lord in the air. (1 Thess. 4:15-17)

The intent and effect of this apocalyptic notion of Christ's Second Coming was to bring Christians heavenward, away from this world and out of history.

But there is also in the New Testament another eschatological perspective on the meaning of the messianic work of Christ. From this point of view, it is the mission of the Risen One not to bear God's people out of the world toward heaven, but to bear God's Spirit into the world and into history. This perspective draws upon a rich strain of Jewish thought concerning the Spirit of God.[2] In the Hebrew Scriptures, the divine power by which God creates and saves is "spirit" (*rûah*), the wind or breath which serves the Holy One's will on behalf of humankind. More dramatically, it is the "Spirit of the Lord" poured out on God's servants which empowers them to effect saving deeds in the history of the covenant people. Various traditions speak differently of the ways by which the gift and power of God's Spirit would be manifested among the people. The prophet Isaiah spoke of a future ideal ruler who would be anointed forever with the Spirit of the Lord. On this messianic king and his council would rest the fullness of God's Spirit (Isa. 28:5ff.). But when the historical house of David fell, Second Isaiah spoke instead of the *ebed Yahweh*, or suffering servant of the Lord, who would lead the Israelites from both political and religious exile (Isa. 42:1-7), restoring justice and salvation to the poor (Isa. 61:1-3). As this messianic tradition unfolded, the prophets began to promise not the bestowal of God's Spirit on the community of salvation alone, but a universal outpouring on all persons and on nature as well. This Spirit of purification (Isa. 4:4-6) and fruitfulness would reestablish the original peace of paradise for all creation (Isa. 32:15-20).

After the return from Exile, the prophets intensified the messianic promise, proclaiming that God would ultimately pour out the divine Spirit "upon all flesh," young and old, men and women, bestowing on everyone gifts of prophetic ecstasy, visions, and dreams (Joel 3:1-2). Indeed this new age would behold the Spirit of the Lord creating "new hearts" in the faithful remnant of the messianic community, making them a "new creature" (Ezek. 11:19; 18:31; 36:26). Then God would fill these transformed hearts forever with divine Spirit so that they might be able to live in the perfection of Yahweh's Law (Ezek. 36:27; 39:29; 37:14; Isa. 61:1-4; Jer. 31:31-34; 32:38ff.). This new age of God's Spirit would climax in the resurrection of the dead (Ezek.37:11-14) and with the realization of the "new heaven and the new earth" suffused with the Spirit of the Lord (Isa. 65:17; 66:22).

It was to traditions such as these that Christians looked to formulate the meaning of Jesus' messiahship. Therefore, Christians came to link his messianic purpose and mission in its various dimensions to the Holy Spirit. This is apparent in the Synoptic Gospel accounts of the life and ministry of Jesus, whose anointing by the Spirit constituted him as Messiah, consecrated him as the Son of God, and reached an unsurpassed fullness in him (Luke 1:35; Mark 1:9-11; Luke 4:1, 14, 18ff.). In his resurrection, Christ Jesus lives according to divine pneuma, and is a spiritual being in and from whom that Spirit overflows to others (1 Cor. 15:45). Because of this exaltation and glorious transformation, to be in Christ is to be in the Spirit, as the Pauline literature so often says (1 Cor. 6:11; Eph. 1:13; etc.).

There is, however, yet another way of understanding the eschatological outpouring of the Spirit, one which describes the messianic task of delivering God's Spirit into history in terms of a separate event following the paschal drama. Whereas for John it was in the resurrection as such that the Spirit was poured out upon the earth for all time (John 7:37-39; 16:7), in Acts this greater anointing happened on Pentecost (Acts 2:4, 33). As a result, the apostles became prophets and leaders of the new messianic community and were given the charisms of preaching and healing (Acts 11:12; 13:9-11; Rom. 15:18-19; 1 Pet. 1:11ff.). Ultimately it was the Spirit poured out on Pentecost which gave life to the Church, inspiring the apostles' choices in its regard (Acts 10:19; 13:2; 15:28; 16:6ff.).

This eschatological point of view contends that with the sending of the Spirit on the Jewish and Gentile Christian communities, the fulfillment of Joel's prophecy had begun (Acts 2:17 re Joel 3:1). The primitive Church lived in the dramatic presence and charismatic possession of the Spirit (Acts 4:31; 1 Cor. 12:4ff.). In this anointed community it was the living Spirit and not the Law which was inscribed on the hearts of believers (2 Cor. 3:2-11), and by this Spirit abiding in the Church the Christian had died and was raised to a new life (Rom. 6:3-11; 2 Cor. 5:17). Indeed, the Church was the body of those born again according to the Spirit (John 3:4ff.; Eph. 2:19), by which they came into possession of eternal life here in this world (John 6:47ff.). Rather than focusing on the future return of the Lord to effect the end of the world, Christians became witnesses to a new world already begun through the recreative presence of the Spirit in the Church.

The Second Coming of Christ did not happen as soon as had been anticipated. Because of the delay the early Christians shifted their focus from the end to the interim, from the future to the present, as the demands and necessities of a rapidly growing movement with many constituent communities caused them to modify their apocalyptic perspective. The interval between the First and Second Appearings of Christ took on a significance of its own as the time for Christian formation (Titus 2:11ff.) and mission (Luke 9:2ff.; Acts 1) during which the Gospel of Christ's advent and the gift of the Spirit were to be universally proclaimed and offered. Moreover, this was the age of the Church (Acts 2:42ff.) which even during the apostolic period, and thereafter, consistently enjoyed along with persecution a steady growth of membership. The success of the mission and the growth of communities fostered a pastoral orientation; it is not surprising, therefore, that a concern about ecclesiology should overshadow eschatology, as the elders sought to ensure the life and authentic Gospel faith of the various churches. The conversion and initiation process was supported by a developing liturgical cult which further modified the eschatological expectation of Christians; the sacraments of the Church were experienced as mysterious rites of union with Christ in the Spirit, who was thereby not absent nor awaited, but really present in the midst of believers.

The Book of Revelation

However much the early Christian community moved away from its expectation of the imminent return of Christ, the notion of the Second Coming has persisted throughout the Christian tradition. Much of its abiding influence is due to the exceptional work of Christian apocalyptic, the Book of Revelation. This scripture appeared toward the end of the first century, even as the Church began to turn from an apocalyptic reading of its eschatological faith. It addressed several communities suffering persecution under the reign of the Roman ruler Domitian, who had recently imposed the demand for emperor worship on his subjects in Asia Minor. As a work of apocalyptic resistance literature, the Book of Revelation is an exhortation to Christians to stand firm in their faith even to the extreme of martyrdom: the triumph of God begun in the life of Jesus must be continued in faith, longed for in hope, until Christ came again in glory.

The Book of Revelation establishes a haunting visionary context for the eschatological event of Christ's imminent return. The *parousia* brings to a climax the catastrophic drama of history in which the heavenly hosts battle the anti-Christian Beast and his allies. After the great war, the dragon (Satan) is chained for a thousand years while peace reigns on earth. But after this millennium of tranquillity (Rev. 20), Satan is released again, briefly, to threaten war on the world for the last time. As the course of history thus rushes to its climax, the divine character, Christ, at once the Son of Man and the Lamb, initiates the last judgment of humankind. The vision culminates in an image of the ultimate cosmic transfiguration of creation — the old heavens and earth now passed away and the new ready to receive the descent of God's heavenly city in which Christ the Lamb reigns forever in glory (Rev. 21). The revelation ends with a promise of Christ's imminent *parousia* and an exhortation to believers to cry out earnestly for the Lord's return (Rev. 22).

The Book of Revelation has had tremendous influence whenever Christians turned to the questions of eschatology, since it provided vivid and powerful images to support the expectation and hope for Christ's ultimate triumph in history. But its vision did not rekindle throughout the Church a vibrant hope for Christ's return. Indeed, it was unable to redirect early Christianity's movement toward a more long-range settlement in history. The apocalyptic hope and fervor it stimulated was neither sanctioned nor supported by the larger Church which was moving toward a different world view. During the next phase of Christian history, the accent of faith moved from an expectation of the Second Coming of Christ to more immediate ecclesiastical concerns. For a while, the pressing theological discussions centered on the incarnation of Christ, leaving aside questions regarding the eschatological Spirit. But, throughout the course of Christianity, whenever these questions resurfaced, Christians would turn once again to the Book of Revelation for inspiration.

SUBSEQUENT CHRISTIAN HISTORY

The Patristic Church
As the Church moved out from Judaism into the Gentile world of Hellenism, its eschatology lost much of its historical and collective perspective, focusing on more personal or moral eschatological issues, such as the immortality of the soul, personal survival after death, and a developing preoccupation with the heavenly realm as the locus and destiny of human fulfillment. The concern for individual salvation also brought with it a moralistic orientation which recast apocalyptic events such as judgment and resurrection in terms of reward and punishment for personal behavior in this life. Gradually the primitive Christian hope for the imminent return of Christ in glory to manifest the victory of God's Spirit in history was spiritualized, its power absorbed and neutralized by a pastoral strategy that favored the establishment of permanent communities in this world. In the East these communities came to flourish in a theological environment which stressed the sanctifying role of the Holy Spirit and gave rise to a mystical expression of Christianity. In the West the theological milieu would underscore the redemptive role of Jesus Christ, giving rise to a moral expression of Christianity. In both cases the more original eschatological hope was significantly altered.

Christianity, therefore, came to see itself as an abiding religion instead of a temporary movement anticipating the reign of God, and as an enduring organization which relied on unity in orthodoxy for its survival. Under the pressure of a growing Church membership and the urgency to achieve and preserve an official doctrinal consensus, the attention of Church leaders, particularly in the West, shifted from the charismatic experience of the Spirit in the communities to dogmatic agreement about the person of Jesus Christ. As the Church Fathers became increasingly preoccupied with christological controversies during the second and third centuries, the biblical language of the Spirit to describe the significance of Christ gave way to the Hellenistic language of Logos philosophy. The question of the ontological nature of Christ obscured his pneumatological task, as Christianity more and more developed into a cult of Jesus Christ rather than of the Spirit of Christ. Furthermore, the eventual adoption of Christianity as the imperial religion of the Roman Empire in the fourth century modified and weakened the Church's original eschatological posture, since to some of the Fathers (such as the official Church historian Eusebius of Caesarea) it seemed that with establishment, the millennium, or thousand-year peace in prelude to Christ's Second Coming, had actually begun in history.

The tensions posed by such a dramatic shift in the eschatological understanding so central to original Christian faith were extreme. The eschatological consciousness of the patristic Church was not able to sustain creatively the dualities (present/future; individual/collective; historical/transcendent; earthly/paradisal) which had developed in the early centuries. The polarities broke into dichotomies, and what could not be accounted for in the present was projected to a distant future or an alternative heavenly realm. There remained speculation about the Second Coming and the ultimate victory of God's Spirit, but passion for it faded. As Moltmann has noted, eschatological concerns were consigned to barren isolation at the end of Christian dogmatics, unrelated to the central themes of faith and therefore perceived as irrelevant. Furthermore the critical and militant character of the eschatological impulse so threatening to the new alliance between the Roman State and Christian Church was now left to fanatics and revolutionaries.

> Owing to the fact that Christian faith banished from its life the future hope by which it is upheld, and relegated the future to a beyond, or to eternity, whereas the biblical testimonies which it handed on are yet full to the brim with future hope of a messianic kind for the world, — owing to this, hope emigrated as it were from the Church and turned in one distorted form or another against the Church.[3]

Heterodox Christian Movements

Although the lively expectation of Christ's imminent and glorious return was not maintained by orthodox Christianity after the second century, the hope was, nevertheless, kept alive in a variety of ways throughout the history of the Church. In fact the sheer number of such witnesses, sects, and movements is so vast and their eschatologies so varied and complex that it would be impossible here to enumerate every one of them adequately. Yet it is interesting to note that within many of these groups there is a curious affinity and at times even a fusion of residual apocalyptic fervor and radical pneumatology, as if these two sometimes unintegrated components of Christian faith were essentially related. A brief outline of such groups will serve to enhance further the background against which Shakerism will be explored.

For the sake of clarity and consistency in terminology, "millennial" will describe that variety of pneumatological eschatology which refers to the final age that is the new situation occasioned by the Spirit's victory in history. The term "millen-

nial" will be used rather than "chiliast," which connotes catastrophe, and rather than "apocalyptic," which connotes the end
of history. Mindful, therefore, that for the Shakers the notion of
parousia linked eschatology with pneumatology, we will survey
Christian history with an eye to the various expressions of millennialism which explicitly highlight the Spirit as the hallmark
of the Second Coming.

Millennial themes were evident in several writers of the ante-
Nicean Church — both heretical and orthodox — among them
Cerinthus, some Ebionites, Papias of Heiropolis, Tertullian,
Justin Martyr, Irenaeus, Lactantius, Victorinus, Cyril of
Jerusalem, and Commodian.[4] But only Montanus "linked the
concept of the millennium with the idea of a Third
Dispensation, and Age of the Spirit to succeed those of the
Father and the Son."[5] Around 170 C.E., perhaps in reaction to
the loss of apocalyptic fervor in the Church at large, Montanus
began to proclaim to his disciples that he was a prophet, the
mouthpiece of the promised Spirit who would teach and guide
the Christian faithful. Two women, Priscilla and Maximilla,
joined him and together they delivered portentous and sometimes obscure oracles, usually in a state of ecstasy, speaking not
in their own persons, but that of the Spirit.[6] Their "New
Prophecy" echoed familiar millennial themes: they promised the
imminent return of Christ, who would soon establish the New
Jerusalem — in the town of Pepuza in Phrygia. In light of this
expectation, marriage was discouraged while a rigorous asceticism of prayer and fasting was fostered as preparation for the
parousia; thus the movement had a moral vigor and purity reminiscent of the primitive Church. But the real theological innovation of the Montanists was their notion that in the dawning
of the *parousia,* the Spirit more dramatically suffused the community, becoming its authority and a vibrant presence which
awakened believers to the eschatological age.

The New Prophecy spread rapidly through Asia Minor, Syria,
Antioch, and was even known in Rome and the West within a

decade. However, Montanism was condemned by the first syn-
ods of the Church which were convened by the bishops of Asia
Minor specifically to consider "the Phrygian problem." It was
tolerated in the West for a while by Zephyrinus, the Bishop of
Rome (199-217), who later, in Tertullian's words, "put to flight
the Paraclete."[7] Montanism survived only in North Africa
where it seems to have been a movement within the Church,
developing as a sect only later, and surviving there until the
time of Augustine of Hippo.

Augustinian Revision

Augustine is the greatest revisionist of the *parousia* hope of
patristic Christianity. Early in the formulation of Christian
eschatology the expectation of the Second Coming became
identified with millennialism, a conviction that the promised
kingdom would be realized in history.[8] It was this millennialism,
particularly in its apocalyptic varieties, that Augustine decisively altered. Initially persuaded by the eschatological optimism of the Eusebian perspective, which linked the destinies of
Rome and the Church in God's historical plan, Augustine later
abandoned a hope for the glorious climax of history after the
sack of Rome by Alaric in 413. He concluded that the City of
God could not be realized within history; it was rather the desti-
nation beyond time to which Christian pilgrims journeyed.

Augustine reinterpreted the notion of the millennium as a
function of the incarnation rather than of the *parousia*, defining it
as the time of the Church prior to the eschatological last judgment
on the Day of the Lord. With the birth of Christ, an invisible
community of salvation had come to life in the world, living as
Church, making its way through unavoidable crisis and conflict in
the earthly city, to the celestial City of God. In this way

> Augustine defused the power inherent in the notion
> of the millennium by inverting its original sense and
> purpose. Claiming it had begun with the Incarnation,

he relocated the focus of hope to the past and not to the future, thereby undermining an optimistic view of secular history. The *saeculum* — that aging world — was doomed to incompletion, for its fulfillment could never be realized within time.[9]

Therefore, Augustine posited all eschatological hope for the ultimate victory of the Spirit beyond history into a spiritual, celestial realm. In his revision of Christian eschatology, the Second Advent would not introduce a new age of the Spirit into history, since at the *parousia*, time would come to an end. The interval between the First and Second Appearings of Christ was one of waiting for history to run its course. There were no significant events or innovations to expect; rather the purpose of this age was the gathering of souls into the Church wherein to await the life of heaven. In consequence of the enormous influence Augustine had on the orientation of subsequent theology, the powerful eschatological ideas of the millennium and *parousia* in orthodox faith were spiritualized and placed beyond the range of history into a supratemporal and heavenly realm.

The Middle Ages

Even though the Augustinian recasting of millennial faith became normative Christian eschatology in the Middle Ages, there still lingered various kinds of the more primitive hope for the realization of God's reign in history, though, for the most part, without a markedly pneumatological character. The eschatological tradition was kept alive in the many commentaries on the Apocalypse by Bede, Walafrid, Anselm of Laon, Bruno of Segni, and others. It also was explored by more speculative writers, such as Honorius of Autun, Hugh of St. Victor, Adam of Whitehorn, Gerhoh of Reichersberg, Anselm of Havelberg, Rupert of Deutz, Eberwin of Steinfeld, Hildegard of Bingen, Joachim of Fiore, John of Parma, Gerard of Borgo San Donnino, and Bonaventure.[10]

As early as the seventh century millennial expectation had undergone significant adaptation which intensified its political rather than explicitly spiritual character. In response to the rise of militant Islam, there surfaced a Christian myth of the Last World Emperor, a messianic figure who would drive the Muslims back into the desert and free the Empire by contending with Antichrist, whose demise would announce Christ's Second Coming.[11] This early medieval Syriac legend is important because it returned to Western Christianity an image on which to focus its millennial hope, now in the form of a new political savior. Furthermore, the myth of the Last World Emperor, who would rule from Jerusalem, influenced the crusading spirit of the eleventh century, intensifying its apocalyptic orientations.[12]

In the religious ferment of the Middle Ages a host of other sects and societies arose, filled with millennial fervor and crying for Church reform. Some called for a return to the spiritual purity of the primitive community, others for an advance to the spiritual purity of the anticipated eschatological community. Many decried the abuse of wealth and power by the hierarchy in their witness to radical poverty: the Franciscans and other mendicant movements, the Albigensians, Waldensians, Beguines, Beghards, various groups of Fraticelli, Apostolic Brethren, Guglielmiti, and the Brethren of the Free Spirit. It is among these various movements of reform during the Middle Ages that there emerged the several types of "Spirituals," those who represent the conjunction between the eschatology and pneumatology which is of interest here.

Although the charismatic demand for an *ecclesia spiritualis* thrived in medieval Christianity, it was most clearly articulated in the widely circulated eschatology of the Calabrian monk Abbot Joachim of Fiore. His vision became very influential among the various millennial groups of the thirteenth century since it provided a complex mystical vision of history's progress toward the ultimate Age of the Spirit. According to Joachim, the Age of the Father, revealed in the Old Testament and exemplified in the married state, was followed by the Age of the Son, revealed in the New Testament and exemplified in the clerical state, to be followed by the Age of the Spirit, revealed by the Eternal Gospel of the new pneumatic being, exemplified in the monastic state. Joachim anticipated an invisible Church without hierarchy, sacraments, or external worship, whose hallmarks were instead poverty, peace, a spiritual understanding of Scripture, and very often, celibacy. Moreover, Joachism encouraged a lively eschatological expectation because it reasserted, against the Augustinian formulation, the primitive Christian hope that the fullness of God's promise was as yet in the historical future, indeed, in a compelling event which must rouse the believer to vigilance, discipline, and hope.

More than any other Christian writer, Joachim identified the eschatological age within history with the advent of the Spirit. In effect he articulated a theology of the eschatological person of the Trinity: the Holy Spirit. As Marjorie Reeves has noted, the genius of Joachim's theological imagination was in projecting the full manifestation of the Third Person of the Trinity into the future, therefore definitively breaking with the dominant Augustinian consensus. Furthermore, Joachim provocatively suggests that in this millennial Third Age of the Spirit the work of the Second Person of the Trinity — Christ — will be embodied in a secret or middle advent to precede the final glorious Advent.[13]

It is not necessary here to explore the spiritualist influence of Abbot Joachim on medieval and subsequent Christianity, except to say it was substantial.[14] It was especially so among the Franciscans, whose own particular eschatology had great influence in the Middle Ages, since Francis was thought by many Spirituals to be the form of Christ's "middle advent," and forerunner to the ultimate *parousia*.[15] But the eschatological visions of the medieval Spirituals had a revolutionary character and force as well, driving their influence beyond the Church, to the social order.

The complexity and instability of social, political, and economic life for medieval Europeans made them quite susceptible to chiliastic phantasies and movements. The grim, apocalyptic prelude to various millennial stirrings was the Black Death (1348-1349), which seemed to portend the end of the world before the *parousia* for which numerous millennial sects prepared by self-flagellation and other extreme ascetical practices. Against this background, many millennial groups became movements for social reform attracting the poor, as seen in the Jacquerie (1358), the Peasant Revolt in England (1381), and the Taborite movement (1441), a revolutionary offspring of the Hussites which incorporated an intense expectation of Christ's Second Coming. Furthermore, in the fourteenth century, a political form of Joachism can be seen in charismatic leaders like Savanarola, who prophecied that the Last World Emperor and the Angelic Pope would join forces in the battle against Antichrist, whose defeat would bring the millennial regeneration of Christianity.[16]

In all these various expressions, the Middle Ages witnessed a resurgence of eschatological hope for Christ's Second Coming which again reinstated the millennial age into history, linking it more explicitly than ever before to a fuller experience of the Holy Spirit.

The Reformation

Hope in the Second Coming of Christ was certainly a dominant feature of Reformation Christianity, not so much among the magisterial Reformers — whether Lutheran, Reformed, or English — but rather among those diverse and complex movements which comprise the Radical Reformation: Anabaptists, Spirituals, and Evangelical Rationalists.[17] Whereas Protestants sought an ecclesial renewal somehow in continuity with the old Church, the Radicals espoused a fundamental rupture with all the religious forms and institutions of the past and were intent on assembling a new Church in the power of the Holy Spirit, all with an eschatological fervor far more intense than anything found in normative Protestantism or Catholicism.[18]

This strong millennial expectancy had some familiar features of an earlier medieval variety. Among certain Radicals, Joachism resurfaced, especially in the visions of Michael Servetus and several others who believed that the new Age of the Spirit had definitively dawned in a new moment of crisis and promise, signaled by the impending fall of the post-apostolic Church. Other Radicals, represented by Thomas Muntzer, John Hut, and Melchior Hoffman, saw the fulfillment of Daniel's prophecy of the four empires (of which the Roman Church was the last), leading to a Fifth Monarchy or Age, in which Christ would reign over the saints. Yet others of a separatist type were inspired by the figure of the "woman of the wilderness" in Revelation 12:6 to withdraw into holy conventicles and await the millennium.

In the enormously variegated eschatologies prevalent among these Radicals, one predominant strain is especially significant for this inquiry. Everywhere about them Radicals experienced the outpouring of the Spirit promised by the prophets for the end of the age. They laid particular stress on a sense of divine immediacy by way of the inner Word, or a Spirit possession which drove them to enact the presence of that eschatological kingdom which they sought to realize. In general they met in separate conventicles, renouncing traditional sacraments and ordinances. All were convinced that they were "uniquely summoned as instruments of the Holy Spirit to usher in the social righteousness of the millennium under the fifth age of Christ or the third age of the Holy Spirit."[19]

But the Radical Reformation was an abortive revolution, subject to violence and persecution from both Catholic and Protestant sides. A new consensus was shaped by the various mainstream Churches of the magisterial Reformation, which agreed with Rome in rejecting both the high eschatology and the pneumatology of the Radicals. Once again hope for a new

Age of the Spirit — a millennium in time — was confined to the borders of Christendom, where it gave impetus to various forms of sectarian Christianity.

Post-Reformation English Protestantism

Protestants and Catholics fought over the new boundaries of faith for over a century and a half throughout Europe. England was in particular turmoil during the protracted period of its religious reformation. The Anglicanism set in place by the Elizabethan settlement was soon challenged by a more aggressive form of Protestantism, namely Puritanism. Consequently, religious strife led to civil war as these two exponents of English Protestantism struggled for dominance over each other and over the Romanism which periodically threatened to reassert itself with the ascendance of a Catholic monarch.

During the period of extreme turmoil in mid-seventeenth-century England, sectarian religious movements multiplied greatly, among them the social utopian Levelers, Ranters, and Diggers; the millennial Fifth Monarchy Men; and the mystical Seekers and Finders. But the most significant of these groups for religious history in general and Shaker history in particular, was the Society of Friends, more commonly called Quakers, in derision of their dramatic manifestations of the long awaited millennial outpouring of the Holy Spirit.

The Quakers had their birth in the religious experience of George Fox (1624-1691), who after a long search for spiritual transformation in consultation with various ministers, found the mystical encounter he had sought in a radically inward personal experience. Opening his heart to a direct revelation of the Spirit, Fox discovered the illumination of the "Inner Light" which he believed led him to the fullness of spiritual truth. In consequence he saw that revelation is not confined to Scripture, which remains the word of God, but rather is given directly and interiorly to believers, leading them to inward transformation. Consequently, the outward forms of religious life all but disappeared for Fox as he rejected association with any of the major Churches, with the professional ministry, the sacraments, oath taking, and tithes. For the Friends, the only authentic expression of faith was a transformed and consecrated life which turned one from warfare and slavery to the pursuit of peace and reconciliation.

However, hostility toward the Quakers was strong. Their highly exercised meetings, in which they shook and quaked and trembled under the influence of the eschatological Spirit, and their habit of breaking into the worship services of various Churches, calling congregants to forsake the "steeple house" and join the living Church of Christ, drew them into conflict with the law. Arrests by the thousands, and even executions, galvanized the sect into a formidable religious society which began a bold missionary campaign in several countries. Some Quakers eventually sought freedom in the New World, far from the religious intolerance of Europe, under the guidance of William Penn (1677).

Fox and his followers — the "Children of Light" — had not intended to form a new sect, but believed that they represented the revival of authentic, primitive Christianity through the discovery of the principle of the Inner Light of the Spirit. They hoped that this grace would be accepted everywhere and transform the world, gathering everyone — believers and non-believers alike — into the universal embrace of the Spirit. This work, which had begun in the early Church, was now in its eschatological phase and would soon climax in the realization of Christ's kingdom.[20] With this faith the Quakers joined a type of millennial eschatology with a radical pneumatology, recognized by later Shakers to be kindred to their own.[21]

Along with the Quakers, Shaker sources acknowledge another group as their direct forebears, namely, the French Prophets or Camisards.[22] Louis XIV's revocation of the Edict of Nantes in 1685 culminated two decades of increasing harassment and inaugurated the supervised transition of the Huguenot minority to the status of "new converts." The effect was virtually to dismantle French Protestantism within a year. However, clandestine assemblies of radical Calvinists of Languedoc and Dauphiné resisted attempts by the Catholic state to bring them to the "new conversion." Instead they met for midnight worship in wilderness assemblies where preachers interpreted their present trials as the necessary prelude to the approaching millennium. The first prophets — all children — appeared among them in 1688,[23] announcing from a sleeplike trance the presence of the Spirit and the nearness of the final Pentecost. Soon these young *inspirés* became more numerous and public, and their somnambulant agitations more violent — shaking, choking, and falling as they uttered the prophecies of deliverance from the crown's oppression and the world's precataclysmic millennial judgment.

For the next decade and a half the Cévennole prophets grew more numerous and daring, inciting their followers to violence against the emblems of Catholicism. Reprisals were swift and harsh. By 1701 over 350 *fanatiques* were in prison or slavery, with as many more driven into the mountains of the Cévennes to become apocalyptic guerrillas. The Camisard revolt[24] which ensued lasted about two years, with troops of about two thousand men and women resisting government forces and was ended only by an intensive military operation. By 1704 the revolt was crushed, with many of the refugees fleeing to Germany and Switzerland for sanctuary; but it was in England that the movement drew new vigor from the millenarian climate thriving there.

It was 1706 when three missionary Camisard prophets — Elie Marion, Durand Fage, and Jean Cavalier — came to London where various expectations of the end of the world, the millennium, and the Second Coming were long-standing.[25] In this milieu, it only took a few years for the French Prophets to attract several followers with their seizures of millennial and Spirit-filled prophecy, among them John Lacy, Sir Richard Buckley, Thomas Cotton, Richard Roach, and Sir John Phillips.

But the millennial faith of the French Prophets underwent significant change in its new environment. Under the influence of its English adherents, believers moved from a cataclysmic notion of the Second Coming to a more deliberately Pentecostal and communal one. Their faith saw the nearness of the Second Coming evidenced in a renewed outpouring of the gifts of the Spirit, creating the true Church in their midst. In this new attitude, the French Prophets undertook a vigorous mission to the Continent where they were further influenced by quietists and pietists who stressed the indwelling Spirit. Furthermore, they traveled extensively through Britain, retaining circles of believers in Bristol, Birmingham, and Manchester. Several decades later in an obscure way they would inspire the ecstatic, spirit-possessed millennialists who became the Shakers.[26]

Characteristic of the French Prophets was the influential and predominant role afforded women in the various assemblies — a practice that would pass on to the Shakers. In fact the Prophets finished their approximately fifty-year dispensation of millennial faith guided by the leadership of women. Under their tutelege, the Prophets came to the consensus that the basic metaphor and attitude of their eschatological faith was waiting — waiting in the Spirit for the Second Coming of Christ.

By 1730, French Prophet Hannah Wharton of Birmingham introduced what she called a new season for the various congregations of Prophets by insisting that the millennium would dawn in an inward Pentecost: "although these were the very last days, the personal reappearance of Jesus would be made known mildly at first and to the inward self."[27] Soon, under the influence of another woman, a new millennial metaphor would emerge — past the waiting, to the advent itself. Ann Lee was to announce the end of anticipation — the inward event inaugurating the long-awaited millennium had happened in her.[28]

NOTES

1. John J. Collins, *The Apocalyptic Imagination: An Introduction to the Jewish Matrix of Christianity* (New York: Crossroad, 1984), pp. 207ff.

2. For a relevant anthropological and historical sketch of "spirit possession" in the Jewish and Christian antecedents of the Shakers, see Clarke Garrett, *Spirit Possession and Popular Religion from the Camisards to the Shakers* (Baltimore: Johns Hopkins University Press, 1987), pp. 1-12.

3. Jürgen Moltmann, *Theology of Hope: On the Ground and Implications of a Christian Eschatology* (New York: Harper and Row, 1967) pp. 15-16.

4. Bernard McGinn, *Visions of the End* (New York: Columbia University Press, 1979), pp. 14-25.

5. Marjorie Reeves, "The Originality and Influence of Joachim of Fiore," *Traditio* 36 (1980): 272.

6. Williston Walker et al., *A History of the Christian Church*, 4th ed. (New York: Charles Scribner's Sons, 1985), p. 69; Garrett, *Spirit Possession and Popular Religion*, pp. 8-9.

7. Tertullian, the North African Father, was Montanism's most famous convert. Walker et al., p. 70.

8. McGinn, citing Jean Daniélou, in *Visions of the End*, p. 17.

9. P. Brown, "Saint Augustine," in *Trends in Medieval Political Thought*, ed. Beryl Smalley (New York: Barnes and Noble, 1965), p. 11.

10. The thirteenth-century Calabrian abbot Joachim of Fiore, particularly, brought this anagogical form of reflection to new levels, since he not only added insight to the work of periodizing history and speculating on its progress and eventual conclusion, but with the exception of Hildegard of Bingen, he alone reinserted the Seventh Age into time and also introduced the notion of a qualitatively new Age of the Spirit to precede the Second Coming of Christ (see Reeves, "Originality and Influence," pp. 276-278).

11. Ibid., p. 274.

12. *New Catholic Encyclopedia,* 1967-1974, s.v. "Millennialism and Eschatology," by J. P. Dolan.

13. Reeves, "Originality and Influence," p. 293.

14. For extensive references to works by Joachist scholar Marjorie Reeves, see bibliography.

15. Even in its most spiritual form, however, Franciscan eschatology remained basically christocentric and reformistic. For a more thorough reading of the eschatological role of Francis and the movement he inspired, see works by Ewert Cousins, E. Randolph Daniel, and Bernard McGinn noted in the bibliography.

16. Reeves, "Originality and Influence," p. 307.

17. See George H. Williams, *The Radical Reformation* (Philadelphia: Westminster Press, 1957).

18. Ibid., pp. 857-858.

19. Ibid.

20. Hugh Barbour and Arthur Roberts, eds. *Early Quaker Writings, 1650-1700* (Grand Rapids: William B. Eerdmans Publishing Company, 1973), pp. 14-15; Douglas Steere, ed., *Quaker Spirituality: Selected Writings* (New York: Paulist Press, 1984), pp. 8-9, 20-21.

21. Although scholars debate the relationship and influence of Quakerism on English Shakerism, confluences can be argued. See Hugh Barbour and J. William Frost, *The Quakers* (Westport: Greenwood Press, 1988), pp. 11-18, 33; Garrett, *Spirit Possession and Popular Religion*, pp. 46-47, 141-142.

22. Hillel Schwartz, *The French Prophets* (Berkeley: University of California Press, 1980), pp. 17ff. For another perspective, see John Symond, *Thomas Brown and the Angels* (London: Hutchinson, 1961).

23. Garrett, *Spirit Possession and Popular Religion* pp. 15ff.

24. The word "camisard" either refers to the "night attack" (obs. Fr. *camisade*) or comes from the term for "white shirt" (*camisole*) which they wore in battle. Hillel Schwartz, *French Prophets*, p. 23.

25. Ibid., pp. 37ff.; Garrett, *Spirit Possession and Popular Religion*, pp. 40ff.

26. Garrett, *Spirit Possession and Popular Religion*, p. 58.

27. Hillel Schwartz, *French Prophets*, p. 197; Garrett, *Spirit Possession and Popular Religion*, pp. 57-58.

28. Hillel Schwartz, *French Prophets*, p. 215.

2 The Birth of Shaker Eschatology: The Second Appearing of Christ in Mother Ann

Shaker eschatology had its birth in the religious experience of Ann Lee. In 1770 Ann suffered a profound mystical experience of union with Christ, out of which emerged her conviction that Christ had come again. Since she was the founder of the United Society of Believers in Christ's Second Appearing, the "Millennial Church," her own "experience" of the Second Coming and its effect on the lives of the original Believers were of great significance in the earliest phase of Shaker eschatology.

Ann Lee left no writings expressive of her own life, however, so the theologian is faced with a problem analogous to the "quest for the historical Jesus." The most significant records of her spiritual story are the testimonies of her earliest followers, whose own lives were utterly changed by their encounter with her, and which were recounted to, for, and by later Believers. These testimonies, like the canonical Gospels, serve better as proclamations of faith in Ann Lee and her messianic role among Shakers than as a record of her own faith.

Nevertheless, a deliberate rendering of these earliest written testimonies of the Shakers offers an explicitly textual route to their original understanding of Christ's Second Appearing. These documents demonstrate that the Believers' millennial belief was founded on Lee's maternal ministry among them: her spiritual maternity was at once the source and object of their primitive proclamation of eschatological faith. Therefore, special attention will be paid to the "Mother" kerygma at the center of the earliest Shaker Gospel in order to comprehend its soteriological, christological, pneumatological, and eschatological meaning.

By way of beginning, what is known of the Ann Lee of biographical history will be examined as preparation for what the *Testimonies* will present of the Mother Ann of Shaker faith, whose very eschatological motherhood becomes the primary metaphor for Shakerism's earliest stated understanding of Christ's Second Appearing.

ANN LEE OF HISTORY

Lee's Social Background

Most of what is known about Ann Lee comes from Shaker sources which are saturated with faith and long removed from the events they report. Yet, it is possible to reconstruct the broad strokes of her biography.[1] Ann Lee, the second of eight children, was born on February 29, 1736, in Manchester, England, into the family of John Lees,[2] a blacksmith. Her birthplace was one of the first cities in England to experiment with industrialization, and during her youth Ann participated in the seminal phase of the project as a laborer in the cotton textile mills.[3] At twenty, she worked in Manchester's new infirmary for the sick poor, serving as a cook. Two years later, in 1758, she embarked on a religious quest which brought her into the lively current of spiritual awakening at work in Lancashire.

Lee's Religious Background

Manchester in Lee's time offered many options for religious seekers. The Anglicans and Presbyterians were the two dominant and rival Churches of English Christianity, appealing mostly to the town gentry and new merchants of the large metropolis.[4] Roman Catholics were few in Lee's city, Quakers and Jews even fewer. But there were other religious influences in eighteenth-century Manchester, notably of the quietist and enthusiast variety. The former was a diverse and rich religious subculture developed from the visionary and millenarian influences of various Catholic mystics, especially the seventeenth-century German Jacob Boehme, the Moravians, and the Swedenborgians.[5] The latter were the Methodists and Baptists, with their new-styled evangelicalism which appealed to the weavers, spinners, and craftspeople at the humble end of the social scale. These offered, especially to the poor, a vital spiritual alternative to the more stagnant established Churches.

Where Ann Lee fit into this religious complex cannot be clearly documented. Andrews discovered the record of her private baptism in the Anglican Cathedral of Manchester, dated June 1, 1742.[6] But it is most likely that she was one of the great numbers of those awakened by the radical evangelicalism of George Whitefield and the Wesleys, who visited her district regularly during her formative years. The Shaker sources explicitly note that Lee was one of Whitefield's "hearers." From 1749, he had made Manchester a station on his northern revival circuit. Indeed, Whitefield's influence on Shakerism was enormous and far reaching.[7] Not only were Ann Lee's English associates affected by his powerful preaching, but his transatlantic itinerancy brought the same fires of revival to New England, where Shakerism would ultimately flourish.

At the heart of Whitefield's gospel was the indispensable necessity of the "new birth" for all those who sought salvation. This new birth was achieved instantaneously, at the moment of conversion, in a radical awakening of the human spirit to the Holy Spirit, accompanied by a variety of enthusiastic behaviors, from trances and spasms to speaking in tongues. The new birth was, in Whitefield's preaching, a total renovation which opened one to the possibility of the sinless life, imparting "new principles, a new understanding, a new will, and new affections, a new conscience, a renewed memory, nay, a renewed body."[8]

Ann Lee and the Shaking Quakers

Sometime during the 1750s, while still in her teens, Lee came under Whitefield's influence. Shaker sources record her response to him as an authentic prophet endowed with "great powers and gifts of God," but with whom she later became disenchanted because he had taken protection under the British crown.[9] It is not clear whether she attended Methodist meetings in Manchester where a society had been formed during her youth. But in 1758, Lee's radical evangelical piety definitively led her out of Anglicanism and into association with the separatist charismatic sect led by Jane and James Wardley, whose enthusiastic worship and quest for perfectionist rebirth clearly situated them in the flow of popular religion coursing through Britain and emboldened by the Methodist Awakening.[10]

The Shaker sources do not mention the Methodist link, portraying the Wardleys instead as a small group of radical dissenters who allegedly had withdrawn from the Society of Friends during the 1740s in search of a more expressive experience of the Inner Light than was possible in the Quaker Meeting. Shortly after, Shaker sources claim they came under the influence of the highly charismatic and millennial French Prophets who, as we have noted, combined radical Calvinism with ecstatic spirituality and apocalyptic chiliasm.[11]

Like the Friends, the Wardleyites had a conviction of Inner Light and liberty, a reliance on the Spirit as the primary experience of God, a rejection of all sacramental forms, a liberal approach to Scripture, total pacifism, and refusal to take oaths or directly participate in government. Like the French Prophets, they exhibited an ecstatic, charismatic temperament, vividly dramatized in various physical manifestations from shaking and whirling to speaking in tongues. But the most significant inheritance from the Cévennole prophets was the millennial conviction of the imminent return of Christ. From both traditions they received an openness to the spiritual leadership of women and a belief in the power of the eschatological Spirit shaking the age in preparation for the millennium. Thus the Wardley group, derisively called the Shaking Quakers, felt that they were heralds of this new age. An important Shaker text from the nineteenth century recounts these events:

> About the year 1747, a small number who were endowed with the spirit of these witnesses were led by the influence of the Divine Spirit to unite themselves into a small society, in the neighborhood of Manchester, under the ministry of James and Jane Wardley.... This infant society gave itself up to be led and guided entirely by the operations of the Spirit of God. They boldly testified that the second appearing of Christ was at hand...they were seized by mighty tremblings...with singing, shouting, dancing...with great agitations of body and limbs...while under the influence of these spiritual signs. From these exercises...they received the appellation Shakers. (Green & Wells, *Millennial Church*, pp. 4-5)

The primacy of women as leaders in the Wardley sect placed them in the long English tradition of religious leadership by female charismatics.[12] Mother Jane Wardley is remembered for her vibrant evangelism as she exhorted her followers to

> amend your lives. Repent. For the Kingdom of God is at hand. The new heaven and new earth prophesied of old is about to come. The marriage of the Lamb, the first resurrection, the new Jerusalem descending from above, these are even now at the door. And when Christ appears again, and the true church rises in full and transcendent glory, then all anti-Christian denominations — the priests, the church, the pope — will be swept away.[13]

The sect's apocalyptic, anticlerical, and anti-institutional character gave them an affinity to the Radicals of the Reformation whose influence was still being felt throughout English Christianity. Powerful millennial prophecies filled the Wardleyites; in their own religious meetings, they prepared for the imminent return of Christ by such charismatic exercises as shaking, barking, whirling, quaking, and by public confession of sin. The evangelical quest for liberation from sin and for perfection was the hallmark of their eschatological belief.

Ann Lee's Marriage

Ann Lee joined the Wardleys in September of 1758, when she was twenty-two years old. The intensity of their faith and the fullness of their testimony greatly appealed to her and she gave herself wholeheartedly to the tiny sect. It was not uncommon for women deeply engaged in religion to resist marriage past the period of social expectation, as Ann had done, but her family was anxious to lead their daughter away from the heresies of the Shaking Quakers. Thus, yielding to the social and economic pressures imposed on her by her family, Ann married Abraham Standerin, a Manchester blacksmith who probably worked for her father, on January 5, 1762.

By all Shaker accounts, her husband Abraham was good-natured but unsuited to Lee's intense, high-strung religious temperament. This spiritual incompatibility with regard to matters which meant most to her in life was probably the cause of Ann's severe marital distress. It is likely, too, that Lee felt marriage itself inhibited her search for perfection when the demands of the flesh apparently conflicted with those of the spirit. However, the most explicit and documented crises were her several maternities. During the first years of her marriage, in rapid succession and with great physical difficulty, she bore four children, all of whom died at birth or early childhood. Each tragedy deepened her guilt and suffering, gravely damaging her psychological and physical health. The birth of her last child,

Elizabeth, almost took Lee's life, and left her in a severe and chronic depression.[14] Thereafter, she avoided all sexual relations with her husband and engaged in exhaustive spiritual exercises in order to be released from the impasse sexuality had become for her.

Ann Lee's Celibacy

Evidently, sex had been an issue for James and Jane Wardley and other members of their sect even before Ann Lee's association with them. The *Testimonies* (1816) say that when Ann related some of her own agonizing experiences to Jane Wardley, she was quietly directed to practice the celibacy already in vogue among some members of the sect.

> Some time after I set out to live up to the light of God manifested to me, through James and Jane Wardley, I fell under heavy trials and tribulation on account of lodging with my husband; and as I looked to them for help and counsel, I opened my trials to Jane. She said, "James and I lodge together; but we do not touch each other any more than two babes. You may return home and do likewise." (*Testimonies* [1816], chap. 6, sec. 21, p. 49)

By the early 1770s, Lee had a series of visionary experiences convincing her that lust was the root of all evil and celibacy its cure. This protracted conversion took nine years, but when her spiritual labor was done, for the first time Lee experienced the release of the new birth promised in the revivals. She emerged from her difficult crisis full of conviction that celibacy was the only means to this new life.

Ann Lee's Leadership of the English Shakers

After the death of her last child, Lee achieved prominence among the Shaker sect and began proclaiming her gospel of celibacy among them. Her charismatic influence led the Shakers to believe that the new birth was achieved by total sexual abstinence, and furthermore, that this new way of living brought one into the intimate union with Christ which was the desired Second Coming. She was thereafter acclaimed the leader of the society, and bore the charismatic title "Mother Ann."

With Ann Lee's ascendancy as the zealous, charismatic leader of the group, harassment and ridicule became increasingly hostile and violent. The Shaker sect had always endured persecution because of the wildly dramatic nature of their worship; they were often fined or arrested for disturbing the peace. But under Lee's direction they came into conflict with civil and ecclesiastical authorities because of their practice of deliberately upsetting the liturgy of various churches. In Manchester and the nearby towns of Bolton, Chesborne, and Mayortown, they engaged in "Sabbath-breaking," noisily interrupting the formal worship of churches in order to denounce every institutional religious organization as belonging to Antichrist, and to announce the nearness of the new age to be inaugurated at Christ's Second Coming.

When several attempts were made on Lee's life,[15] and because of a powerful vision she had, Ann and eight Believers left England and sailed for America on May 19, 1774, settling in New York on August 6. Later she told her disciples:

> I knew by the revelation of God, that God had chosen a people in America: I saw some of them in vision; and when I met them in America, I knew them. I had a vision of America: I saw a large tree, every leaf of which shone with such brightness as made it appear like a burning torch, representing the Church of Christ which will yet be established in this land. (Frederick Evans, *Shakers: Compendium*, p. 138)

The Shakers in America

In 1776, after two years of extreme poverty and working various jobs to support themselves, the tiny band moved to the wilderness of Niskeyuna, north of Albany, New York.[16] During the next three years of isolation and intense labor, they established a communal homestead where they awaited the converts Lee had envisioned. These years were very trying for the tiny band. Their pacifism and English origins made them suspect as subversives during this Revolutionary period, and they were frequently harassed on suspicion of treason, pacifist agitation, and abetting the enemy.[17] Nevertheless, they "set their hands to work and their hearts to God,"[18] planting and building and readying themselves for the Gospel work they believed was entrusted to them.

Shakerism found the American religious psyche particularly fertile for its eschatological Gospel. The same spirit of evangelical revivalism which had provided the impetus for English Shakerism was flourishing in the New World when Ann Lee and her disciples arrived. Whitefield's transatlantic preaching circuit was one link of evangelical continuity between England and New England in the mid-eighteenth century. The evangelical Gospel he so dynamically proclaimed in the Lanchashire revivals was echoed likewise in revivals throughout the Connecticut Valley and along the eastern seaboard, resonating deeply in the souls of American religious seekers.[19] Revivals resumed after Whitefield's departure, and one of them, in upstate New York near the Massachusetts border, is particularly significant in the annals of Shakerism.[20] While stressing the regular themes of new birth and perfection, this particular revival was characterized by an extraordinary millennialism. Indeed, its participants clearly expected that Christ would soon return in their midst.

> In the year 1779...a remarkable revival of religion commenced in New Lebanon and the adjacent towns. Many...testified that the day of redemption

was at hand, that the second coming of Christ was
nigh. (Green, *Millennial Church*, p. 23)

The revival aroused the eschatological expectations of the
people, but it was unable to fulfill their hope for Christ's return
and the dawn of the millennial kingdom.

Opening of the Shaker Gospel

In 1780, some of the revivalists who left the meetings in profound disillusionment came upon the Shakers in Niskeyuna by
chance and asked for hospitality. While there they heard
Mother Ann proclaim that the Second Coming had already
commenced and was open to all who would suffer the new birth
of regeneration which, as redefined by the Shakers, could only
be attained by a laboring state of ongoing conversion, inaugurated in the confession of sin and adoption of celibacy. This was
the opening of the Gospel in America in which the unique
Shaker doctrine of the eschaton was proclaimed to the many
religious seekers who desired the ultimate experience of rebirth
and union with Christ.

Ann Lee's Shaker Mission

In the next few years, Mother Ann and the other elders set out
on missionary tours to other revival sites throughout New
England, with Lee focusing her efforts on Massachusetts, particularly at Harvard, and sending others to southern Maine and
New Hampshire. The strategy for conversion rested heavily on
Mother Ann's charismatic personality, especially as one who
could effectively bring a person through rebirth and into that
experience of union which was believed to be Christ's Second
Appearing.[21] Public meetings were held two or three times a day,
but the most effective conversion technique was the private
"interview" with the elders. Centering on the issue of lust and
carnal relations, these highly personalized encounters permitted

the charismatic leaders to work on the potential convert in an atmosphere charged with drama and intimacy.

Ann Lee's Death
Mother Ann and the elders, already exhausted by their missionary journeys, suffered further from violent persecution because of suspicion of witchcraft, heresy, and fomenting Church schism. Although these three years had been most fruitful for gathering large numbers of Shaker converts, the demands of such labor soon took their toll. In the spring of 1784, Lee's brother William died, and then on September 8, Mother Ann herself died, at the age of forty-nine, from both exhaustion and injuries inflicted by a Harvard Township mob. With their deaths, the first season of American Shakerism came to a close.

Founding the Millennial Church
The burden of leadership passed to Lee's young English disciple, James Whittaker. Confronted with the challenge of supporting and guiding the numerous random associations of Shakers, Whittaker endeavored to gather the Believers into self-sustaining communities. He set out to establish the model Shaker Society at New Lebanon, New York, where he engaged Believers in a vigorous building campaign. But within three years, in 1788, he too died of exhaustion upon the completion of the meetinghouse. This time the lead was passed to Joseph Meacham who, with Lucy Wright, succeeded in completing Whittaker's task of establishing the Shakers into several highly organized, self-sufficient communes linked to a central authority at New Lebanon. Between 1785 and 1797, the Shaker leaders turned from their conversion campaigns to focus exclusively on securing the life of the Society in all its spiritual and temporal aspects. They formed it into vital, stable, flourishing communities, and they declared it the Millennial Church.

MOTHER ANN OF FAITH

The "Testimonies" Tradition

These remarks concerning the Ann Lee of history provide some
bearings for the task of discovering the Mother Ann of faith in
whom is found the controlling metaphor of primitive Shaker
eschatology. While there is no single expression explicitly
offered by the earliest Shakers as a summary of their eschatological understanding, a persistent theme is discernible in the official documents on nineteenth-century Shakerism. The single
most important clue to the earliest Believers' understanding of
Christ's Second Appearing is the motif of motherhood. In the
imagination of Believers, it is Ann in her role as spiritual
mother who brings them to the Second Appearing of Christ. In
rich and complex feminine metaphors of marriage, motherhood,
and birth, the Shakers proclaim her messianic labor of giving
them life in the Millennial Church.

The earliest written evidence of the Mother Ann of faith is
the *Testimonies* material, a collection of the personal accounts,
memories, testimonies, and stories which originally circulated
orally among the Shakers.[22] The subject of this prototheological
remembrance is Ann Lee and the elders — their sayings, gospel,
and acts. The interviews with Believers, upon which the
accounts were based, began about 1808, and for the next thirty
years Elder Rufus Bishop collected "Mother's Sayings" for the
young generation of Shakers who had not known her in person.
While Bishop gathered material at New Lebanon, Seth Youngs
Wells did the same from Mother Ann's contemporaries at
Watervliet. These materials were then augmented by correspondence. Later, these sources were used as the basis of the four
texts which make up the *Testimonies* tradition:

Testimonies of the Life, Character, Revelations and Doctrines of Our Ever Blessed Mother Ann Lee, and the Elders with Her (1816);

Testimonies Concerning the Character and Ministry of Mother Ann Lee and the First Witnesses of the Gospel of Christ's Second Appearing (1827);

Sayings of Mother Ann and the First Elders and Incidents Related by Jemima Blanchard of Her Experience and Intercourse with Mother Ann and Our First Parents (1845?); and

Testimonies of the Life, Character, Revelations, and Doctrines of Mother Ann Lee and the Elders with Her (1888).

The 1816 *Testimonies* have as their purpose the preservation of the founding spirit and the instruction of second-generation Shakers. Since they provide the earliest description of Christ's Second Appearing, only the collection from 1816 will be presented. Their contents are arranged according to the format of the title, *Testimonies of the Life, Character, Revelations and Doctrines of Our Ever Blessed Mother Ann Lee*, with forty-three chapters divided into sections dealing with these various components. For the purpose of clarity and brevity, only those passages which bear direct relevance to the theme of Ann Lee's eschatological motherhood will be considered.

The Revelation of Mother Ann
The Shaker kerygma formulated in the early nineteenth century concerning Mother Ann is rooted in the understanding of her religious identity as it was revealed to her and to the Shakers in a vision Lee experienced in a Manchester jail. The incident took place at the height of Lee's desire to achieve the new birth,

at the end of her nine years of severe physical and emotional suffering, marital stress, and sexual confusion. The event is described in the 1816 *Testimonies:*

> In this prison and at this time Mother received great revelations of God. Many deep and important mysteries were there revealed to her; and by the power and authority of the Holy Ghost, she was there commissioned to take the lead of this society which, till then, had rested with James and Jane Wardley. (Chap. 8, sec. 47, p. 62)
>
> But when she was released from this last imprisonment she...collected the Society together, and opened her revelations, with the most astonishing power of God. Here it was seen, at once, that the candle of the Lord was in her hand, and that she was able, by the light thereof, to search every heart and try every soul among them. From this time Mother took the lead of the society and was recognized and acknowledged, as the first pillar of the Church of God upon the earth. (Chap. 8, sec. 48, p. 63)

This event had the character of a revelation to Ann Lee and her disciples, that is, the disclosure of something radically new. For years, she had sought an understanding of the source of the Fall from grace and how restoration should take place. In this vision, Ann Lee beheld that sin's roots were in the disordered sexual instinct; its healing was perceived to be celibacy. With this conviction experienced as revelation, she was at last released from the spiritual imprisonment she had so long suffered. After nine years of anguished labor, Lee was delivered beyond the second birth into an even greater intensity of spiritual life. Furthermore, Lee believed that she had been anointed for the special task of proclaiming the Gospel of Christ's Second Appearing in the lives of all who would be reborn through a life of celibate perfection.

The Shakers witnessed in her not simply a new charismatic leader, but the first instance of a new possibility for human being lived in eschatological consciousness. They acknowledged her as the cornerstone of a new Spirit-filled assembly which was the Church of the millennial age. This was the hitherto unknown light she brought to her Believers.

> The light and power of God, revealed in Ann, and through her, administered to those who received her testimony, had such sensible effect, in giving them power over all sin, and filling them with visions, revelations and gifts of God, that she was received and acknowledged as the first spiritual Mother in Christ and second heir of the covenant of life in the New Creation. Hence she received the title Mother. (Chap. 1, sec. 15, p. 7)

This passage from the 1816 *Testimonies* announces the theme of Lee's eschatological motherhood and underscores its significance for the early Shakers. She was given the honored title Mother because of her manifest spiritual authority. But more importantly, she was acclaimed Mother because a new kind of life became available to the Shakers through her ministry.

According to Shaker accounts, Ann Lee believed that Christ had come again in a deeply personal and transformative experience of union by which she was born into the New Creation. In this New Creation there was no longer sexual but only spiritual union among persons. Therefore, celibacy was the singular expression of eschatological life. Not only did Lee preach this gospel, but by the intense labor of her charismatic ministry she was actually able to deliver others into an eschatological consciousness analogous to that which she herself experienced. Her disciples sensed that the eschatological dimension of spiritual life was no longer projected into the distant future or the hereafter: through Ann Lee, God had made the eschaton available in the present age. In collaboration with Christ Jesus, Shakers believed, Lee became "the second heir of the covenant of life" through whom the anticipated New Creation could at last begin. The eschatological age now had its messianic analogue in the female, who would enact her millennial role by being Mother to the true Church of God.

From this revelatory event in the Manchester jail, the seminal insight of Ann's eschatological motherhood would root deeply in the imagination of Shakers and give impetus to the growth of a tradition — a tradition that would have to account for Ann's motherhood throughout the various phases of Shakerism's theological life.

Mother of Christ's Second Appearing

In calling Ann Lee "Mother," the early Believers document their experience of her as their personal, spiritual mother.[23] However, this simple word implies complex and multivalent processes and relationships for the one so named. Every mother must first be a spouse, and by union with her mate, must conceive by him, must carry, then labor, to bear her offspring. Then she must nurse and nurture her children, guide and teach them, secure her family, leave an inheritance. This is the organic metaphor at the root of the religious metaphor of spiritual mother. Therefore, the stages of natural motherhood will be used in order to structure and interpret the way in which Shakers spoke of Ann Lee's spiritual motherhood in the relevant texts of *Testimonies*.

Biblical messianic prophecy often adopts a nuptial idiom to describe the ultimate union God means to effect with the people of covenant through an anointed one, a messiah.[24] Particularly in the New Testament, the messianic age is described in marital terms, with Christ portrayed as the sacrificial Bridegroom who has come, and will come again, to espouse his collective Bride, a chosen people or Church.[25] Christ's union with the corporate spouse inaugurates a new era of human possibility and meaning and ushers in the millennial age of God's victorious reign.[26]

There is a rich residue of these diverse biblical images in the *Testimonies* which suggests that the wedding feast of the messianic age has begun in Ann Lee's ministry. In these texts, Lee is implicitly cast in an eschatological light, with Shakers evolving a new messianic category beyond the eschatological Bride of the Lamb, namely the eschatological mother of the true Church. This rich maternal metaphor embraces a range of eschatological themes present in the *Testimonies:* Ann's millennial virginity; her marriage to the Lamb; her fruitful union with Christ; her messianic birth pangs; her millennial motherhood; the messianic feeding of her children; her millennial family making. These facets of Lee's eschatological motherhood will be explored for their relevance to Christ's Second Appearing.

Eschatological Virginity

The New Testament links virginity and messianic expectation in several instances.[27] In the Book of Revelation especially, the faithful virgins are the companions of the Lamb who is to marry his Bride, thereby heralding in the eschatological age.[28] Although this tradition of celibacy has a long history in monastic Christianity, particularly in the Roman Church, it is most unexpected to hear the evangelical Mother Ann call Believers to celibacy as the only means of eschatological rebirth, not just for some, but for all. In several places the *Testimonies* recall Mother Ann saying to married people:

> You must forsake the marriage of the flesh, or you cannot be married to the Lamb, nor have any share in the resurrection of Christ; for those who are counted worthy to have part in the resurrection of Christ, neither marry nor are given in marriage, but are like unto the angels. (Chap. 3, sec. 6, p. 17)

Celibacy, therefore, stands as the cornerstone of Shaker millennial faith, because by it, Believers claim to pass from the old creation of sin in the disordered flesh to the new creation of perfection by forsaking sexual relations. Celibacy will bring the Believer to the angelic life of the realized kingdom, and is the prerequisite for sharing in the resurrection of Christ in this world.

Celibacy, then, is the core of Mother Ann's gospel, experientially revealed in her own agony and then liberation in relation to sex. Shakers insist that eschatological celibacy alone can ready one for the union with Christ effected in the spirit. Furthermore, celibacy is the eschatological sign which evidences one's incorporation into the resurrection. Therefore, Shakers see Mother Ann's millennial celibacy as the deeper spiritual context for the dramatic union with Christ that the *Testimonies* claim for her.

Eschatological Marriage

One lives the virgin life as the precondition and context of the eschatological marriage to the Lamb: so says the Book of Revelation; so says Mother Ann.[29] The enigmatic figure of the apocalyptic Bride stands collectively for Christ's chosen, the true Church.[30] But in Shaker understanding, this Bride with whom Christ consummates the eschatological marriage that inaugurates the New Creation is none other than Ann Lee: she is both the personification and the promise of the collective bridehood of the eschatological Church. The *Testimonies* are rich with her implicit claim to this designation.

> She spoke with great power, and said, "I am married to the Lord Jesus Christ! He is my head and my husband; and I have no other! I have walked, hand in hand, with him in heaven! (Chap. 23, sec. 24, p. 211)
>
> Mother often said, that Christ was her Lover; that he had promised her his love, and she had promised him her love, and that they were lovers together. She

also said that she saw Christ and conversed with him,
face to face.... "What shall separate us from the love of
God in Christ Jesus!" (Chap. 23, sec. 27, pp. 211-212)

Her marriage to Christ was understood to have effected a
unique union with Him, a union so profound and sensible that
she was led to conclude that Christ had come again. But in the
imagination of Shakers this Second Coming had a subtle and
unique meaning: Christ did not appear as the bodily person of
Jesus, but as the intimate, intense, and indwelling presence of
the Christ Spirit in union with the person of Ann Lee.

> "The Lord...has redeemed my soul. I hear the angels
> sing! — I see the glory of God as bright as the pre-
> sent with me, as sensibly as I feel my hands together!
> — My soul is married to him! — He is my Husband!
> — It is not I that speak; It is Christ who dwells in
> me!" (Chap. 23, sec. 2, p. 205)
>
> At Watervliet...Mother expressed her great love
> to Christ, saying, "He is my Lord and Lover; I feel
> great union with him, and walk with him in union,
> as with a lover. I see the opening of the heavens, as I
> see the heaven of heavens, as it were glory beyond
> glory; and still see that which does excel in glory!"
> (Chap. 23, sec. 35, p. 213)

This unique mystical union with Christ as a lover and husband made Ann a spiritual virgin, which, paradoxically, left her
fruitful in the Spirit. The implicit logic of these *Testimonies* suggests that by this union Christ Jesus and Ann spiritually conceived the Millennial Church and became its parents, as later
Shaker theologians explicitly argued. Here we simply encounter
her claim to privileged union with Christ.

Eschatological Birth Pangs

What Ann conceived in union with Christ Jesus was not born without an intense and painful labor analogous to His passion. The sufferings of carrying and bringing forth the Millennial Church — the eschatological family — were remembered by the early Shakers.

> As she was ordained of God, as her followers believe, to be the first Mother of all souls in the regeneration, she had, not only to labor and travel for her own redemption through scenes of tribulation, and to set the example of righteousness, and mark out the line of self-denial and the cross for her followers, but also to see and feel the depth of man's loss, and the pain and judgement which every description of lost souls were under. (Chap. 1, sec. 10, p. 4)

> Hence she was destined to pass through inexpressible sufferings for their redemption. Sometimes for whole nights together, her cries, screeches and groans were such as to fill every soul around her with fear and trembling, and could be compared to nothing but the horrors and agonies of souls under sufferings for the violation of the laws of God, whose awful states were laid upon her, and whose various agonies she was, by turns, made to feel. (Chap. 1, sec. 11, p. 4)

These passages from the *Testimonies* are reminiscent of the biblical descriptions of the birth pangs accompanying the messianic age,[31] and they appropriately evoke the sense of travail Ann Lee suffered to bring Believers into the faith of Christ's Second Appearing. These passages become all the more poignant when we remember how difficult Lee's natural labor at childbirth had been; her travail to bring forth spiritual children was no less an agony. The particular attention she paid to each convert and the exhausting labor to bring Believers into the new birth intensified the character of her maternal ministry.

Eschatological Mother

There is, at the heart of the maternal metaphor in the *Testimonies*, a weighty theological claim which discloses the radical import of Ann Lee's eschatological motherhood. Indeed, Shakerism's most primitive kerygma about Christ's Second Appearing is to be found in this theological understanding of her motherhood:

> Christ did, verily, make a Second Appearance in Ann Lee...she was chosen, a Witness of God, to usher in a new dispensation of the Gospel; to rend the veil of the flesh, which separates the soul from God; to enter into the Holy of Holies and become the first spiritual Mother of all the Children of the Resurrection. (Preface, p. vi)

Here is encountered the Shaker apocalypse: the Second Appearing of Christ disclosed in Mother Ann. This theological sentence is packed with many of the themes which were to preoccupy later Shaker writers: the new Gospel dispensation; the triumph of spirit over flesh; the availability of the resurrection life in this age. But the most controversial and fundamental issue presented here is the proclamation that "Christ did make a Second Appearance in Ann Lee."

This theme, with its particular christological import, made Shakerism distinct from all other forms of Christianity, even of the sectarian variety. In this one sentence the Shakers had shifted the ground of eschatology, christology, and soteriology from a masculine to a feminine base. To be sure, the assertion that the messianic return of Christ had been realized in a woman was problematical from the beginning, even among Believers. Yet the dynamic logic of their claim that the Second Coming was achieved through Ann Lee's revelation and ministry makes such a conclusion almost unavoidable. The *Testimonies* record the way the difficult kerygma was received.

> Mother was...under great sufferings of soul. She came forth with a very powerful gift of God, and reproved the people for their hardness of heart, and unbelief in the Second Appearance of Christ. "Especially, (said she,) ye men and brethren! I upbraid you of your unbelief and hardness of heart." (Chap. 23, sec. 2, p. 205)
>
> She spoke of the unbelieving Jews, in his first appearance. "Even his own disciples, (added she) after he arose from the dead, though he had often told them that he should rise the third day, believed it not. They would not believe that he had risen, because he appeared first to a woman! So great was their unbelief that the words of Mary seemed to them like idle tales! His appearing first to a woman, showed that his second appearing would be in a woman! (Chap. 23, sec. 3, p. 205)

The Believers' clever reading of Scripture supported them well as they defended their testimony of Ann Lee's messianic nature to nonbelieving detractors. In response to the often posed Pauline objection to female leadership in the Church, the Shakers began to evolve their characteristic pneumatic christology. By identifying the christic anointing of Ann Lee as a salvific function of the Spirit for the redemption of a people, they freed it from exclusive and confusing identity with the person of Jesus. In this way they made room for Lee's messianic vocation.

> One evening, afterward, two men came to dispute with Mother, one of whom was called Colonel Smith. They went into the room where Mother Ann and the Elders were, with a number of Believers, but did not know Mother. Smith asked, "Is there not a woman here that is the head of the Church?" "Nay,

Christ is the head of the Church," replied Mother. Elder William Lee said, "We do not allow man nor woman to be the head of the Church, for Christ is the head of the Church." "But," said Smith, "there is a woman here that teaches, is there not — We must not suffer a woman to teach." Father William Lee replied, "We do not suffer man nor woman to teach except they have the spirit of Christ in them, and Christ teaches through them, and then either man or woman may teach." This answer so confounded the Colonel that he had no more to say, but soon went away. (Chap. 15, sec. 19, p. 134)

Perhaps the most imaginative and subtle apology for Ann's headship of the Millennial Church was occasioned by the challenge of Joseph Meacham prior to his conversion to Shakerism. How is it, he asked, that a woman claims headship in the Church against the Pauline injunction? Lee's answer established the foundations of Shakerism and recapitulates the themes of her messianic motherhood, her headship of the eschatological community, and her very specific and unique christological identity. She brings all these issues together in the typical Shaker habit of speaking of the spiritual order by analogy to the natural order. The effect is to offer a firm basis for her claim to lead the Church of the final age. The *Testimonies* report that she replied:

The order of man, in the natural creation, is a figure of the order of God in the spiritual creation. As the order of nature required a man and woman to produce offspring; so where they both stand in their proper order, the man is first and the woman the second in the government of the family. He is the father and she is the mother, and all the children, both male and female, must be subject unto the parents; and the woman, being second, must be subject to her husband, who is first; but when the man is gone, the right of government belongs to the woman: so it is in the family of Christ. (Chap. 4, sec. 3, p. 21)

The *Testimonies* continue:

This answer opened a vast field of contemplation to Joseph, and filled his mind with great light and understanding concerning the spiritual work of God. He clearly saw that the New Creation could not be perfect in its order, without a father and a mother: that, as the natural creation was the offspring of a natural father and mother; so the spiritual creation must be the offspring of a spiritual father and mother. (Chap. 4, sec. 4, p. 22)

He saw Jesus Christ to be the Father of the spiritual creation, who was now absent; and he saw Ann Lee to be the Mother of all who were now begotten in the regeneration; and she, being present in the body, the power and authority of Christ on earth, was committed to her; and to her appertained the right of leading, directing and governing all her spiritual children. (Chap. 4, sec. 5, p. 22)

This is the most comprehensive expression the *Testimonies* offer to support the thesis of Ann Lee's millennial motherhood. The cosmology imagined here implies two interdependent and analogous creations. The natural creation makes visible the corresponding processes, relations, and order of the spiritual creation; the natural creation serves the spiritual. Likewise, the anthropology implies two interdependent and analogous functions for the male and the female in both the natural and spiritual orders. There is also a hierarchy of authority suggested: the parents over the children, the husband over the wife. However, in absence of the man, leadership goes to the woman — "so it is in the family of Christ." As a soteriological statement, it likewise bears a twofold character. Jesus had the salvific task of fathering the New Creation by his life, death, and resurrection. Analogously, in the second, eschatological phase of redemption, a woman would perform her particular messianic task of mothering the New Creation.

Ultimately, this statement from the *Testimonies* leads to and rests on a unique christological understanding. Like all the other Shaker theological insights, it implies a twofold christology. The messianic work of Christ would be realized in two persons who receive two different anointings. Initially, Jesus was anointed by God to bring forth the New Creation out of the old by his cross of celibacy against the flesh. In this way he became the potent source of resurrection life for all his offspring. He was, therefore, the father of the spiritual creation, and indeed of all its children. But there could be no spiritual children without the messianic labor of a mother. Therefore, Christ's messianic work would have to be completed by a woman — Ann Lee.

Without explicitly saying so here,[32] the Shakers shift the basis of their christological understanding from emphasis on the person of Jesus to emphasis on the pneumatic anointing that made him the Christ. In this way Ann Lee could likewise be seen as one anointed with the power and authority of Christ. As later writers would make clear, Christ's appearing on earth requires a living body to make visible the presence of God's salvation and to bring forth the family of the resurrection. Mother Ann was the embodiment of this millennial redemption, and through her messianic labor the new family was born.

In these statements, the *Testimonies* present how the Shakers understood Ann Lee's spiritual motherhood as a revelation of Christ's Second Appearing, and how her maternity was the fecund source of Shakerism's life.

Messianic Nurture

Ann Lee's motherhood was in service to the children of the New Creation whom she had brought forth. Her maternal care of her spiritual family was evidenced in many ways: by her witness, exhortations, instruction, governance, healing, and prophetic ministrations. But one ministry bears particular significance for her spiritual motherhood: the feeding of her children.

As biblical messianic literature is full of allusions to the feasting of the new age,[33] so are the *Testimonies* rich in various images where Mother Ann is cast in the mythic role as source of miraculous and sometimes mystical nourishment for her Church.

> Sometimes the people were ordered by Mother, to sit down upon the floor, or on the ground, and a small quantity of bread and cheese, or some other kind of provision, was served round to the multitude, much in the same manner as Christ fed the multitude, with a few loaves and fishes; and the power and blessing of God evidently attended them, so that a small portion sufficed for a large number, and all were satisfied. (Chap. 16, sec. 8, p. 137)

> One particular instance of this kind which took place in the winter, is well recollected, by many. There being a very large collection of people from various parts, and scarcely anything to eat, Mother called on the family to give the people something to eat. (Chap. 16, sec. 9, p. 137)

> They answered, "There is no victuals to give so many people." Mother again said, "Give them to eat." The people were then ordered to sit down, and a very small quantity of bread and cheese, cut into small pieces, was served around to the multitude, of which they all partook, and had aplenty. After they had eaten, Mother said, "It is by the miracles of God that you have been fed, as when Christ fed the multitude, O ye of little faith!" (Chap. 16, sec. 10, p. 138)

These passages are clearly reminiscent of Jesus' feeding the multitude. As he ushered in the messianic age by fulfilling the biblical banquet prophecies, so Mother Ann is envisioned as ushering in the millennial age by reenacting similar signs. Jesus inaugurated the promised kingdom with new spiritual food, so now Mother Ann is perceived to inaugurate its realization by miracles of feeding and spiritual nurture.

There are other images of Mother's nurturance in the *Testimonies,* which offer a more subtle insight into the importance of food symbolism in Shaker spirituality.

> One morning, Mother raised her window and, looking out, said, "I have had new fruit to eat this morning; such as I never had before! I am full, like a vessel that is ready to burst! My soul is running over! O, that souls would come and partake!" (Chap. 23, sec. 32, pp. 212-213)

This passage is interesting for several reasons. First, it must be noted that Shakerism has no sacramental system. The Eucharist is particularly rejected because it is the memorial of Christ's death until the Second Coming in glory, while the early Shakers believed the Second Appearing of Christ had already commenced in their Church. For them, the sacrament of communion gave way to the reality of union; the sacrament of Christ's body was replaced by the reappearance of Christ's body in the true Church. Yet, however much the Shakers bypassed the sacramental forms of spiritual nurture and eucharistic awareness, there was a rich spiritual food tradition evident in the early *Testimonies* which underscores Mother Ann's ministry of faithfully offering her children heavenly nurture.

Second, this passage illustrates how insistent the spiritual food tradition of Christianity is and how the early Shakers supported this tradition without ritual forms. For them, Ann as Mother was the source of their spiritual nourishment; it was she who fed them with the fruitfulness and abundance of her anointing. And, faithful to the feminine imagery of maternal feeding, she called her children to come and nurse from her fullness.[34]

The Millennial Family

The metaphor of eschatological motherhood stands to serve the fundamental ecclesiological claim of Shakerism: the offspring of Ann Lee are the Millennial Church, the community of Christ's Second Appearing. Mother Ann makes clear that her messianic work was to bring forth the true Church of the last age, as the *Testimonies* recall:

> Mother prophesied to Samuel Fitch, at the time of his first interview with her, saying "After I have done my work in this world, there will be a great increase of the gospel. It will be like a man's beginning the world, and raising up a family of children, gathering an interest and then dying, and leaving his interest with his children, who will improve thereon and gather more." (Chap. 23, sec. 15, p. 218)

There is a curious gender inversion unaccounted for in this text, as Mother likens herself to "a man" raising up a family. Perhaps the real focus here is on the "interest" or wealth to be bequeathed to the children, since inheritance has traditionally been considered "patrimony" — derived from the father. In any case, the primary concern is the birthright Ann gives her children, namely to inherit the fullness of salvation in the present age. Her bequest not only meant the Shakers gained salvation from sin, but more positively, that they inherited the resurrection life of eschatological union with Christ in this world. The Believers remembered Elder James' testimony:

> After this Elder James came forward, and said, "My name is James Whittaker; I have prayed to God for

you, as earnestly as I ever prayed for my own soul."
He then spoke of the great loss and fallen state of
man; and of the necessity of a restoration through
Christ, in order to find salvation and redemption
now offered through the medium of the gospel. "The
time is fully come," said he, "according to ancient
prophecy, for Christ to make his second appearance,
for the redemption of lost man. This is the Second
Appearance of Christ, and we are God's true witnesses, through whom Christ has manifested himself,
in this day of his second appearing; and the only
means of salvation that will ever be offered to a lost
world is to confess and forsake their sins, take up
their cross, and follow Christ in the regeneration.
(Chap. 20, sec. 7, p. 174)

The bold and startling claim that "this is the Second
Appearing of Christ" is the climax of the mother metaphor of
earliest Shaker eschatology. By its own inner logic, the maternal
motif is oriented toward a fulfillment beyond itself — in offspring, in a family. As the primary primitive metaphor of
Christ's Second Appearing, the focus of Ann Lee's millennial
motherhood does not center on her exclusively, but widens to
embrace the family born through her.

In his testimony, Elder James Whittaker insists that the Shakers
as a corporate reality "are God's true witnesses, though whom Christ
has manifested himself, in this day of his Second Appearing." By
this he underscores the importance of the collective and manifest
character of the event. The Second Appearing, like the first, must
happen in a human body. But now that body is not individual, but
social. Nor is it simply in Mother Ann, but rather it is begun in her
and by her labor, and fully realized only in her family. David
Meacham's testimony also expressed this sense of the corporate
Second Appearing of Christ with simplicity and clarity:

When he arrived among them and beheld in their worship, the extraordinary operations of the invisible power of God, he was fully convinced that Christ had made his Second Appearing in these people. (Chap. 3, sec. 8, p. 23)

CONCLUSION

Shakerism's earliest stated eschatological understanding was that "Christ had made his Second Appearing in these people," they who were the Millennial Church. But it seems apparent that at the heart of what would later become a highly developed articulation of ecclesiological eschatology, there is a clear and persistent motif of the millennial mother. It was Ann Lee's maternal ministry that brought the Shakers into the faith of Christ's Second Appearing. Because she gave birth to the Church in whom Christ had come again, she was the threshold of the eschatological event and its first realized instance.

By examining the texts of the 1816 *Testimonies*, I have tried to make explicit the implicit logic and coherence of these various maternal images used to describe Ann Lee's relation to Christ's Second Appearing in the imagination of the early Shakers. What becomes clear is Mother Ann's christological and ecclesiological meaning for the first Believers in relation to the issue of the Second Coming. Christologically she is portrayed as the female analogue of Christ Jesus, similarly anointed by the Spirit to undertake a redemptive labor on behalf of God's people for the final age; therefore, there is a certain, but as yet only implicit, pneumatology present in this early phase. Ecclesiologically, she is herself the spiritual mother of this people, who are the corporate and manifest Second Appearing of Christ, the Millennial Church.

Out of this originating experience of Ann Lee's spiritual motherhood on behalf of Christ's Second Appearing, later Shaker theologians evolved a rich and complex rendering of their eschatological faith. But at its heart was always Mother Ann, "this extraordinary female whom her followers believe God had chosen, and in whom Christ did visibly make his Second Appearing" (chap. 1, sec. 1, p. 2).

NOTES

1. The events and dates of Ann Lee's life are found in many Shaker sources and repeated in a standard way without much change throughout the literature from the eighteenth to the twentieth centuries. The oldest and best construction of Ann Lee's life and the history of Shakerism is Edward Deming Andrews, *The People Called Shakers* (New York: Dover Publishing, 1953). This remains the classic work on Shaker history and will be the basis for the biographical sketch drawn here regarding dates, events, and actors. Though extensive in its research and reliance on primary material, it fails to note in the text its original sources. Since the data woven into a coherent narrative by Andrews are found but piecemeal scattered throughout the original sources, Andrews only will be cited here. However, much of the original material has been surveyed and recorded in the extensive reading of primary Shaker works included in the bibliography. Where others have offered reconstructions and interpretations and stressed other influences concerning Ann Lee's life and the early days of the movement, these will be cited directly.

2. Although her family name was Lees, it was shortened after the Shakers came to America, and all the Church's documents refer to her as "Ann Lee."

3. There is much controversy surrounding the influence of industrialism both on Ann Lee and on Shakerism. The nineteenth-century socialists Robert Owen and Friedrich Engels saw Shaker communes as social and economic alternatives to the ravages of industrial capitalism, and this analysis has influenced some contemporary discussions of Shakerism. The social scientist Henri Desroche has offered a Marxist understanding of Ann's life and religious temperament, depicting her as the victim of industrial oppression and violence. He uses these social facts as the explanation of her admitted abhorrence of sex, her spiritual sublimation, and her sense of industry which were the roots of later Shaker communism. But this theory has lately been challenged by Henry Rank, a religious historian from Manchester, and others who suggest that during Ann Lee's early life industrialism was in its primitive, more benign phase. However psychologically painful to a sensitive young person the poverty and exploitation of her social situation may have been, it does not of itself explain her singular religious intensity. See also Garrett, *Spirit Possession and Popular Religion,* p. 143.

4. A large urban center, Manchester consisted of a town and a cluster of townships whose population in Ann's childhood was 24,000; by the time she had reached maturity it was 70,000.

5. Henry Rank, "Establishment, Evangelicals, and Enthusiasts in Eighteenth-Century Manchester," paper presented at the Institute for Shaker Studies, Sabbathday Lake, Maine, July 1984.

6. Andrews, *People Called Shakers*, p. 5; Garrett, *Spirit Possession and Popular Religion*, pp. 140-159.

7. Stephen Marini has offered the best analysis of Whitefield's influence on early Shakerism in *Radical Sects of Revolutionary New England* (Cambridge: Harvard University Press, 1982); see also Garrett, *Spirit Possession and Popular Religion*, pp. 74-147.

8. George Whitefield, *Eighteen Sermons* (London, 1771), p. 22, quoted in Marini, *Radical Sects*, p. 13.

9. R. Bishop and S. Y. Wells, eds., *Testimonies of the Life, Character, etc.* (Hancock, MA: J. Talcott and J. Deming, 1816), p. 64; Garrett, *Spirit Possession and Popular Religion*, p. 143.

10. John Hocknell, one of the members of the Wardley group, and later, one of the original Shakers, had been a Methodist, and it is possible that Ann Lee herself had some Methodist connections. See Andrews, *People Called Shakers*, p. 7; Garrett, *Spirit Possession and Popular Religion*, pp. 143-145.

11. See Marini, *Radical Sects*, p. 75; Garrett, *Spirit Possession and Popular Religion*, pp. 101, 141ff.

12. Stephen Marini, "Charisma, Gender, and Tradition in Mother Ann's Ministry," paper presented at the Institute for Shaker Studies, Sabbathday Lake, Maine, July 1984.

13. Cited in Andrews, *People Called Shakers*, p. 6.

14. For a study of the psychosexual features of Lee's religious experience and the unique celibate society to which it gave rise, see Lawrence Foster, *Religion and Sexuality: Three American Communal Experiments of the Nineteenth Century* (New York: Oxford University Press, 1981); and Louis Kern,

An Ordered Love: Sex Roles and Sexuality in Victorian Utopias — The Shakers, the Mormons, and the Oneida Community (Chapel Hill: University of North Carolina Press, 1982). See also Henri Desroche, *The American Shakers: From Neo-Christianity to Presocialism* (Amherst: University of Massachusetts Press, 1971); and Robert Lauer and Jeanette Lauer, *The Spirit and the Flesh: Sex in Utopian Communities* (Metuchen, NJ: Scarecrow Press, 1983).

15. Andrews says the early legends and tales of mistreatment of the prophetess were exaggerated, but are significant as examples of the persecution complex which characterized the early years of the Shaker testimony (*People Called Shakers,* p. 11).

16. The original Shakers were William Lee (Ann's brother), James Whittaker, James Shepherd, John Hocknell and his son Richard, Mary Partington, and Nancy Lees and her mother. Later, John Hocknell's wife and John Partington joined them.

17. Andrews, *People Called Shakers,* pp. 32-34.

18. Bishop and Wells, *Testimonies* (1816), p. 46.

19. Marini, *Radical Sects,* p. 11.

20. This revival, known as the "New Light Stir," will be discussed in more detail in Chapter 3.

21. Marini, "Charisma."

22. See Appendix, "Profile of the *Testimonies.*"

23. Thomas Swain discusses the development of Shaker faith

regarding Ann Lee in the use of the titles "Mother," "Mother Ann," and "our blessed Mother" in his article, "The Evolving Expressions of the Religious and Theological Experiences of a Community: A Comparative Study of the Shaker *Testimonies*," *Shaker Quarterly* 12 (Spring 1972). He notes a pattern which emerged that correlated with a time factor: the further the text from the actual period of original experience, the more abstract the representation of Ann Lee became. The statements from the "eye and ear wit-nesses" of the earliest *Testimonies* referred to her as "Mother," expressing their experience of her as their per-sonal, spiritual mother. The 1845 *Testimonies* (Grosvenor) reflected this also, but introduced references to her as "our blessed Mother," a title which arose during the spiritualist stage of Shakerism and meant to differentiate her from "Holy Mother Wisdom," the Mother-analogue of the Godhead. By 1888, most references to "Mother" or "Ann Lee" became "Mother Ann." Swain contends that with this specific and formal designation for Ann Lee, the charis-matic and spiritual import of "Mother" tended to become lost. The meaning and feeling of motherhood that Ann Lee expressed to the first Shakers was gone (p. 49).

24. Jer. 30:17; 31:2-4, 21-22; Ezek. 16:53-63; Isa. 49:14-21; 50:1-2; 51:17-52:2; 54:1-10.

25. John 3:25-30; Matt. 5:1-13; 9:14-16; 22:1-14; Eph. 5:26; Gal. 4:21-31; 2 Cor. 11:1-3.

26. Rev. 19:6-10; 21:1-2, 9-14.

27. Matt. 5:1-13; 19:12; 1 Cor. 7:25-38.

28. Rev. 14:1-5; 19:9; 21:1-5; 22:3-4.

29. Rev. 14:1-5.

30. Rev. 21:1-9.

31. Micha 4:9-10; 5:1-4; Isa. 66:7-15; Rev. 12:2.

32. Shakerism's pneumatic christology will be developed by later theologians. See Chapter 3.

33. Isa. 55:1-3; 65:13; Ps. 23; Matt. 14:15-20; 15:32-38; 16:1-12; 22:2-14; 25:1-3; Mark 6:37; Luke 6:21-25; 14:12-24; John 2:1-12; 6:1-12; Rev. 3:20-21.

34. The song tradition of Shakerism is rich in images of Mother Ann as source of mystical food. It is interesting to note that, in keeping with her maternal ministry, she mostly invites her children to "come and drink." See *Millennial Praises*; Andrews, *The Gift to Be Simple*; Patterson, *The Shaker Spiritual*. In a less theological vein, some ex-Shakers of the time and detractors claimed excessive drinking among the early Believers who may have used alcohol to induce visionary experience and which may have also contributed to Ann Lee's rather early death. See Garrett, *Spirit Possession and Popular Religion* pp. 197ff.

3 The Growth of Shaker Eschatology: The Second Appearing of Christ as the Millennial Church

INTRODUCTION

In the early nineteenth century, Shaker eschatology grew beyond the original metaphors of new birth and motherhood for the experience of Christ's Second Appearing to more developed ecclesiological ones. This is the period during which Shakerism's most noted theologians presented the faith of Believers to the Society itself and the world at large. Theirs was an interpretive project whose purpose was to articulate a profession of faith regarding Christ's Second Appearing, and to this end they set out to express systematically the essential issues of Shakerism for Believers and nonbelievers alike.

Here we see the Shakers explicitly doing theology by attempting to render their understanding of Christ's Second Appearing in new terms. The theological consensus which they achieved clearly affirmed that the Second Appearing of Christ was manifested in the Millennial Church. Therefore, the prime eschatological metaphor to emerge in this period was essentially ecclesiological, and by it these theologians, each in his own way, sought to bring coherence and order to the various constituent features of Shaker faith.

The reading of the four leading theologians of this phase — Meacham, Youngs, Dunlavy, and Green — uncovers in their writings the explicit or implicit definition of Christ's Second Appearing. What are the notions used by them to bring others to an understanding of Shakerism's millennial faith? What are the fundamental consistencies, the essential logic, the particular innovations of these writers as each contributes to the foundations of Shaker theology? These questions guide the task of exposition, analysis, and interpretation of the major theological works of nineteenth-century Shakerism and help to make explicit the internal coherence of these texts by exposing the dominant metaphor for Christ's Second Appearing in each. In this way, the growth of Shaker eschatology can be reviewed through the works of these theologians who recast the Believers' eschatological faith in dramatically ecclesiological terms.

In order to understand the theological intention of these early nineteenth-century Shaker writers, some attention to their religious and cultural context is necessary. The Shakers represent one of the several radical sects of early American Christianity which derived their impetus from revivalism. Like other revivalists, the Shakers participated in the process of developing new religious options and expressions for the born-again, and during the late eighteenth and early nineteenth centuries, Shaker writers labored to translate their unique spiritual experience into a coherent theological form.

This process was influenced by a number of external and internal forces. Externally, traditional, Old Light Calvinism evoked from Shaker writers a bold, corrective argument to the deterministic doctrines of the absolute sovereignty of God, innate human depravity, limited substitutionary atonement of Jesus Christ, and predestination. In place of these, Shakers outlined a doctrine of God's benevolence, human perfectibility, universal nonpenal atonement, and grace freely given to all people of faith. Internally, powerful convictions concerning celibate perfectionism, freedom of the will, and universal salvation motivated the Shakers to recast traditional scriptural exegesis and theological rhetoric in support of their own realized eschatological christology, ecclesiology, and soteriology. By the second decade of the nineteenth century, the early American converts to Shakerism had reformulated the teachings of Mother Ann and the Elders into a comprehensive, albeit sectarian, systematic theology.[1]

MEACHAM'S CONCISE STATEMENT: THE SECOND APPEARING OF CHRIST AS A PEOPLE

The Pioneer of Shaker Theology

The pioneer who gave subsequent formal Shaker theology its orientation was Joseph Meacham, who in 1790 published *A Concise Statement of the Principles of the Only True Church.* This work, though very brief, established the foundation of nineteenth-century Shaker eschatology. As a writer, and in his other labors as well, Joseph Meacham deserves his designation as the American founder of Shakerism. His influence on Shaker eschatology was enormous, and it justifies the attention given here to his life.

Joseph Meacham was born during the Great Awakening in Enfield, Connecticut, on February 22, 1741.[2] His father, who was awakened by the famous sermon of Jonathan Edwards delivered there, founded its first Baptist Church and society. By the 1770s Joseph himself became the leading lay preacher of the denomination at New Lebanon, New York, where he lived with his wife and sons. In the revivalist tradition of the New Lights,[3] he emerged as one of the most eloquent exhorters of experimental faith and of the sensible experience of conversion to Christ.[4]

In 1776, after an internal Church conflict, Meacham set off on a spiritual pilgrimage that lasted several years. His Shaker biographer Calvin Green notes that at this time

> His penetrating mind could not be satisfied with the old beaten track of religious and formal customs of professions and ceremonies among any of the standing orders: for he saw that they were all lacking of

salvation. Hence, his mind was much exercised in labor after an increase of light, and to know more perfectly the way of God: to find the work of full salvation. (Green, *Biographical Account*, chap. 1, sec. 5)

By 1779 he had reached New Lebanon, New York, just before the outbreak of the "New Light Stir."

Meacham and the New Light Stir

The New Light Stir was the most significant religious event of Revolutionary New England, and represents once again the profound influence George Whitefield has had on American religion and especially Shakerism. One of the truly enduring effects of Whitefield's preaching tours was to set in motion the cyclical spasms of mass revival, beginning with the Great Awakening in 1739 and lasting into the nineteenth century. The New Light Stir was such an awakening from which Shakerism emerged in America.

Between 1776 and 1783 a great revival swept the hill country of western New England and Maritime Canada, beginning in certain townships of Nova Scotia, moving southward into the Connecticut River Valley.[5] The rural preachers accented the standard revivalist themes encouraging the new birth, dramatic "exercises," separation from the world, and the movement to become a gathered Church. But the unique element of this particular revival was the intensity of its millennial and perfectionist concerns, which stressed that these days of revolutionary Armageddon were surely the long prophesied Last Days for salvation and grace and the prelude to Christ's Second Appearing.

The torches of this New Light revivalism were carried all over the northeast regions of Canada and New England by several inspired itinerant preachers. Its fires swept the Berkshire Hills and the Taconic Range, and were particularly intense at New Lebanon, New York, where the settlers gathered into a highly charismatic, millennial sect to await the imminent return of Christ. The leader of the sect was Joseph Meacham.

Meacham explicitly set the stage for the Second Coming of Christ during the revival: this was its centerpiece, its anticipated denouement. The intense millennial fervor aroused many extraordinary charismatic manifestations among participants, such as visions, prophecy, tongues, and various physical exercises, which seemed only to validate their conviction that these were indeed the Last Days of the eschatological Spirit. But Christ did not come in the sudden, apocalyptic way he had expected, and Meacham's biographer remembers the severe disillusionment and depression which befell him and the other revivalists.

> But before the end of this year, the extraordinary gifts and power manifested in this work died away, and left the subjects of it destitute of that salvation which they had fervently sought, and of which they had prophesied. In this state they were greatly troubled & filled with inexpressible tribulation; & while in their meetings they would often call out to Elder Joseph (naming him first) to come forth and lead them into the kingdom but this he confessed with the rest, he was not able to do; having himself come, as it were, directly against a wall, where he could see no further way, being hedged up in everyside. He however, still kept his faith that he should yet find that kingdom for which he sought and see the travel of his soul and be satisfied. (Green, *Biographical Account,* chap. 1, sec. 11)

Meacham and the Shakers

Two of Meacham's disillusioned colleagues, Talmadge Bishop and Reuben White, left the revival in the eastern part of New Lebanon Township, journeying westward.[6] On their way, they happened upon Mother Ann's community at Niskeyuna, where they received hospitality, witnessed the worship, and heard the testimony that the Christ whom they awaited had already made an appearance in the Shakers. Furthermore, they learned, the perfection of the sinless life was available in the power of the resurrection. This resurrection was not a catastrophic, apocalyptic event to break in suddenly and end history. Rather it was the progressive experience of personal regeneration within history, inaugurated in the act of confession of sin, and sustained by a commitment to celibacy, whereby one was born into the eschatological life of the Christ Spirit whose presence would gradually fill the whole world.

The revivalists returned immediately to New Lebanon and recounted their amazing discovery to Meacham, who delegated Calvin Harlow to investigate the peculiar people. Thereafter Meacham himself ventured to Niskeyuna and encountered the Shakers.

> Elder Joseph's labor was to measure his light with theirs, to see whether they had in reality the spirit of Christ in his Second Coming or not. At length, he was fully convinced that these strange people possessed the spirit, kingdom, and work for which he had prophesied.... His last great objection was that a woman should govern or stand at head of the Church which was so diametrically opposed to the doctrine of St. Paul....
>
> Father James mentioned the above named objection to Mother; upon which she directed an answer thus, "Tell him (Joseph) that in the natural state, the man is first in the government of the family; but when the man is absent the government belongs to the woman." By this wise answer, Father Joseph easily caught the beautiful idea, that Christ Jesus in his first appearance, being present, in the body verry [sic] properly took the lead, but now Jesus being absent from the earth and the real likeness of Christ exemplified as his second appearance in a woman; it was

her right to lead and govern the family, or children of
the new creation, which constitutes the true Church
of God on earth. He was fully satisfied that Mother
Ann was the Bride, the lamb's wife, and soon after he
became a faithful member of the society. (Green,
Biographical Account, chap. 1, sec. 14)

The daylong encounter between the Believers and the delegation on May 19, 1780, inaugurated the first public opening of the
Gospel of Shakerism.[7] During the intensive "interviews" with
the Elders and the worship sessions, Meacham was convinced
that the charismatic signs witnessed among the Shakers were the
millennial evidence of Christ's Second Appearing and proof of
the sinless life for which he had so long sought. Therefore, he
and many New Lebanon revivalists joined the Believers, initiat-
ing a period of tremendous growth for early Shakerism.

It was clear to everyone that Meacham would someday have
a place of prominence among the newborn Church. There are
even apocryphal accounts in which Mother Ann herself named
him "the wisest man that has ever been born of Woman in 600
years" whom God had "called and anointed to be a Father to all
his people in America." Furthermore, she is said to have pro-
nounced, "Joseph is my first Bishop; he is my Apostle in the
Ministry...what he does, I do."[8]

Upon her death, Mother Ann's English spiritual son, James
Whittaker, succeeded to leadership among the Shakers. After some
exhausting missionary endeavors, he "closed the Gospel" for a season,
suspending the conversion campaigns and laborious interviews with aspi-
rants, in order to deepen the life of the gathered members.[9] His regime
was short-lived, and at his death in 1787 the candidates for leadership of
the Shakers were Joseph Meacham, his younger brother David, and
Calvin Harlow. The decision was made with characteristic Shaker
reliance on the Spirit: during a discernment meeting the teenage Job
Bishop received by inspiration the confirmation of Joseph Meacham.[10]

Meacham's New Millennial Order

On taking the lead, Meacham immediately addressed the institutional crisis facing the Shakers in the 1790s and early 1800s. In order to unify the loose charismatic associations of the faithful, Meacham formed "The United Society of Believers in Christ's Second Appearing" by formally gathering "The Millennial Church" in to what he termed "Gospel Order" — that is, he founded a utopian community. In so doing, Meacham fashioned a bold and ingenious communitarian ecclesiology which became his most enduring and significant contribution to Shakerism.

From the very beginning, Ann Lee and her disciples were convinced of the value of living apart from the world. The hostility engendered by their vigorous gospel and witness of celibate perfectionism made communal living a necessity. Even while Mother Ann was involved in her New England mission tour, her followers had begun to organize into "family" units, consecrating their goods to the religious project and entertaining their converts at "free cost." Yet, Ann Lee herself had no clear institutional program to offer her adherents, and it is unlikely that the early disciples realized the implications of communal living. Nevertheless, the positive experience of free-style community and the negative experience of persecution led the Believers inevitably toward alternative social arrangements.

However, it was the organizational genius of Joseph Meacham that fashioned the Shakers into the most creative and enduring utopian society in American history.

> About this time Elder Joseph received the immediate revelation of God to gather the church into Gospel Order. He saw by Divine revelation that the time was fully come for the Church of Christ's Second Appearing to be gathered in the order of his ever lasting kingdom for the foundation of the second gospel temple to be laid. He also saw by the same revelation, the commission to go forth and lay the foundation

and to complete it in his day as far as he was able.
(Green, *Biographical Account,* chap. 1, sec. 23)

By "Gospel Order" Meacham attempted to make visible the intrinsic and essential spiritual relationships which characterized the new, regenerated community of Believers. By relating and conforming every detail of daily life to the Shakers' eschatological faith, Gospel Order expressed a communal society conscious of itself as the Millennial Church. Indeed, Gospel Order, with its penchant for making visible the personal and social effects of the resurrection in all the sublime and mundane features of human existence, succeeded in modeling a United Society which Shakers believed to be the corporate manifestation of Christ's Second Appearing.

Meacham's genius was to design a communal organization which supported the fundamental religious values of Shakerism: celibacy, confession, community of goods, and sexual equality in leadership and govenance. Committed to the enduring consequence which the Second Appearing in Mother Ann would have for all Shakerism, Meacham was determined to have the Millennial Church mirror the new relation between the sexes which he believed to be the sign of the eschatological age.

> Soon after the Church began to be gathered, Father Joseph saw that a spiritual union must be gained between male and female before gospel order should be established in the Church; that "the man was not without the woman, nor the woman without the man in the Lord," — that without this spiritual union in virgin purity being gained in a joint body, which is directly contrary to the union and works of the flesh, a real travel out of the fallen nature of the flesh could not be experienced, nor the spiritual order of Christ's kingdom be made — that this spiritual order must first be made manifest in the visible parentage of the

Church, before it could be gained in the body...Father Joseph having received this gift, & seeing that the time was fully come for the joint parentage of the church to be visibly established, put numbers of people to labor for a gift to know who their visible Mother was in the spiritual order of the church. And soon manifestly, by the moving of the spirit they spontaneously felt & declared it was Lucy Wright. (Green, *Biographical Account*, chap. 1, secs. 28-29)

In September 1787, Joseph Meacham and Lucy Wright, who had been Mother Ann's protégée, were recognized as the "beloved Parents in Church relation, and first in relation to the whole visible body of Believers."[11] They undertook the organizational task of establishing the Gospel Order which they believed would manifest the truth of Christ's Second Appearing. Patterned after the biblical temple in Jerusalem, the Church was designed on a three-court structure comprising different kinds of celibate families, each signing different covenants.[12] The inner, sacred court was comprised of mature Believers who had made the total, irrevocable consecration of themselves and all they owned to the community; the second, or junior, court comprised those young persons who were in a process of formation or who still had worldly obligations; and a third, outer court comprised older or infirm persons who were selected to carry on the labor of gathering in new Believers and conduct business with the outside world.

Meacham designed the New Lebanon Society as the model for all the other societies, and as the center of authority for the whole Church. The New Lebanon community was divided into several autonomous groups, called "families." Each family had a collegial pastorate of two elders and two eldresses who took the spiritual lead, while two deacons and two deaconesses cared for the families' temporal needs. The several families of New Lebanon were presided over by the Ministry, which was also comprised of two elders and two eldresses and functioned as a collegial episcopate. These several families in a particular locale were collectively designated a Society, and soon the various Shaker settlements — in Massachusetts, Maine, Connecticut, and New Hampshire — all conformed to the model established at New Lebanon, which remained the Church's center until the twentieth century.[13]

In his organizational effort, Meacham established an ecclesial structure whose basic metaphor was the regenerated human family. Its polity was comprised of male and female spiritual elders who governed the life of the Gospel family of brothers and sisters with strict but benevolent parental authority. In 1795, Meacham drafted the first written covenant solemnizing what had formerly been an oral agreement among the Shakers to share one joint community of goods. Additionally, Meacham was the authority for the "Millennial Laws" of the United Society. Originally in oral form, this perfectionist code for right behavior was drawn from the writings of Father Joseph and the pronouncements of Mother Lucy. It was compiled for use in the various Societies only after the death of the First Parents. Father Meacham also undertook a progressive reform of Shaker worship. He transformed the spontaneity and extravagance of revivalist practices — such as the jerks and barks, rolling, shaking, whirling, stamping, jumping, and other impulsive, involuntary behaviors — into the highly disciplined spiritual exercises of the sacred dance, which became Shakerism's most characteristic form of worship.[14]

With this structure and reform in place, Gospel Order was established, and the outward visible gathering of the Church, begun by James Whittaker, was fully realized. Thereafter, the Gospel was again opened to the world, as Shakers sought and received new members. Now the testimony of the Second Coming was presented by and as a Church in manifest union in the Christ Spirit. At Meacham's death in 1796, the Shakers were well-founded in the strength of his millennial vision: a society bearing witness to the presence of Christ's Second Appearing. Furthermore, subsequent Shaker theologians had an experiential knowledge of and context for the ecclesiological images they would present and defend as the manifestation of Christ's Second Appearing.

Meacham's Ecclesial Eschatology: A Concise Statement

Meacham's written legacy to the Shakers is entitled *A Concise Statement of the Principles of the Only True Church, according to the Gospel of the Present Appearance of Christ. As Held to and Practiced upon by the True Followers of the Living Saviour, at New Lebanon.* Sensitive to the essentially charismatic nature of Shakerism, Meacham was reluctant to authorize forms or laws or printed statements which might later be absolutized into a static tradition.[15] However, in 1790, at the request of a deaf man, he wrote what was the first theological statement of the Society to the world, and its first printed document. Although very brief, *A Concise Statement* manages to sound all the fundamental millennial themes which second-generation theologians would develop into a coherent statement of Shakerism's eschatological vision. With its obviously ecclesiological intent, Meacham's *Statement* clears the ground for the theological task of this period.

While Shaker religious experience itself provided the subject matter and suggested the method for developing a systematic theology, Meacham did not invent a formal structure to organize the elements of Shaker faith. For this he turned to the "history of redemption" paradigm, popularized in the evangelism of Jonathan Edwards, George Whitefield, and others. In a survey of biblical history, the revivalists outlined three distinct soteriological dispensations with their doctrinal corollaries: from the fall to the incarnation, concerning creation, sin, and the Law; the incarnation to the resurrection, concerning Christ's nature and atonement; the resurrection to the end of the world, concerning regeneration, ecclesiology, and eschatology.[16] Meacham adopted this format of biblical dispensations to make Shakerism's first eschatological profession of faith.

Meacham describes his work as "a short information of what we believe of the dispensations of God's Grace to Fallen Man." Set as a theological motif, this theme of "dispensation" becomes central to the Shaker understanding of revelation. It also places them in that apocalyptic tradition, extending from the Book of Daniel to Jonathan Edwards, which divided the history of redemption into discrete periods. For the Shakers, however, unlike some other apocalyptists who periodized history, the revelation or work of God from age to age is continuous, each successive phase building on the former. Furthermore, Meacham's work makes explicit the Shaker notion that salvation is always the work of Christ in whatever age it is offered. Therefore, the foundation for ultimate, eschatological redemption is set at the very beginning of salvation history as it progresses toward its own inevitable fulfillment in the eschatological Christ.

This sense of graded progress in the mystery of Christ's eschatological salvation is likened in *A Concise Statement* to the water of the prophecy in Ezekiel 47. Here the four historical stages of salvation's unfoldment are symbolized by waters to the ankles, then to the knees, then to the loins, and finally complete submersion into the life of Christ in the Second Appearing. In the format of progressive unfoldment,[17] Meacham introduces the basic eschatological themes of the Christ Spirit, celibacy, people of God, perfection, resurrection, and regeneration. Faithful to the notion of progress, the *Statement* ends on a note of certitude that the final dispensation will, in time, be universally realized. In this way, Meacham gives the structure to all subsequent Shaker theology: the progressive revelation of the Christ Spirit unfolding its ultimate millennial plan in the Church of the Shakers and moving toward universal recognition and acceptance.

The First Dispensation: Salvation by Promise

In the first dispensation, salvation is seen to arise gradually as God's free gift to sinners — in stages, beginning with the first light of "promise."

> We believe that the first light of salvation was given or made known to the patriarchs by promise; and that they believed in the promise of Christ, and were obedient to the command of God made known unto them, were the people of God and were accepted of God as righteous, or perfect in their generations; according to the measure of light and truth manifested unto them; which was as waters to the ancles [sic] signified by Ezekiel's vision of the holy waters.[18]

Promise is a very important category for Meacham, since by it he is able to situate this first dispensation in light of the several eschatological themes noted above. He clearly states that this first phase of salvation was as complete as it could be, though not powerful enough to effect the regeneration of the race because this power belonged to the eschatological Spirit of Christ alone. But Meacham does manage to introduce a seminal ecclesiology even in this first dispensation under the rubric "people of God." It is this ecclesiological motif which will progressively unfold in the subsequent dispensations to realize its eschatological perfection. Furthermore, Meacham introduces a theme which surfaces in different ways throughout the *Statement,* namely, "the body" — in this instance, "the body of sin."

> And although they could not receive regeneration or the fullness of salvation, from the fleshy or fallen nature in this life; because the fullness of time was not yet come, that they should receive the baptism of the Holy Ghost and fire for the destruction of the body of sin and purification of the soul.

The "body" is problematic for Shakerism since it is at once the ground of both sin and salvation. The fundamental root of humanity's disorder was its bondage to fleshly nature — more explicitly, sexual relations. But liberation from carnal disorder would be progressive; therefore Abraham was received into covenant relation with God by promise, sealed by the rite of circumcision. This sign was seen by Meacham as a test of obedience which made explicit "the principal seat of human depravity" yet which "was but a sign of the mortification and destruction of the flesh by the gospel in a future day." In this sign, Meacham sees both the bodily wound inflicted on sinful flesh and the foreshadowed healing of eschatological celibacy.

As the prototype of salvation, Abraham stood in relation to Christ, as forebear of the eschatological people of God. He therefore had universal significance for "all the families of earth." Within this category of promise, therefore, Meacham has introduced his basic millennial themes from the fall to universal transformation, and has situated these in the context of a corporate, that is both bodily and communal, salvation.

> So that Abram, though in the full faith of the promise; yet, as he did not receive the substance of the thing promised, his hope of eternal salvation was in Christ, by the Gospel to be attained in the resurrection from the dead.

The Second Dispensation: Promise Yields to Law and Obedience

The second dispensation, which Meacham barely treats, "was the law that was given of God to Israel, by the hand of Moses; which was a further manifestation of that salvation which was promised through Christ by the gospel." The law addressed more explicitly the wayward carnal nature of humanity, offered moral guidelines, and sought to curb its licentiousness. With this increase the water of redemption come "to the ancles."[19] As salvation came by promise in the first dispensation, "blessing was promised unto them in the line of obedience" in the second. With greater awareness of the nature of sin came greater culpability. Therefore, the perfection of this dispensation was expressed in obedience to the saving law of God.

> For while they were obedient to the command of God, and purged out sin from amongst them, God was with them, according to his promise. But when they disobeyed the command of God, and committed sin, and became like other people, the hand of the Lord was turned against them; and those evils came upon them which God had threatened; so we see that they were wholly obedient to the will of God made known in the dispensation, were accepted as just, or righteous.

Noting the brevity of this dispensation, Meacham reiterated the Pauline argument about the ultimate powerlessness of the law which stands only as a mirror of human sinfulness and of prefigurement of a more efficacious salvation.

> Yet, as this dispensation was short, they did not attain that salvation which was promised in the gospel; so that as it respected the new-birth, or real purification of the man from all sin, the law made nothing perfect, but was a shadow of good things to come; their only hope of eternal redemption was in the promise of Christ, by the gospel to be attained in the resurrection from the dead. (Acts of the Apostles 26: 6, 7)

The Third Dispensation: Law Yields to the Body or the Flesh of Christ

The third dispensation "was the gospel of Christ's first appearance in the flesh," which brought the tide of salvation "to the loins." In this phase salvation was not effective merely in promise, nor in mere obedience, but "in the flesh" of Christ:

> And that salvation...took place in consequence of his life, death, resurrection, and ascension at the right hand of the father being accepted in his obedience, as the first born among many brethren.

The First Appearing of Christ has explicit reference to the flesh of Jesus, whose incarnate, bodily nature becomes a revelation of the possibility for regeneration which is available to all who would imitate his faithfulness to the cross of celibacy. Because of his obedience Jesus becomes exemplar and firstborn of a transformed humanity.

> He received power and authority to administer the power of the resurrection and eternal judgment to all the children of men: so that he has become the author of eternal salvation to all that obey him; and as Christ has this power in himself, he did administer power and authority to his church at the day of Pentecost, as his body.

In this third dispensation, Meacham again plays with the multivalent notion of "body" of Christ: in one sense, referring to the corporeal source and particular incarnation of the saving power of the resurrection in Jesus; in another sense, referring to the communal locus of his enduring life, in the Church. But after the ascension, the emphasis on the particularity of Christ's flesh in the First Appearing yields to the more subtle ecclesiological image of Christ's corporate body, in which he indwells and anoints a people. These Christ empowers

> with all the gifts that he had promised them, which was the first gift of the Holy Ghost, as an in-dwelling comforter to abide with them forever; and by which they were baptized into Christ's death; death to all sin; and were in the hope of the resurrection from the dead, through the operation of the power of God, which wrought in them.

The First Appearing of Christ brought God's people closer to the realization of eschatological redemption because in Jesus, the salvific power of the Holy Spirit had been embodied in human flesh, and had wholly transformed bodily nature. In this dispensation "they had received the substance of the promise of Christ come in the flesh, by the gift and power of the Holy Ghost," thereby establishing the essential relationship between the substantive revelation of Christ, who is the anointing Spirit, and the body in which the revelation "appears." The stress on the Spirit's embodiment first in one and then in the many is a hallmark Shaker theme which recurs in the *Statement* and then becomes normative for the later tradition. But what must be noted is the identity of Christ primarily with the Spirit and not with the person of Jesus.

Furthermore, as Believers are incorporated into the power of the redeeming Spirit of Christ by following the way of Jesus, they "become entirely dead to the law by the body of Christ, or power of the Holy Ghost, were in the travel of the resurrection from the dead; or the redemption of the body." This sentence perfectly balances the essentially reflexive terms which always imply each other in Shaker theological usage: "the body of Christ" is the manifest locus of "power of the Holy Ghost." Union with this power effects "resurrection from the dead" which for Shakerism is nothing more or less than "redemption of the body."

The fundamental revelation of the First Appearing was the power available for human transformation and eschatological perfection to those who "took up a full cross against the world, flesh, and devil," a reference to the indispensable obedience of lifelong celibacy. However,

> The mystery of God was not finished; but there was another day prophesied of, called the second appearance of Christ, or the final and last display of God's grace to a lost world; in which the mystery of God should be finished as he has spoken by his prophets since the world began: which day could not come except there was a falling away from that faith and power that the church then stood in; in which time anti-Christ was to have his reign.

With this, Meacham begins a brief discourse on a theme familiar to Protestantism: the establishment of false religion and the eclipse of the true Church with the rise of medieval Roman Catholicism. During this protracted phase "the witnesses of Christ have prophesied...under darkness," and at the expense of their own lives. Meacham offers this mark of distinction between the true and false Churches: one is the persecuted, the other, the persecutor. Even the world is in the grip of this demonic power, and Meacham envisions the messianic task of Christ in the Second Appearing to be an eschatological struggle in which Antichrist is vanquished and the kingdom is established on earth. As he closes his reflections on the third dispensation, Meacham anticipates the corporate way in which God will realize the next phase of this salvific work: "the revelation of Christ must be in his people, whom he has chosen to be his body, to give testimony of him and to preach his gospel to a lost world."

The Fourth Dispensation: Flesh Yields to Spirit

The fourth dispensation "is the second appearance of Christ, or final, or last display of God's grace to a lost world, in which the mystery of God will be finished and decisive work, to the final salvation, or damnation of all the children of man." Parenthetically, Meacham says the prophetic calculations set the beginning of the fourth dispensation in the year 1747, the date of the gathering of the Wardley sect. The inauguration of this eschatological era is suffused with Pentecostal light, as it happened "in the manner following":

> To a number, in the manifestation of great light —
> and mighty trembling by the invisible power of God,
> and visions, revelations, and prophecies; which has
> progressively increased, with administration of all
> those spiritual gifts, that was administered to the
> apostles at the day of Pentecost: which is the com-
> forter that has led us into all truth: which was
> promised to abide with the true church of Christ
> unto the end of the world, and by which we find bap-
> tism into Christ's death; death to all sin, become
> alive to God, by the power of Christ's resurrection,
> which worketh in us mightily; by which a dispensa-
> tion of the gospel is committed unto us; and woe be
> unto us if we preach not the gospel of Christ.

The Christ Spirit makes an appearance in the eschatological community of faith which for Meacham is the Shakers. With them the final phase of salvation is introduced into history. Meacham, therefore, announces the Second Appearing as an ecclesiological event — that is, Christ embodied in the community as the corporate manifestation of salvation and not in one member only. More specifically, Meacham nowhere even mentions the eschatological role of Mother Ann in the *Statement*. Given his personal relationship to Lee, and her tremendous spiritual influence on him and all the early Believers, his omission of her in connection with the fourth dispensation has very clear and deliberate theological significance. As the earliest written document of Shaker faith in the Second Appearing, the *Statement* radically underscores the Believers' faith that Christ had come, not in a person but in a people. The Second Appearing is neither the return of Jesus nor the advent of Ann, but the gathering of a Church for the final redemptive work of gathering all men and women into the eschatological community of the resurrection.

At this point, the several eschatological themes Meacham addresses reach full development. The good news of this final dispensation is precisely the universality of God's will for the salvation and perfection of each and every one who would confess and forsake all sin, bear the cross of celibacy against the world, flesh, and devil, and be reborn in the regenerative power of the resurrection. The eschatological work of the fourth and final dispensation is to be universalized not in the sudden, castrophic way imagined by many premillennialists, but in the characteristically Shaker way, gradually, for as Meacham taught Believers, "the work of God is progressive."[20]

Underscoring his original rubric of progressive unfoldment, Meacham maintains that justification is found "in believing and obeying the light and truth of God, revealed or made known, in the day or dispensation in which it was revealed." When the fullness of grace is made available, only that fullness is ultimately redemptive; the graces of the former dispensations have been subsumed and transformed. Thus in the fourth dispensation, salvation can no longer come from faith in Jesus Christ alone, but only in the fullness of Christ's Second Appearing, emphatically located in the corporate body of the Millennial Church.

> In short, as we believe, and do testify, that the present gospel of God's grace unto us is the day which in the scripture is spoken or prophesied of, as the sec-

ond appearing of Christ to consume or destroy anti-Christ, or false religion, and to make an end of the reigning power of sin (for he that committeth sin is the servant of sin and satan) over the children of men: and to establish his kingdom, and that righteousness that will stand forever: and that the present display of the work and power of God will increase until it is manifest to all; which it must be in due time: for every eye shall see him.

Although Meacham was convinced that "every eye shall see" Christ in the Second Appearing, he was equally convinced that most of those who were presently looking for the event were ignorant of its true place and nature. The description of the revelation summarized by Meacham in the *Statement* is supported and nuanced by his "Word Respecting the Millennium or Work of Christ's Second Appearing," remembered by his biographer Calvin Green. In these remarks ascribed to Father Joseph, Green makes very clear that only those in the event can discern its truth and meaning.

Many in this day are looking for the commencement of the Millennium or latter day of glory, when Christ will be set up & established on earth...But the order & manner of the commencement & establishment of the kingdom of Christ on earth, is not, neither can it be understood by any, but by the revelation of Christ, either immediate in their own souls, or by those who have it. (Green, *Biographical Account*, "Father's Word Respecting the Millennium or Work of Christ's Second Appearing," chap. 4, sec. 1)

He underscores the novelty of the eschatological event of Christ's Second Appearing as "a new and further dispensation of

God to his people." Like all dispensations of grace it "is revealed by one to others;" and can only be understood by those who have received it since "creatures must be in the very work to understand the true meaning of the work of God in their day." Furthermore, "the second appearing or work of Christ in the latter day" is non-denominational or non-confessional in its realization and intent, neither will it "be in the order or manner of any kingdom," but in its progress will consume all." This "work of Christ in his Second Appearing is already begun," as evidenced for Meacham in contemporary political upheavals. However, the eschatological transformation of the world will be preceded by the eschatological transformation of God's Church and this "work of God is progressive" (Green, *Biographical Account,* "Father's Word Respecting the Millennium or Work of Christ's Second Appearing," chap. 4, secs. 1-8).

These then are the guidelines for discerning the authenticity of the Shaker claim to be in the reality of Christ's Second Appearing. Meacham insists that knowledge of the millennium comes only from participation in the event, not in observation, speculation, or analysis of it. Only those who personally experience the Second Appearing can realize how radical and new this dispensation is and how it surpasses and subsumes all antecedent revelations.

As each of the previous dispensations had a particular mediator — Abraham, Moses, and Jesus — this final phase is also "revealed by one to others," a reference to Ann Lee, who is, however, not explicitly named. Meacham consistently diverts attention from the controversial Mother of Christ's Second Appearing to the family her ministry brought into being. It is clearly this eschatological community, fashioned by Meacham into the Millennial Church, which is the locus of Christ's Second Appearing.

But Meacham did not intend simply to found a Church alongside the many others. Rather, the Shaker Church was to be the vanguard community of the new age, whose eschatological labor was to proclaim and model the new situation of Christian life in the millennium. Similarly, the Kingdom of God progressively realized through the life of the Millennial Church stands in sharp distinction to the kingdoms of the world. Meacham suggests that the new societies which comprise the corporate expression of Christ's Second Appearing are indeed the seminal forms of the new reality which will eventually "consume all" existing kingdoms in the progress of the millennium. It is the Church, as the eschatological people who comprise Christ's Second Appearing, which must proclaim the Kingdom to the world, and this is indeed what Meacham prepared the Shakers to do.

Meacham ends the *Statement* on an exhortatory note. In the name of the Believers he pleads with the world to repent:

> We desire therefore that the children of men would believe the testimony of truth, and turn from their sins by repentance, that they might obtain the mercy of God, and salvation from sin before it is too late.

The spiritual crisis occasioned by Christ's Second Appearing was an invitation — a call to conversion, not damnation; to repentence, not punishment. While Meacham's eschatology, then, retained a subtle apocalyptic cast, he viewed the Second Coming as a gradual process rather than a sudden, cataclysmic event: its import creative rather than destructive. Meacham's earlier apocalypticism had obviously been tempered by years of lived faith in Christ's Second Appearing as a corporate and unfolding phenomenon. Calvin Green remembers Meacham saying, perhaps about himself,

> that those who had a prophetic sight of the work that would be effected in the great day of God so much looked for in the world, greatly erred in setting the time too soon for it to be accomplished, they mistook the beginning for the end. (Green, *Biographical Account*, chap. 2, sec. 12)

The eschaton inaugurated in the people of Christ's Second Appearing, therefore, was not the end, but the new beginning of the world, the age in which the human community intended by God at creation was to be ultimately achieved, a transfiguration from flesh to spirit by the labor of the cross of celibacy. In this dawning age, the human family would mature beyond the foundations of biological relationship to the new and universal foundations of spiritual relationship. The millennium, therefore, would progress by the inward work of awakening to the presence of Christ in the fullness of redemptive power, beginning with a few and then eventually comprising the whole world. This ultimately universal millennium inaugurated by Christ's Second Appearing in a new body or Church was the core of Meacham's *Statement,* which became normative for the entire Shaker tradition. In this very brief work, Father Joseph managed to expose those fundamental issues of Shakerism — from the nature of sin to universal eschatological redemption — which would preoccupy all subsequent Shaker theologians.

YOUNGS' TESTIMONY: THE SECOND APPEARING OF CHRIST AS THE CHURCH BORN OF WOMAN

Missionary of Shakerism

Benjamin Seth Youngs was born in Schenectady, New York, on September 17, 1774, to Seth Youngs and Martha Farley. In 1794, when he was twenty, he and his family joined the Shakers at Watervliet, New York. By the early 1780s, when the Church resumed its active proselytizing after a period of withdrawal, Youngs had clearly been identified as one of the most promising preachers in the Society. As such, he was sent with several of his companions to the various sites of revival.

Beginning in Pittsfield, Vermont, in 1802, Youngs and a companion, Issachar Bates, traveled the revival circuit through Guilford, New Hampshire, to Otsego, New York, and by year's end 1,600 Believers had been gathered into Shakerism. It was evident to the Society's leadership that the widespread growth of their movement depended on enlisting the converts of these regional awakenings. Therefore, the Ministry followed the progress of the revivals very carefully, intent upon having Shaker missionaries, such as Youngs and his colleagues, carry and proclaim the Believers' testimony as the fulfillment of revivalistic expectation. Since Mother Ann herself on several occasions had prophesied that the next opening of the Gospel would be in "a great level country in the Southwest,"[21] the protracted and extraordinary Kentucky Revival, begun in 1799 at the famous Cane Ridge camp meeting, was watched with particular interest, especially by Benjamin Seth Youngs.

The Opening of the Shaker Gospel in the West

The Kentucky Revival opened an important chapter in the annals of Shakerism. Just before the end of the eighteenth century, revivalism visited the sparsely populated farming and lumbering settlements of Ohio and Kentucky, where protracted and intense camp meetings were often the only centers of social and spiritual gathering. At Cane Ridge and elsewhere, Methodist, Baptist, and Presbyterian preachers, each in their turn, labored to awaken the souls of their hearers to the eschatological promises of Christ being realized in their day. Their audiences responded to the dramatic preaching with even more dramatic exercises of body and spirit, heightening the religious excitement and reputation of the revival. Indeed, even before the arrival of the Shakers, the Cane Ridge participants had already joined an acute awareness of the Second Coming with the usual charismatic expressions of enthusiastic religion.

Several years into the revival, however, reaction set in. By 1803, denominational rivalries and doctrinal controversy had factionalized the movement, resulting in a schism among the Presbyterians. From this crisis there emerged a new sect variously called the New Lights, Schismatics, or simply "Christians," who withdrew from the jurisdiction of the Kentucky Synod to form the Springfield Presbytery. In 1803, under the leadership of John Dunlavy, Barton Stone, Richard McNemar, Malcolm Worley and others, they established their headquarters at Cane Ridge, Kentucky.[22] By freeing themselves from the restrictive authority of the Presbyterian system, the New Lights hoped to establish Scripture as the "only rule of faith and practice, the only standard of doctrine and discipline."[23]

At the dissolution of the Springfield Presbytery a year later in 1804, only the radical sect called the Schismatics endured. With McNemar and Worley among the leadership, this sect developed a new church which practiced general confession of sin and encouraged the wild and frenzied excitations of religious response, such as the barks, jerks, shakes, rolls, trances, and dances which characterized their worship, all of which were believed to foretoken the Second Coming. The advent of Benjamin Seth Youngs and his colleagues would kindle anew this still-smoldering ember of the Kentucky Revival.[24] By the light of the Believers' fiery preaching, the Schismatics would come to recognize the Shakers as the fulfillment of their own millennial hopes, and they in turn would fulfill Mother Ann's prophecy of opening the Gospel to the West.

Elders David Meacham, Amos Hammond, and Ebenezer Cooley of the New Lebanon Ministry confided the historic mission to the West to Issachar Bates, John Meacham (Father Joseph's eldest), and Benjamin Seth Youngs. On January 1, 1805, the missionaries set out, going on foot from Peekskill, in search of an open door to Shakerism among the religious enthusiasts. On March 22, after a journey of more than 1,200 miles, they found their welcome in the home of Malcolm

Worley at Turtle Creek, in southern Ohio. He became the Shaker's first convert, followed by Richard McNemar, at whose church the following Sunday the missionaries read a letter from the Elders, which said in part,

> altho we had been a people greatly wrought upon by the Spirit of God, and were looking for the coming of Christ, yet the light manifested in the witnesses showed us that we were unspeakably short of salvation and had never travelled one step in the regeneration towards the new birth; for it showed us that it was impossible for them who lived in the works of natural generation, copulating in the works of the flesh, to travel in the great work of regeneration and the new birth.
>
> And as these witnesses had received the revelation of Christ, in this last display of the grace of God, which is a way out of all sin, in the manner following.
>
> First. To believe in the manifestation of Christ and in the messengers he had sent. Secondly, to confess all our sins; and thirdly, to take up our cross against the flesh, the world, and all evil....
>
> We have had a great desire that some of you might have visited us before now, as we have been waiting for some time to know the mind of God in relation to you: we now out of duty to God and our fellow creatures, have sent three of our brethren viz., John Meacham, Issachar Bates and Benjamin Youngs, who we trust will be able to declare these things more particularly and open the way of eternal life unto you, which is the way out of all sin....Receive them, therefore, as messengers of Christ and friends to your salvation.[25]

The Shaker testimony was enthusiastically received, first by the leaders of the local churches — most notably McNemar, Dunlavy, and Stone[26] — and subsequently by large numbers of their congregations who were attracted by its concrete, experiential character. The Shakers did not offer "mere speculation" about new life and salvation but, as convert Richard McNemar wrote: "things that had for many years been reduced to practice, and established by the living experience of hundreds."[27] That is, the Believers did not merely preach the Second Coming as had the revivalists, but rather celebrated its realized presence in their community. It was this eschatological event, with its power of salvation and grace for living the life of perfection, which seemed now to be made manifest in the coming of the Shakers. And within the next several years, the Shaker missionaries and their new converts developed the nuclei of several new societies which soon became flourishing centers of the new eschatological faith.[28]

Toward a Shaker Bible

In 1806, the eastern Ministry realized that these new converts required some authoritative expression of Shaker faith, since now the majority of Believers were unfamiliar with the personal testimonies of the first witnesses. Therefore it was decided that the various teachings of Ann Lee, James Whittaker, and Joseph Meacham, as they had unfolded in the lived experience of Believers, should be drawn together in a comprehensive expression of Shaker belief. Benjamin Seth Youngs was chosen for the task and undertook the first authoritative work on the theology of the United Society. The plan was approved by Mother Lucy Wright, who wrote to Youngs and his colleagues:

> (Canaan) 9th 10 mo. 1806
> Beloved Brethren —
>   ...I am sensible that what you have written is the

Gift of God.... I have felt & experienced consider-
able with Father Joseph in relation to writing, &
making more fully known to the world the foundation of our Faith — We have always felt the time
was not come — But now I feel satisfied, the time is
come & the gift is in you and with you to accomplish this work — I am sensible your Gift & calling
that you are called to in the present opening of the
Gospel, brings every gift clear & plain that is necessary for the full accomplishment of this work.

These few lines from your Parent in the
Gospel....I hope & trust you will consider well &
not get anything printed but what you are willing to
Live by & die by.[29]

The first edition of Youngs' *Testimony of Christ's Second
Appearing* was published in 1808, an astonishing accomplishment given the book's length, his many duties as Elder, and
the crude circumstances in which he worked — a "spare attic
room in the recently completed Turtle Creek dwelling."[30] It
was published again in 1810 and in 1823 with few changes.
However the extraordinary spiritual phenomena which swept
the Society in the 1830s, called "Mother Ann's Work,"[31]
caused Youngs to add large blocks of new material to the
fourth edition in 1856. I have used the 1823 edition of the
Testimony for our discussion of Youngs' theological contribution because it represents the first comprehensive statement of
early Shaker eschatology.

Testimony of Christ's Second Appearing

Aim and Purpose

Youngs, like all of the theologians under consideration, was an
apologist for Shakerism. More particularly, he was an ecclesiol-

ogist committed to presenting and defending the weighty eschatological claims of the Millennial Church in its soteriological plan and purpose, its theological source and telos, its historical matrix, and its realization. Youngs offers Shakerism's first systematic development of its theology, christology, and ecclesiology by sketching a finely detailed diptych drawn from the biblical images of the first and second creations. By means of this binary paradigm, Youngs achieves a bold and imaginative synthesis of Shakerism's eschatological vision.

Known among Believers as "The Shaker Bible," *The Testimony of Christ's Second Appearing* is an elaborate exegesis of Old and New Testaments and subsequent Christian history as they prepared for the eschatological event which is Youngs' subject. Because his concern is the interpretation of writings and happenings which demonstrate the authentication of Shaker theological claims, Youngs uses those features of the panorama of Christian history which in some way prefigured, anticipated, or promised an eschatological resolution in the Second Coming. Furthermore, Youngs does so with characteristic Shaker commitment to the notion of progressive revelation.

> Seeing then that the whole of God's work is considered like links of a chain, and that one thing riseth out of another in an increasing line from beginning to end; it will be proper to treat of things in their true and natural order, as they rise from age to age; from which the appearing of Christ, first and last, may be understood in its true nature and design. (Pt. 1, chap. 1, sec. 23)

In these introductory remarks Youngs presents both his thesis and his method: to understand the nature and design of the first and last Appearings of Christ by examining the process and modes of their particular manifestations. Indeed, this compact sentence at the beginning of the *Testimony* provides a device for structuring the exposition and analysis of Youngs' very lengthy treatise and for interpreting the *Testimony* in particular and Shaker theology in general. Youngs says God's work is (a) gradually and progressively unfolding; (b) within history; (c) according to a divinely intended order; (d) rooted in the natural, created world; (e) manifested in a perceptible design, particularly of a binary or dual sort. These elements will provide a principle of limitation for selecting the material from the *Testimony* to be discussed and as a schema for its analysis.

Structural Plan: The Order of Correspondences

The recurring motif throughout the *Testimony* is the notion of "order," one of Shakerism's highest values. For Youngs this term has a bivalent significance and connotation, implying an order of balance, harmony, perfection, and symmetry in the structure of the divine world as reflected in the natural world, and an order of history related to the progressive, successive, and gradual nature of revelation. Youngs' sense of order, therefore, establishes an interrelationship and structural correspondence between history and nature, time and space. Yet more subtly he penetrates to the bivalences even within each of these, to the divine and human, eternal and temporal dimensions which establish the polarities of all reality. Youngs' intricacy is deliberate as he uses this dyadic schema of correspondences as the structural principle for his monumental work. What the Shakers did in the highly detailed twofold ordering of their existence — in their architecture, their song and worship, their living arrangements, their labor, their cultural, emotional, and intellectual habits — Youngs did for their theology in the *Testimony*.

As we trace the design of the *Testimony* we can see Youngs laying out the blueprint of correspondences between the old and new, the human and divine, the original and eschatological. At the base of all these pairings, Youngs reveals the cornerstone of his theological construction: the fundamental pair of male and female. It is this paradigm — the human couple — which Youngs sets as his archetypal foundation and upon which he builds his entire eschatological argument.

It is man and woman who symbolically reflect the constituent features of sacred order, which was first made known and given form in the male line through Adam, and after him, in Eve. Analogously, the New Creation in Jesus Christ will at last be completed by a subsequent and derivative New Creation in the female line, through Mother Ann. By faithfulness to this analogical and binary metaphor, Youngs achieves an expression of Shakerism's most peculiar eschatological claim. His particular innovation is precisely his insistence that the Second Appearing or "finishing work of the new creation" rests upon the theological significance of woman. Indeed, the novelty which constitutes this dispensation as specifically eschatological is nothing less than the disclosure of the feminine analogue of God in Holy Mother Wisdom, of Christ in the anointing of Ann Lee, and of the Church through its new birth in the messianic ministry of the eschatological woman, Mother Ann. By means of his analogy of correspondences, and especially of sexual correspondence, Youngs develops an impressive systematic theology for Shakerism which serves to bring his eschatological ecclesiology into view, namely his understanding of Christ's Second Appearing as the eschatological Church born of Woman.

To understand the subtlety and depth of Youngs' eschatological ecclesiology, it is necessary to survey briefly the corresponding orders of reality which he perceives. I begin with Youngs' implied theological anthropology since when it is made explicit, his subsequent soteriology and eschatology become more clear. And rather than following the historical outline of his own exposition, I will treat the issues he raises in the order of the following theological topics so as to highlight his understanding of Christ's Second Appearing: the First Creation; the New Creation; christology of the First and

Second Appearings; ecclesiology of the Second Appearing; theology of the Second Appearing.

The First Creation

Theological Anthropology

As a preamble to his eschatological thesis, Youngs considers the "state of man in his first creation" (pt. 1, chap. 2, sec. 5), and by employing his analogy of binary correspondences, develops a foundational theological anthropology. Spiritual human nature is to Youngs, "matter the most refined," where

> in the union of soul and body, every part or sense of the body must be occupied by a corresponding part or sense of the soul. (Pt. 1, chap. 2, sec. 15)

In the bipolar creation of the human, the natural self was created for time, the soul for eternity. The very ontology of human persons, therefore, was essentially dual, and this situation constituted their existential promise and crisis.

> But the living soul of man was united to a material and natural body, which was of earth, and which was possessive of its own animal and earthly instinct; and this constitutes his state of trial, and placed him as it were between two worlds, between life and death. (Pt. 1, chap. 2, sec. 28)

Furthermore, this binary nature penetrated and divided the human person into a being of two complementary modes.

> Thus man was formed into two parts, male and female. These two, as to their visible form were distinct; but in point of nature and species they were one, constituting one entire man complete in his order. (Pt. 1, chap. 2, sec. 21)

The sexual symmetry of the human pair is a constantly recurring motif throughout the *Testimony* and is the corner-stone of Youngs' order of correspondences. The male and female were equal in nature, but according to the Bible, the male had temporal priority in the order of creation since he was formed first. Woman was second in order of creation, since she was taken from the man according to the myth of Genesis. She was, therefore, "second as to headship" and was "depen-dent on him for her counsel and instruction" (pt. 1, chap. 2, sec. 23). This question of the order of the sexes, although very subtle, is of paramount importance for Youngs' unfolding eschatological vision, for he demonstrated that she, who was ordered to follow the lead of her spiritual counterpart in the first creation, would herself take the lead in the second.

Linking the dynamic notion of process to the static one of corresponding order, he claims that the created nature of man and woman is progressive "and ...must of necessity advance into some higher order." Humans are preordained to a process of self-transcendence by which they progress to greater stages of per-fection. For Youngs, humanity "was created in a probationary state in order to subserve a higher purpose," namely the univer-sal rule of order and progression (pt. 1, chap. 2, sec. 11). To fail or refuse this divine order of progression is sin. The fall, there-fore, is the chaotic disharmony and regression of the human being, the effect of which is disorder and ultimately death.

The Fall of the First Creation

The *Testimony*, however Shaker in idiom, recounts the cre-ation in traditional terms: it tells of the fall and of the first sin, but it is the creation with a Shaker twist. The fall is the disor-der of the correspondences, especially between soul and body, male and female, which establishes itself in the primary, or originally superior, element.

> By the fall of man, is not meant any change in the
> position of his body, but of his soul...his soul fell
> from God in disobedience. By yielding to the influ-
> ence of an inferior attraction, he was (in the weaker
> part) deceived and drawn out of his proper order, in
> which he had been placed by the fountain of
> truth...and being drawn out of his proper order he
> loosed the bond of his union and relation to
> heaven, and being loosed he fell into that which
> attracted him, and in that, he is a fallen creature;
> yet still remaineth his former capacities, which all
> of the fancied pleasures of his fallen state can never
> fill nor satisfy. (Pt. 1, chap. 3, sec. 1)

Humanity was to subdue and have dominion over inferior
things, but these inferior things subdued and took dominion of
humanity instead. The lived dialectic of choice between the
superior and the inferior is precisely humanity's "state of trial"
(pt. 1, chap. 3, sec. 8). The root of all disorder and suffering
and oppression is therefore humanity's obedience to an enslav-
ing power, because "in obeying his inferior he became servant
of that over which he had been placed ruler" (pt. 1, chap. 3,
sec. 9), thereby breaking the law and order of God.

This inversion began in Eve, the second in creation, "the
weaker" (pt. 1, chap. 3, sec. 13), since in her "a contrary sense
of the order of things began to take root in her animal nature
and to promise something more delightful than what she had
apprehended from the order and counsel of God" (pt. 1, chap. 3,
sec. 13). In the traditional Christian way, Youngs underscores
the particular culpability of the woman in the disordering of
human nature, since allegedly in her the sexual appetite was
wrested from the order in which it had been created. Therefore,
however nuanced his language, Youngs clearly perceived sex as
such as constituting the fall, since its disorder ruptures the har-

mony of existence. In likening human sexual nature to a tree, he is careful to affirm the goodness of its fruit when it is properly ordered (pt. 1, chap. 3, secs. 20-21). Yet he concludes:

> Thus it was an undue, unseasonable and inordinate desire of the knowledge of that nature, excited by the subtlety of the serpent, through which the female was allured and led away out of her proper order, instead of being led by the gift of God, vested in the male, who was her proper head. (Pt. 1, chap. 3, sec. 23)

Finding the source of disorder in the sexual function, Youngs traces the inevitable ramifications for the successive generations of humankind:

> Thus the foul and deceitful nature of the serpent set up its growing influence in the first part of man, (i.e. the male) through the second, (i.e. the female) and by their obedience to the serpent, their nature became corrupt at the root...and all fruit afterward was corrupt...till the evil influence was broken by obedience to Christ. (Pt. 1, chap. 3, sec. 26)

It is clear to Youngs that since the female played so significant a role in the fall, she must therefore play as significant a role in redemption. What begins as a conventional Christian rendering of the fall becomes an unconventional Shaker rendering of salvation. Indeed Youngs will insist that it is precisely the restoration of order between the sexes which constitutes eschatological salvation, and that restoration must be initiated in and by a woman.

> As the first covenant between the male and female was broken, and the whole creation thereby marred;

so no restoration could take place without a new covenant relation between male and female. And therefore it was necessary both in the purpose of God, and in the order of things, that Christ should make his first appearance in the male and his second in the female. (Pt. 7, chap. 5, sec. 20)

Toward Redemption

For the Shakers the new covenant of redemption between men and women began where these two had become disordered, namely in their sexual relation. For Youngs, particularly, there is a profound congruity between the natural and supernatural creations: "the natural [is] a figure of the spiritual" (pt. 7, chap. 6, sec. 27). So "as man and woman are terms used to express the joint body and relation in the natural creation of man; so they are used in regard to the spiritual work of God" (pt. 7, chap. 6, sec. 26). Sexuality, then, as the dynamic bonding and fruitful relation between man and woman, has a spiritual analogue to its physical expression, the discovery and commitment to which in celibate union is the matter for Shaker redemption.

In a survey of biblical texts, Youngs contends that salvation history anticipates the renovation of human sexuality in the covenants of Abraham and Moses, as they prepared for the ultimately renovating covenant of Christ. Yet however much each progressive phase of salvation oriented God's elect toward the fullness of redemption, "all of them, patriarchs and families, kings and prophets, priests and people, from Adam to Christ, were destitute of the real internal power from all sin" (pt. 1, chap. 10, sec. 64). This work of spiritual empowerment was reserved for Christ in the New Creation. And, we shall see, even Youngs' image of Christ exhibits the binary character of reality; even here the bisexual analogy of the human couple informs the highly innovative christology which he develops as the foundation of his eschatology.

The New Creation

Christology of the First Appearing

In Shakerism, Christ is the divine Spirit of anointing for salvation: "not a man or woman, but the unction or anointing of his Holy Spirit" (pt. 7, chap. 5, sec. 3).

> Neither is the anointed one member, but many: not a particular person only, but a body of people. And as everything must have a foundation or first cause, so the body of the anointed originated from one, and this one must be considered as the foundation pillar or first father of all who constitute that body. (Pt. 7, chap. 5, sec. 3)

Shakers always see Christ in corporate terms, that is, in relation to a body and comprising many members: "the body of the anointed." Therefore, there is a very close identity between Christ, God's economic function of salvation as Holy Spirit, and the Church which is at once the continuation and the body of that anointing in history.

The Christ of the First Appearing had its foundation or first cause in Jesus, the father of the New Creation, the Church.

> Hence the Church is called the body of Christ, which signifies the body of the anointed, or the body of those who have received the Holy Spirit, and have been baptized into the one spiritual body; therefore the Church of Christ is the Church of the anointed. Christ Jesus was not the body of the anointed, but the Head, and as the body hath many members, so also is Christ, or the anointed. These members are those human beings in which the anointing spirit hath its abode. (Pt. 7, chap. 5, sec. 2)

What Youngs proposes is a corporate christology which is virtually interchangeable with ecclesiology. The Christ is Christ by virtue of the task of convening the new community of the saving Spirit. Against this ground the significance of Jesus' saving work comes into view.

The christologic or redemptive labor of Jesus was to inaugurate the salvation of humankind. First, Jesus initiates the first stage of the soteriologic work of the Christ Spirit, and second, he does this by constituting the Second Adam of the New Creation.

> The man Jesus, through the medium of a woman, inherited the seed of Abraham, the nature of human depravity (Heb. 2:16,17) with which he entered the world, and in all things he was made like unto his brethren; yet, by perfectly following the divine light, he was, in every sense taken out of, separated from, and placed above (John 8:29) every correspondent attachment to all that was carnal in woman, which came by the fall.
>
> And by the energy of that eternal word, which he received from his Father, he overcame the spirit and power of human depravity, and was sanctified and set apart in the work of redemption, as the first born in the new creation. (Pt. 7, chap. 6, secs. 18-19)

Here Youngs' analogical imagination proposes a process for the New Creation which corresponds to the old creation. In the original creation there is a primordial being, Adam, from whom the male and female are drawn and differentiated. Because of the fall, the divinely ordered relation of man and woman was violated and in need of renovation. Therefore, the new creation of redemption needed to repeat, on a higher plane, an analogous creation process wherein the two would be called out, again, from a new christic Adam. The images and metaphors Youngs uses to make this critical transition in his work are quite subtle. Indeed, it is the very nuance of his thought here that is essential to his unfolding eschatological vision, as these several points will illustrate with respect to Jesus as the new christic Adam and also as head of the body, the Church.

First, Youngs needs to describe how, in the first appearing of Christ, Jesus is constituted as the new christic Adam. It is clear he is not created so, because he shared "the nature of human depravity" which was the disordered sexual relation to "all that was carnal in woman." The means by which Jesus "separated" from this carnal attachment was a total renunciation of sexual relation to woman. Therefore, Jesus was the first witness to the necessity of a reorientation from flesh to spirit by what Shakers term "the labor of the cross of celibacy." It was this death of the flesh that merited the anointing of the Spirit. Since Jesus succeeded in breaking through the fleshly into the spiritual dimension of being by his cross of celibacy, he became for any who would follow his lead the source of the indwelling Spirit available now in the restored harmony which is the primacy of spirit over flesh.

Second, Youngs needs to suggest how in the First Appearing, Jesus' christological function of headship yields to the greater ecclesiological function of ordering a body of salvation. Following the analogy of the renovated Adam, the body has been brought into right relation with the spirit, which has headship. This has been accomplished through the redemptive labor of celibacy, both in Jesus and in his disciples.

> And such of the apostles as had wives, when they came to follow Christ in the spiritual work of regeneration, had nothing more to do with works of natural generation ...and all his followers without exception, took up their cross and abstained from every carnal gratification of the flesh. (Pt. 2, chap. 4, sec. 12)

> As long, therefore, as any were under the neces-
> sity of making any provision for the flesh, it was an
> evidence that the affections and lusts of the flesh
> were never yet crucified, nor destroyed by the bap-
> tism of the Holy Ghost and fire, with which the
> apostles and all the true and real followers of Christ
> were baptized. (Pt. 2, chap. 3, sec. 47)

As the disciples of Jesus came into the experience of the Holy
Spirit by the same suffering labor of celibacy, they formed the
anointed body of Christ's First Appearing, the Church.

> Here then was the true institution of the Primitive
> church; even the Spirit of truth and revelation of
> God given to the apostles, as the foundation upon
> which the church was built: The anointing of the
> Holy Ghost, that is, Christ himself, being the chief
> cornerstone; Christ dwelling in his people, and they
> in him, according to promise. (Pt. 2, chap. 3, sec. 47)

Youngs affirms that the soteriological economy had been
established in the Church alone, "the only medium through
which the gospel of salvation and eternal life could be admin-
istered" to humankind (pt. 2, chap. 6, sec. 39).

> Christ (that is, the Anointing with which Jesus was
> anointed) alone knew the Father, being a quicken-
> ing Spirit, one with the Father; it is evident that no
> man can know the things of Christ, but the Spirit of
> Christ which is in his truly begotten
> followers...therefore it is impossible for any other
> place, or through any other medium, than through
> the Church, or saints, the true members of his body,
> in which he dwelt. (Pt. 2, chap. 6, secs. 29-30)

But the primitive Church simply prefigured the fuller ecclesi-ological mystery yet to be revealed in the completing work of the New Creation. As the original Adam was incomplete with-out his corresponding human analogue, Eve, so is the masculine Christ, in head and body, incomplete without his feminine ana-logue, in head and body. For this reason the original true Church of Christ's First Appearing existed only in remnants throughout history, unable to increase and multiply for want of its feminine counterpart. When this feminine counterpart was called out from Christ Jesus her head, she could then enter into that life-giving union with him which would bring forth the eschatological community of ultimate redemption.

> Then the Church, which was the body of Christ in his first appearing, did constitute one new man, consisting of man and woman; but that body alone could not increase and multiply, after the order of the new covenant, any more than the body of the first male and female, while in the state in which God first cre-ated them, when he called their name Adam until spiritual woman was taken out of the spiritual man, and placed in her own proper order and correspondent relation to her spiritual head. (Pt. 7, chap. 6, sec. 21)

Christology of the Second Appearing

Eschatology of the Woman

Christ Jesus was indeed the beginning of God's New Creation, but its realization required a corresponding female to complete the soteriologic project "that the new covenant might stand between them both, for the increase and glory of the new cre-ation" (pt. 7, chap. 5, sec. 11).

> The first man was created male and female jointly, but neither was male or female separately,

until the woman was taken out of the man; so in the first appearing of Christ, that spirit of anointing which constituted Christ, was male and female jointly, but separately in visible order: nor could any abiding or perfect spiritual relation exist in order, between the sexes, until the woman was raised up, in her appointed season, and anointed to complete the order in the foundation of the new creation, for the redemption of both man and woman. (Pt. 7, chap. 5, sec. 12)

The woman was the first in the transgression, and therefore must be the last out of it, and by her the way of deliverance must be completed. (Pt. 7, chap. 5, sec. 14)

Through the analogy of correspondence to the first creation, Youngs looks into the new and spiritual creation which was "intended to display the glory of God in a superior manner" (pt. 7, chap. 6, sec. 11). As in Genesis, the female was brought into her rightfully created order out of the primordial Adam, likewise in the new Genesis, the female must be drawn out of Christ, the Second Adam, into separate existence and correct relation with the male. Echoing Mother Ann's testimony to Joseph Meacham, Youngs affirms:

As the first man was not without the woman, nor the woman without the man in the natural creation, so neither is the man without the woman, nor the woman without the man in the Lord. Man cannot exist without woman… Christ Jesus in his first appearance did not exist without a woman. He was made of a woman, and from the natural and visible correspondence between man and woman, he received the attributes of man. (Pt. 7, chap. 6, sec. 14)

And as no higher order of woman existed than

natural, he could be known only as a natural man; but as a spiritual man, and one standing alone in the beginning of a new and spiritual creation, he could not be revealed or known, in reality without a spiritual woman, any more than the first natural man could, in reality, have been declared as such, when God created male and female, two in one, and called their name Adam, in the day when they were created. (Pt. 7, chap. 6, sec. 15)

As Jesus became exemplar of the new spiritual man in the line of the male, so it was necessary that a new spiritual woman

set the example of righteousness for all woman, and in her proper order is, the Lord our Righteousness, or the manifest of God, according to the promise of the latter day.

And therefore, as the righteousness of the latter day was to be infinite, comprehending both He and She, Male and Female, it could enter but by something new and strange: as it is written of the new creation by the same prophet, "the Lord hath created a new thing in the earth: a woman shall compass a man (Jer. 31:22)." (Pt. 7, chap. 8, secs. 13-14)

Since Christ's First Appearing was in the line of the male only, neither was the mystery of inequity fully revealed nor was salvation fully realized, since the new spiritual woman had not yet manifested the Second Appearing. It was necessary that in correspondence to the man, the work of God would "reveal the mystery where it first entered...to separate the woman from her correspondent relation in the flesh" and to place her in her "proper order as a spiritual woman, according to the new covenant, in correspondent relation to the first spiritual man" (pt. 7, chap. 6, sec. 23). In that way, in her, and by her, the glory and perfection of the spiritual man Christ Jesus was revealed (pt. 7, chap. 6, sec. 24).

It hath been observed, that the perfection and glory of the natural creation was not completed until the woman was taken out of the man, and placed in her proper order. Whatever essential glory man might have possessed, yet could not have been declarative, so long as it existed alone. That is, it could not have been declared, revealed or manifested, without a suitable correspondent object, to declare and exhibit his glory. And therefore the Lord God said, "It is not good that the man should be alone; I will make him a help like to that (order which is) before him."

Upon the same principle it was not good for Christ Jesus to be alone in the glory of his kingdom, and the perfection of that victory which he gained over the spirit and power of the fall. Nor could the true glory of what he gained ever have been declared, or made manifest, without a correspondent object united to him in joint-relation. (Pt. 7, chap. 6, secs. 12-14)

Therefore, in the fullness of time, according to the unchangeable purpose of God, that same Spirit and word of power, which created man at the beginning — which dwelt in the man Jesus — which was given to the Apostles and true witnesses as the Holy Spirit and word of promise, which groaned in them, waiting for the day of redemption — and which was spoken of in the language of prophecy, as "a woman traveling with child, and pained to be delivered," was revealed in a WOMAN.

And that woman, in whom was manifested that

Spirit and word of power, who was anointed and chosen of God, to reveal the mystery of iniquity, to stand as the first in her order, to accomplish the purpose of God, in the restoration of that which was lost by the transgression of the first woman, and to finish the work of man's final redemption, was ANN LEE. (Pt. 7, chap. 5, secs. 26-27)

Christology of Ann Lee

Youngs' christological kerygma further claims that, appointed by Divine Wisdom, the feminine analogue of the masculine Divine Power, Ann, "by her faithful obedience to that same anointing, became the temple of the Holy Ghost, and the second heir with Jesus, her Lord and head, in the covenant and promise of eternal life" (pt. 7, chap. 5, sec. 28). The same "anointing" is none other than her own celibacy, corresponding to the carnal renunciation of Jesus, which achieved for her an analogous christological identity to his.

The Holy Ghost thus signifieth that sin could never be taken away...until Christ should come in the flesh of woman to destroy and take away sin from where it had first entered; and therefore the full and perfect order of confessing sin, once for all, was never established until Christ's Second Appearing. (Pt. 7, chap. 7, sec. 53)

Thus the saving complement of Jesus in the work of redemption is Ann Lee, who as

the blessed Mother of our redemption, in all respects, suffered her due proportion, and died, upon the same fundamental principles that the sufferings and death of Christ were necessary, in his first appearing. (Pt. 8, chap. 6, sec. 30)

By extending his penchant for corresponding analogies to the paschal mystery, Youngs makes an analogy between the types of passion endured by Jesus and by Ann who each in his and her unique circumstances suffered the death of the nature of flesh so "enduring life could come forth in the Spirit" (pt. 8, chap. 6, sec. 13). In consequence of such passage, both were raised to a new christological status.

> And in that she died, she died unto sin, once, as he did, and revived, and rose again and ascended into the same divine nature and everlasting union in the Spirit; and being regenerated, and born out of corrupt nature of the first woman, she was the first-born and first-fruit unto God in the order of the female, having in all points been tempted like as they are; but through the power of God never yielded to the tempter, that she might be able to succor those that are tempted. (Pt. 8, chap. 6, sec. 30)

But how can Youngs make such a claim about Ann Lee — how can he justify such an assertion on the grounds of biblical revelation? It is important to remember that the Shakers are fundamentally eschatologists — people who start at the end rather than the beginning to validate the present. Therefore, in order to support the unorthodox assertion of Ann's christological nature and purpose, Youngs turns to the last book of the Bible, the Book of Revelation, to focus on the familiar eschatological image, the wedding of the Lamb. Without a doubt, the Shakers believed "the marriage of the Lamb is come and his bride has made herself ready" (Rev. 19:6,7). By identifying the figure of the Bride of the eschatological marriage feast, not with the Church corporately, as in traditional exegesis, but with Ann Lee personally, Youngs is able to situate her in an authoritative biblical framework and establish her messianic credentials in an eschatological context.

And, therefore, as it will be granted that the bridegroom was the single person, who contemplated a
marriage or spiritual relation, which should be contemporary with the setting up of his kingdom in the
latter day; so it followeth, beyond any reasonable dis-
pute, that the manifestation of his glory at his second
appearing was to be in this spiritual relation with his
bride; from whom, in a particular manner, the
Church is spoken of as feminine, and that this bride
was to be a peculiar object, a single person, and as
distinct from the body, the church collectively, as
Jesus himself was distinct from his body, the church,
in his first appearing and no more so. To this the law
and the prophets all point from beginning to end and
which is also consonant to the plainest dictates of
reason. (Pt. 7, chap. 8, sec. 57)

Youngs explores the Scripture for other clues to the eschatological identity of Ann Lee. Mindful that in Jesus' own
prophecies he often used the image of "returning in glory,"
Youngs looks afresh at the notion of "glory" and develops a
peculiar feminine exegesis of the term. In a simple, bold cross-
referencing of biblical texts, Youngs declares with Paul, "the
woman is the glory of man" (1 Cor. 11:7). As man is head of
the woman, so woman is his glory,

and as Christ made his first appearance in many, which
was the first part of his manhood, it remained...that
Christ was to make his second appearance in the
woman, the second part of his manhood and this is the
glory in which he was to appear. (Pt. 7, chap. 9, sec. 4)

For Youngs, Ann is the glory of Christ Jesus because of her
unique relationship to him. She alone was elected to suffer

into that union which differentiated their particular soterio-logical identities and conversely into that differentiation which became the bond of an ultimate union with Jesus her Lord. Therefore, she becomes his feminine counterpart as manifestation of the Christ Spirit and complementary "pillar of the new creation" through the renovated relations between the sexes achieved in Jesus and Ann.

> Thus, the perfection of the revelation of God, in this latter day, excels, particularly, in that which respects the glorious part in the creation of man, namely, the woman....
> By the first and second appearing of Christ, the foundation of God is laid completed, for the full restoration and redemption of both the man and the woman in Christ.
> And in this covenant both male and female as brethren and sisters in the family of Christ, jointly united by the bond of love, find each their corre-spondent relation to the first cause of their exis-tence, through the joint parentage of their redemption. (Pt. 7, chap. 6, sec. 32)

Having made his case for the unique christological and eschatological nature and function of Ann Lee by his exegesis of corresponding analogy with Jesus, Youngs must ground her lofty and exalted status in her concrete and specific soteriolog-ical task: to mother the new creation by spiritually giving birth to its corporate embodiment, the family of Shakers.

> As a chosen vessel appointed by divine Wisdom, she, by her faithful obedience to that same anointing, became the temple of the Holy Ghost, and the sec-ond heir with Jesus, her Lord and head, in the covenant and promise of eternal life. And by her suf-

ferings and travail for a lost world, and her union and
subjection to Christ Jesus, her Lord, she became the
first born of many sisters, and the true MOTHER of all
living in the new creation. (Pt. 7, chap. 5, sec. 28)

With this innovative and declarative christology of Ann Lee
in place, Youngs can proceed to work out his consistently
bivalent eschatological ecclesiology — the centerpiece of
Christ's Second Appearing.

Ecclesiology of the Second Appearing

The Church Born of Christic Parents

Youngs' most urgent and motivating concern in the *Testimony*
is to validate Shakerism's claim to be the Millennial Church
— the ultimate community of salvation, by which the New
Creation can at last go forward to manifest on earth the heavenly society. The revelation of the spiritual woman in Ann
Lee is the penultimate circumstance which allows the eschatological event of Christ's corporate body of salvation to be
brought forth. This body is none other than Christ's Second
Appearing, the Millennial Church, which issues from the joint
parentage of the christological couple, Jesus and Ann.

Then the man who was called Jesus, and the woman
who was called Ann, are verily the two visible foundation pillars of the Church of Christ — the two
anointed ones — the two first visible parents in the
work of redemption—and in whom was revealed the
invisible joint parentage in the new creation, for the
increase of that seed through which "all the families
of the earth shall be blessed." (Pt. 7, chap. 5, sec. 32)

Youngs traces over the lines of the natural creation to establish the contours of the New Creation, which is the ecclesial

society of the Millennial Church. As the world of persons sprang from Adam and Eve, so the new world of regenerated persons springs from the joint parentage of Jesus and Ann.

> Then, if the Church, which is called out and sepa-
> rated from the unclean, is composed of sons and
> daughters, they must have both a father and a mother,
> and these must be the first foundation pillars and joint
> parentage of the Church. (Pt. 7, chap. 6, sec. 30)

In this piece of his theology, Youngs typically begins with the concrete facts of life and then moves to their transcendent analogues. There is obviously "the certain existence of sons and daughters, or spiritual children," the growing number of Shakers (pt. 7, chap. 6, sec. 25). And if there are children, there must necessarily be parents bound in fruitful union. Because of the order of correspondences in Youngs' theological universe, union among the millennial offspring points back to a prior and substantially enduring union of their christic parents.

> Therefore, as there was a natural Adam and Eve,
> who were the first foundation pillars of the world
> and the first joint parentage of the human race so
> there is also a spiritual Adam and Eve (manifested
> in Jesus and Ann), the first foundation pillars of the
> Church, and the invisible parentage of all the chil-
> dren of redemption. And as the world, truly and
> properly proceeds from father and mother, in the
> line of generation; so the Church truly and properly
> proceeds from father and mother in the line of
> regeneration. (Pt. 7, chap. 6, sec. 31)

Again, speaking of the spiritual intuition among the Shaker children regarding their christic parents in an analogy to humankind's relationship to Adam and Eve, Youngs declares:

And whether they immediately and personally know it or not, yet, by the spirit of harmony and union flowing through the anointed, there is a relative knowledge of their union; as much as the world relatively know, by experience, the nature and union of their first foundation pillars or parentage, whose image they bear.

And as the order in the foundation of the old creation could not be complete in the man alone; for the man is not without the woman in the Lord, nor the woman without the man. (Pt. 7, chap. 5, secs. 8-9)

Millennial Church: Offspring of the Eschatological Woman

In the *Testimony* Youngs can be seen exploring exhaustively this symbol of parentage for its promising subtle theological possibilities as he describes the Church of Christ's Second Appearing. Sometimes mixing metaphors, he draws upon organic analogies to convey not simply a developmental notion of ecclesiogenesis, but one which features maternity as the unique process of church-making. More explicitly, it is the maternity of Ann Lee, as the eschatological term of christic parentage, which is the sine qua non of the millennial family.

Everything that hath life and growth, from a law in itself, hath its beginning from a seed planted in its proper season; so the work and testimony of Christ is the seed of God, by which the Church is begotten, conceived, and brought forth; and as many as receive the word and testimony of Christ, and are thus begotten and conceived, in any opening of the testimony, are the seed of one distinct body, to be born in due season, in their proper order, as members of Christ.

The Church is compared to the human body,

which hath a head and many members united there-
with; or to a tree, which hath many branches united
to the root: as every part of the tree is first formed
under ground, and the body hath all its parts in the
womb of her that is with child; so the Church is
first formed out of sight by the invisible operations
of the work and testimony proceeding from an
invisible parentage, the joint and corresponding
influence of the two first born in the new creation.
And as there is a travailing and a bringing forth, in
the natural case; so there is in the spiritual. (Pt. 7,
chap. 12, secs. 26-27)

Furthermore, relative to the analogy of natural birth,
Youngs emphasizes that the Church of the millennium is
brought forth at once, as a whole body. That is to say, the
Church lives not in its discrete members, existing in their private, separate ways as they did prior to Christ's Second
Appearing, but now only in a gathered body, visible and
united in a corporate organism.

By this the Church is jointly and invisibly begotten
and conceived, and visibly brought forth, one body,
perfect in its order, and in all its corresponding
parts, as the offspring of God, coming forth from the
invisible order of heaven — rooted, settled,
grounded in the divine nature — sound and
unshakable in her faith — pure and exemplary in
her morals — unpolluted and unstained by the
flesh—and separated and unspotted from the world,
and from all sin. And in the same manner must
every individual be born in and by the Church as
the Mother. (Pt. 7, chap. 12, sec. 29)

With this, Youngs offers a rationale for the social nature of salvation in Shakerism's commitment to communitarianism:

> Hence the work of regeneration and salvation
> respecteth souls in a united capacity; for no individ-
> ual can be regenerated, nor saved in any other
> capacity than in Church relation, any more than a
> hand or foot can be born separate from the human
> body. (Pt. 7, chap. 12, sec. 30)

The Theology of Christ's Second Appearing

The Revelation of the Divine Mother
In the *Testimony,* Youngs searches for the mystery behind the
eschatological revelation of Christ's Second Appearing in the
woman by tracing the bivalent lines of divine procession from
the created world back to their generative sources in the transcendent world.

> It hath been observed, that the universal law of
> nature, established in the first creation of man, hath
> established the order and relation for the increase of
> his posterity after the flesh, by a mutual correspon-
> dence between two; in which it invariably descen-
> deth from generation to generation, proceeding
> from the first Father and Mother, the joint-parent-
> age of all the human race.
> And no less is the law of the new creation estab-
> lished, between two, for the increase of a spiritual
> posterity, by the eternal and unchanging purpose of
> JEHOVAH, according to his Divine and immutable
> perfections, which existed in his divine essence
> before all worlds, which were kept secret through all
> ages and generations; but now are made known
> unto the saints of the present day, for the full and

final accomplishment of all that ever God promised
in Christ, by the mouth of all the prophets, since
the world began. (Pt. 8, chap. 1, secs. 23-24)

He discovers that as the natural man has his christic analogue
in the spiritual man, so the spiritual man has his divine and
generative analogue in the masculine dimension of God made
known through Christ in Jesus as "Father." In parallel fashion,
the natural woman is related to the spiritual or christic woman
whose divine archetype is found in the feminine dimension of
God, revealed through Christ in Ann as "Mother."

The Father is the first in the order of the new
creation, and the Mother is the second, the glory,
wisdom and perfection of the Father...who are one
in essence, nature and union, but two in their office
and manner of operation. (Pt. 8, chap. 1, sec. 25)

With this further depiction of a divine "joint parentage,"[32] we
must not mistake Youngs to be a theological dualist, positing
the inherent reality of a Father God and a corresponding
Mother Goddess.

Yet neither the attribute of Father nor Son, Mother
nor Daughter, existed from all eternity; but derived
their existence from those things which actually
existed in the order of the old and new creation,
which are created by the eternal Word, proceeding
from an everlasting source. (Pt. 8, chap. 1, sec. 26)

Rather, Youngs will argue that the Deity can only be known by
an economic revelation of the Holy Spirit or manifesting principle of God, in recognizable analogues which are the divine self-
communications for the purpose of creation and salvation.

To speak of God's self-revelation implies the "eternal Word," which when spoken into history brings all created being into a bivalently ordered existence. The polarities which undergird the created world are themselves utterances of the constitutive terms of God's power and wisdom. Only against this divinely ordered horizon of bivalent polarities, most clearly beheld in the sexual otherness of man and woman, can any of the economic features of the Deity come into view. The human male, therefore, is a referent to the attribute of divine power, the female to the divine attribute of wisdom, and when the divine Word begins to speak a language of salvation for its own creation, the term of power becomes manifested as redemptive Father, the term of wisdom as redemptive Mother.

But there is a missing element — that is to say, the term which will translate the eternal, transcendent, and bivalent Word of power and wisdom into the historical, economic, still bivalent revelation of Father and Mother. This is the soteriological task of the anointing Spirit who will bridge the gap by manifesting or appearing as Son and then Daughter.

> And in and by the Son and Daughter, or Christ in his first and second appearing, the Father and Mother are both revealed and made known through the mutual influence of the eternal WORD proceeding from both; who are one in essence, nature and union, but two in their office and manner of operation. (Pt. 8, chap. 1, sec. 25)

Therefore Christ — that is the anointing of God poured out upon a man or woman for the sake of revealing a divine truth or enacting a saving task — is the middle term, the center, the bridge between the natural and divine orders. As such, the Second Appearing of Christ is ultimately intended to disclose the other polarity of the bivalent mystery of the Deity, namely the feminine from which proceeds the female order of creation and redemption.

Youngs says that in the fullness of time, the Spirit of God descended and was manifested in the Son, "in whom dwelt the fullness of the Deity, pertaining to man's redemption." Likewise the Spirit did the same in the Daughter, "in and by whom united in a correspondent relation to the Son, the perfection of order in the Deity was made known, and the mystery of God finished, pertaining to the foundation of man's redemption" (pt. 8, chap. 1, sec. 22).

> Therefore, by the first appearing of Christ, in and by the Son, was the revelation of God, pertaining to the true order of the Father, who was everlasting before all worlds; and by the second appearing of Christ, in the Daughter is the revelation of the Holy Ghost, pertaining to the true order of the Mother, who was with him that was everlasting. (Pt. 8, chap. 2, sec. 33)

The ultimate theological significance of Christ's Second Appearing, therefore, is the unfoldment into history of the full mystery of God now completed in the revelation of the Mother. But Youngs has introduced a new subtlety and complexity in the discussion by suggesting that the "Holy Ghost" is somehow a new revelation. Has not the Spirit been disclosing itself all along—indeed, is it not, as the Christ, the very manifesting principle of the First and Second Appearings? Unfortunately, he leaves this very provocative issue without giving it the attention it demands, suggesting that

> before the substance was made known by actual existence of the Son, in Christ's first appearing the Anointing Power (which constituted Christ) dwelt in the eternal WORD, which was communicated to the patriarchs and prophets by the ministering angels; so in the same manner the Holy Ghost was

> given unto the apostles and true witnesses, as a
> Spirit of Promise until the substance should be
> revealed and made known by the actual existence of
> the Daughter, in Christ's Second Appearing. (Pt. 8,
> chap. 1, sec. 21)

Our study of the *Testimony* closes with the explicit conver-
gence of eschatology and pneumatology in Youngs' suggestion
that the ultimate intention of the Second Appearing of Christ
is to reveal the very substance of the Holy Spirit — indeed, to
effect the long-awaited outpouring of the eschatological Spirit.
With this, the pneumatological themes inherent in Christ's
Second Appearing, as Youngs has described them christologically in relation to Ann Lee, and ecclesiologically in relation
to the Church born of her millennial motherhood, are brought
to a crescendo in this dramatic statement:

> The first appearing of Christ, in the simplest terms
> of language, is the Revelation of Father, and the
> second appearing is the Revelation of Mother; but
> for the subject under consideration we have pre-
> ferred the title, "The Revelation of the Holy
> Ghost," as the most forcible and striking of all scrip-
> tural terms, that can be applied to convey an under-
> standing of the fundamental doctrines of Christ in
> the present day. (Pt. 8, chap. 2, footnote)

The theological double helix which Youngs has unraveled
in the *Testimony* began in the primordial creation with Adam
and Eve and moved to the eschatological creation in Jesus and
Ann. Upon these latter two, God's divine Spirit of anointing
was poured out that they might enact each their respective
roles for human redemption. Analogous to Adam, Jesus as
Christ's First Appearing was head and father of the New

Creation by virtue of his victory over the sexual disorder of the flesh. Analogous to Jesus, Ann Lee was Christ's Second Appearing. She, like Eve, was drawn out of her masculine counterpart to deliver and mother the New Creation, in virtue also of her travail out of flesh into spirit. Therefore, the first sense of Christ's Second Appearing is, for Youngs, a statement about Ann Lee's unique christological nature and role in inaugurating the eschatological age of salvation.

However, for Youngs the deeper sense of Christ's Second Appearing is ecclesiological. The christological mission of Ann Lee was precisely to bring forth, by her unique union with Christ Jesus her head, the Body of Christ: the Millennial Church. It is this ecclesiological event of the whole and living body of the Spirit fully manifested and revealed in a regenerated Society of Believers which is truly the Second Appearing of Christ. And it is this elaboration of the eschatological Church born of Woman which is Youngs' most original contribution to Shaker ecclesiology. Furthermore, the interplay of eschatological and pneumatological motives has its climax in the ultimate disclosure of the purpose of the Second Appearing of Christ, namely, to reveal the Mother in God — the very substance of the Holy Spirit — who, through Ann Lee gave birth to the ultimate eschatological family: the Millennial Church.

> Being the seed of the woman, chosen of God to bruise the serpent's head, to keep the commandments of God, and maintain the testimony of Jesus, it is your inestimable privilege to follow the examples of those through whom ye are begotten into the enduring substance of eternal life.... And being called and chosen, be ye faithful...to the promised inheritance, through whom all families of earth shall be blessed. (Pt. 7, chap. 11, sec. 35)

DUNLAVY'S MANIFESTO: THE SECOND APPEARING OF CHRIST AS THE UNION OF BELIEVERS

Evangelist of Shakerism

The next significant systematic work of theology to present an apology for the Believers' faith in Christ's Second Appearing was *The Manifesto; or, A Declaration of the Doctrines and Practice of the Church of Christ,* written by one of Benjamin Youngs' most outstanding converts of the Kentucky Revival, John Dunlavy. A well-educated New Light Presbyterian preacher, Dunlavy was intensely involved in the extraordinary camp meeting revivals of Cane Ridge and directed an enthusiastic congregation at Eagle Creek, several miles east of Turtle Creek in southern Ohio.

As noted, the controversy and factionalism which surrounded the Kentucky Revival led Dunlavy and several colleagues to institute the famous Springfield Presbytery. This ministerial association rejected traditional Presbyterianism in favor of a highly charismatic, evangelical, and explicitly millennial expression of Christianity. Indeed, the faith of many of these schismatics, and Dunlavy's in particular, was so rich in the hope of Christ's Second Coming that they were ready to embrace the Shaker testimony brought by Youngs and his co-missionaries.

By 1806 Dunlavy, with other noted New Lights, had become converted to the new faith. Within several years he put his skill in evangelical persuasion to the service of Shakerism in defense against the intellectual Calvinist divines who thought the peculiar faith at best delusional. In 1817, while chief minister at Pleasant Hill, Kentucky, Dunlavy wrote the *Manifesto*, considered by many to be the definitive treatise on Shaker theology, which further explores the Believers' faith in Christ's Second Appearing. In 1847, after his death, the work was reedited in a clearer format but with few revisions.

Toward a Shaker Manifesto

As the third significant statement of Shaker faith, the *Manifesto* stands apart from the *Concise Statement* and the *Testimony* in several ways. The work clearly bears the mark of being written for "the world" and in an atmosphere of controversy. Therefore, Dunlavy is preoccupied with presenting Shakerism in the categories of strict evangelical faith, refashioning these to illumine his Shaker gospel. Unlike Meacham, who was concerned with dispensational themes, and Youngs, whose interest was in the complementary figures of the old and new creations, Dunlavy is influenced by the stock themes and controversies of evangelical Calvinism more than anything else. Like Youngs, his idiom is clearly biblical, though his usage is more rhetorical.

Most strikingly, nowhere in the *Manifesto* does Dunlavy ever mention the name of Ann Lee, nor does he make reference to her ministry or her significance to the United Society. Only in an appended "Letter to Barton Stone" does he discuss her at all, and here only to answer the accusation that the Shakers have put Ann in the place of Jesus as the Christ. This is particularly significant since Dunlavy was, after all, a convert of Youngs, and it was Youngs who had raised Ann Lee to an exalted christological status in the *Testimony*. Dunlavy had no doubt read Youngs' work, which was considered to be "the Shaker Bible." Whether the *Manifesto*'s silence on the subject of Ann Lee represented Dunlavy's intended strategy for dealing with antagonistic detractors, or whether western Shakerism, in Dunlavy's voice, deliberately sought to modify the significance of her christological role, the effect was to produce an alternative theological expression of Shakerism, particularly in its understanding of eschatology.

In the absence of Ann Lee as the dominant feature of Christ's Second Appearing, Dunlavy was free to explore in greater depth the nature of the Church she had founded. By developing an ecclesiological eschatology with a more pneumatological foundation and focusing on the gathered community of the Millennial Church, Dunlavy offers a theological basis for his assertion that the visible, manifest union of Believers was in fact Christ's Second Appearing.

Manifesto of Union

The theme and category of "union" is for Dunlavy what "order" was for Youngs. This is the richest theological notion woven through the entire *Manifesto,* knitting together its various elements. As Youngs' term "order" had a bivalent significance, Dunlavy's term "union" was multivalent, suggesting the theological relationship of the Father to Christ, of Christ to the Church, and of the members of the Church to one another. Indeed, in Dunlavy's usage the term "union" comprises all the issues of religion: theologically, God is union; christologically, Christ is union; soteriologically, salvation is union; ecclesiologically, the Church is union; eschatologically, the Second Appearing is union. But most importantly for the eschatology here in question, the term "union" always connotes the sense of visibility, of being manifest, perceptible, embodied.

This salvific union is most immediately available to the Believer in the gathered Church which has been called, anointed, and mandated by God to manifest corporately the depth of union willed by God in Christ. Since this call to union is total, absolute, and all encompassing, its social expression is community; therefore Dunlavy's use of the motif of union as it refers to the theological goal and perfection of ecclesial life reveals the Shakers' contribution to and perspective on one of the most significant and widespread religious and social movements of nineteenth-century America: communitarianism.[34]

Manifesto of Community

The issue of community had vital significance to revivalist Christianity, since it offered a solution to the many who wondered what to do with their reborn lives. Some interpreters of

American religion believed, as did the Shakers, that communitarianism was the logical fruit of the personal and social renovation effected by the revival experience. The perfectionist ideology generated by the revivals sought the conditions in which evangelical sanctification could be achieved and, more importantly, sustained. Therefore, the communitarian mode of existence was a complex device which offered its members the possibility of sustaining the atmosphere of revivalist zeal while resisting reabsorption back into a sinful world.[35]

This communitarian ideal was anticipated in some of the radical sects of the Reformation which were among the forebears of the "Free Church" tradition, such as certain Anabaptists, Pietists, and others. Imbued with the conviction that believers constituted a separate and consecrated body distinct from the world, they sought to model human societies of redemption.

Such dreams for new forms of living were transported and transplanted in the New World by religious and social visionaries who found in America an optimal environment for communal experimentation. Indeed, nineteenth-century America became a vast social laboratory where utopians drew upon the revivalism, millennialism, and piety of the American experience, developing them in the unique conditions and exigencies of frontier life and in the optimism generated by a newfound wealth of resources and space. From them emerged a variety of options for communal living which encompassed alternative social arrangements, sexual practices, and relations to wealth, work, property, and the state — among them the Community of the Publik Universal Friend, Amana Society, Harmonists at Economy, Oneida Perfectionists, Aurora and Bethel Communes, Icarians, Cedar Vale Commune, Social Freedom Community, Prairie Home, New Philadelphia, the Owenites, Transcendentalists, and various Fourierist groups.[36]

The communitarian spirit had even influenced some of the Kentucky Revivalists themselves. Prior to their encounter with the Shakers, there had been an effort to found a Church community of the newborn, in anticipation of Christ's Second Appearing, so convinced were they that the eschatological age was about to dawn. Dunlavy recalled a prophecy given during the latter days of the Kentucky Revival "that another summer would not pass before the great day of the Lord would be ushered in and the kingdom of Christ commence" (pt. 4, chap. 1, p. 411). He reminded Barton Stone, onetime Shaker aspirant turned detractor, that the latter's own father had attempted to gather this millennial Church into a visible communal form, but was unsuccessful for want of the true faith in and actual fact of Christ's Second Appearing. It was soon after, in 1805, that Benjamin Youngs and his co-missionaries arrived from New Lebanon "to announce that Christ's kingdom had begun on earth" and that they were living witnesses to it in their visible union as the definitive eschatological community (pt. 4, chap. 1, p. 411).

However, Shakerism's communal form, unlike most religious socialisms, developed of necessity under the pressure of particular conditions. Persecution and the hardship of making a living, combined with their millennial hopes, impelled the Shakers to work toward a communitarian way of life very early in their history. Mother Ann herself was said to have foretold "the gathering of a people into a united body or Church, having a common interest."[37] And her insistence on industry further suggests that Ann thought of the Church as an organization having socioeconomic as well as religious functions.

The forces that drew the Shakers into visible union, and the process itself, are mentioned in the early official histories of the Society. The Shaker chronicler, Calvin Green, tells the story of the Shakers' move toward communitarianism:

> After Mother Ann and her little family arrived in
> this country, they passed through many scenes of
> difficulty, of a temporal nature....
> They were led, however, to make some arrange-

ments, in the first place, for their future residence, where they could be united in the mutual enjoyment of their faith, and wait the call of God to more extensive usefulness. Accordingly, William Lee and John Hocknell went up the river and contracted for a lot of land near Niskeyuna, in the county of Albany, and returned again to New York....

Thus, after passing through many trying scenes, Mother Ann and those who stood faithful to her, were collected together, and in the month of September, 1776, took up their residence in the woods of Watervliet, near Niskeyuna, about seven miles north-west of Albany. The place being then in a wilderness state, they began, with indefatigable zeal and industry, and through additional sufferings, to prepare the way for a faith in peace, amid the tumults of the war, in which the country was then involved. (Calvin Green, *Millennial Church*, p. 14)

Mother Ann died on September 8, 1784, probably of head injuries inflicted by a violent mob during a missionary tour in Massachusetts. The story continues:

The society being now deprived of the visible presence and protection of Mother Ann, Father James [Whittaker] saw and felt, with many others, the necessity of laboring for an increase of the substance of the gospel among the people....

To constitute a true Church of Christ, there must necessarily be a union of faith, of motives and of interest, in all the members who compose it....

The first step was to gather the believers into a body, where they could enjoy all things in common, both of a spiritual and temporal kind, and in which their temporal interest could be united together, and be consecrated to religious purposes....

The gathering of the society began at New Lebanon, in the month of September, 1787, and continued to progress as fast as circumstances and the nature of the work would admit. Elders and deacons were appointed to lead and direct in matters of spiritual and temporal concern; suitable buildings were erected for the accommodation of the members; and order and regularity were, by degrees, established in the society; so that by the year 1792, the Church was considered as established in the principles of her present order and spirit of government. Those who were thus gathered into a united body, were denominated The Church; being a collective body of christians separated from the world, and enjoying, in their united capacity, one common interest. (Green, *Millennial Church*, pp. 14-16, 23-24, 51-52)

With Shakerism, more than any other project, communitarianism made a real impact on American opinion at large, and American history overall. In 1870, the great historian of American socialisms and founder of the Oneida Community, John Humphrey Noyes, remarked:

It is manifest that the Shakers, who discard the radix of the old society with the greatest vehemence, are the most jealous for Communism as the prime unit of organization, have prospered most, and are making the longest and strongest mark on the history of Socialism.

The great facts of modern Socialism are these: From 1776 — the era of our national Revolution — the Shakers have been established in this country...[and] prosperous religious Communism has been modestly and yet loudly preaching to the nation and the world...the example of the Shakers has demonstrated, not merely that successful Communism is subjectively possible, but that this nation is free enough to let it grow. ...Thus it is no more than bare justice to say, that we are indebted to the Shakers more than to any or all other Social Architects of modern times.[38]

By making religious communitarianism the centerpiece of the *Manifesto*, Dunlavy underscores the significance which this movement, particularly as an expression of faith, had achieved among so many American evangelicals. Indeed, Dunlavy will make Shakerism's unique communitarian expression the grounds for the Believers' claim to be the true Church of Christ. Moreover, the *Manifesto* will argue that it is precisely the communitarian character of the Millennial Church (that is, its manifest union in all things spiritual and temporal) which is identified with Christ's Second Appearing.

The Manifesto; or, A Declaration of the Doctrines and Practice of the Church of Christ

Aim and Purpose

A Declaration of the Doctrines and Practice of the Church of Christ is divided into three parts. In the first section, Dunlavy lays his theological groundwork in a conversation with an atheist, a rather philosophical discussion of the being and attributes of God, the motive of creation, the consequences of the fall, and the new divine motive of salvation. In part 2, Dunlavy explores the singular means of salvation which, he argues, is communal life lived in the true Church of Christ's Second Appearing. And finally, in part 3, Dunlavy develops certain consequences and characteristics of life in the community of the saved.

We can see the systematic logic of the *Manifesto* moving from soteriology to ecclesiology and ultimately to eschatology. In other words, Dunlavy's immediate concern is salvation which is to be found in and with the gathered Church of Believers, and ultimately these are to be found only in union with Christ in the Second Appearing. By following this broad schema, in imitation of the broad themes of the *Manifesto,* we hope to represent Dunlavy's unique ecclesiological contribution to Shaker eschatology: the union of Believers as Christ's Second Appearing.

Structural Plan: "The Gospel" of Christ's Second Appearing
Dunlavy sets the foundations for his eschatology of Christ's Second Appearing in the evangelical ground of "The Gospel." This term refers to both the context and controlling metaphor of all the themes of the *Manifesto,* as well as the explicitly evangelical perspective Dunlavy brings to the work. In light of it, he will suggest his theological anthropology, soteriology, and ecclesiology, and by it will be led ultimately to his evangelical eschatology in the symbol of the union of Believers.

Evangelical Anthropology
The foundations of Dunlavy's eschatology are set in a theological anthropology which stresses for his Calvinist readers the explicitly Shaker understanding of creation.

> Thus man was created of God a living being as his representative on earth; in the image of God, as it were, God in miniature, the image and glory of God; God in his sphere, having dominion over all; yet a dependent creature of God; imbued by him in the creation, with the capability of propagating his own species, the offspring of himself in his own likeness. This capability of propagation was found in the cooperation of the organs of the material body in the male

and female; which material body stood in so intimate a relation to the Spirit which came directly from God, that the two constituted in each one distinct person, one man and one woman; so that, by the cooperation of the procreative powers in the male and female a race of beings were propagated and continued...thus mankind are the image and representative of Deity in the world, to this day in a dignity superior to all natural creatures. (Pt. 1, chap. 5, p. 33)

Formulated in the traditional language of Calvinist "decree" theology, Dunlavy states God's creative purpose: to inspire the divine likeness in creatures who would freely, faithfully image it. In that "spirit which came directly from God," the human person is capable of rising to God, and because of it sets forth God's glory "more perfectly than all the material heavens and earth could do besides" (pt. 1, chap. 5, p. 35). This is the original decree of God in humanity's regard, a determination both fixed and unalterable. But the self-evident reality is that "this decree was the law of God which man broke; and by violation of which he fell" (pt. 1, chap. 5, p. 35).

In Dunlavy's discussion of the fall, he makes explicit Shakerism's modification of the traditional notions of human depravity and status of the will. For him the fall is humanity's failure to reflect faithfully the divine image, the free choice of goodness. For "when man fell from God he fell into himself, from the government of the spirit, to that of the flesh" (pt. 1, chap. 5, p. 45). The choice of flesh over spirit constitutes the primal human dilemma which is a kind of slavery to an inferior motive, namely the passions.

But the *Passions* most prominent in human life are those animal sensations, or fleshly appetites and propensities arising from the connection of the spirit of man with the material body in the constitution of animal life. These move inconsiderately and impetuously, and seize with avidity the coveted object...By these mankind are governed in all their pursuits, until they are arrested by something of greater importance presented to the intellect and apprehended by it. All these may, in common language, be comprehended in the general term AFFECTIONS; but the above distinctions are not without their use. And to the last class pertain the affections and lusts of the flesh which all Christians crucify. (Pt. 1, chap. 5, p. 39)

In consequence of the failure of humanity to realize the primordial decree freely to image God (pt. 1, chap. 5, p. 33), there followed the decree of restoration, "executed in Christ, in his first and second appearing" (pt. 1, chap. 5, p. 36). By this remedy, God willed human recovery from the fall and its consequent inversion: the order of spirit over flesh. Therefore, recovery must not merely mend the order of the flesh, but recreate it in the order of Spirit.

Not indeed to restore Adam and his posterity into his first order in the flesh, or to mend that order, but to reinstate them into the favor of God, and in the line of their duty and happiness, in Christ the Second Adam, so much farther on their way — as many as will yield obedience to that plan. This decree is executed in Christ in his first and second appearing. (Pt. 1, chap. 5, p. 36)

Evangelical Soteriology

The issue of salvation has always been a stock theme of evangelical faith and the raison d'être of revivalism. Certainly, getting and staying saved was the singular concern of Dunlavy's own Kentucky Revival, where he and his colleagues circum-scribed the grounds and means of salvation to the gospel. It is not surprising, therefore, to hear Dunlavy reinforcing the cen-trality of traditional evangelical faith for salvation, now in a Shaker idiom.

> When man fell from God he fell from the govern-ment of the spirit to that of the flesh, from the gov-ernment of the judgement to that of the passions, and there he remains until arrested by the Gospel. (Pt. 1, chap. 5, p. 42)

Salvation in the Gospel

The "Gospel" is the comprehensive context in which Dunlavy deals with his soteriological themes. In his usage the term has an eschatological import, because he emphasizes the Pentecostal origins of the Gospel in the First Appearing and its fulfillment in the final age of the Second Appearing when the Christ Spirit proclaims to all the availability of forgiveness which leads to salvation.

> The gospel of Christ is the mean appointed by God for man's recovery and final redemption. It is the power of God to salvation, to everyone that believeth, and by it life and immortality are brought to light. By the gospel is made known who is the salvation of God to the ends of the earth. (Pt. 1, chap. 6, p. 47)

The Gospel alone is the remedy which, when received and obeyed, is calculated to furnish anyone with "power to regulate the affections, subdue the passions and crucify the lusts" (pt. 1, chap. 5, p. 39). By means of the therapy taught by the Gospel, men and women learn once again how to choose the superior motive over the inferior, thereby recovering the exercise of authentic freedom. This restoration is not intended for a few elect souls, but for anyone who would accept its healing power. And Dunlavy devotes much of his book to putting the Shakers on the liberal side of the issues of human depravity, status of the will, predestination, election, salvation by works as well as faith, and the universal availability of salvation.

> The Gospel is the only mean of recovery from all this ruin; and it is sent to the human race on the most liberal terms, excluding none who are willing, or who will be prevailed upon to receive salvation on God's terms. (Pt. 1, chap. 5, p. 45)

Against this ground of "the Gospel" as the only context for evangelical salvation, Dunlavy develops his evangelical christology, ecclesiology, and eschatology. Pursuing a logic that leads to Shakerism, he maps out the way of salvation with its origin in Christ and its terminus in the true Church of the Second Appearing.

> It is the work of God to draw souls to Christ. But it is evident he draws them through the Gospel, or in other words, by Christ himself set forth in the Gospel. Christ is the drawing of the Father, the loadstone by which the Father draws souls to himself. ...Thus the drawing of the Father is treasured up in Christ, and given to his ministers. (Pt. 1, chap. 10, p. 140)

Salvation in the Gospel of Christ/Christological Themes
The Gospel has the power to save because it is the revealed point of access to Christ the Savior.

> In the gospel is all necessary provision for man's salvation, being indeed the power of God to salvation,

> because Christ the power of God and salvation of God
> is therein ministered to men. (Pt. 1, chap. 6, p. 47)

In this evangelical context, Dunlavy takes up the delicate task of reexpressing Shaker christology in terms more acceptable to the orthodox ears of his Calvinist critics who accused the Shakers of supplanting Jesus with Ann. It is not clear whether Dunlavy himself shared their suspicions, but he succeeds in developing a Shaker christology alternative to Youngs' bisexual one, by avoiding all mention of Ann Lee's name. However, Dunlavy remains faithful to some constitutive insights of earlier Shaker christology, namely its pneumatological and exemplaristic features. At the same time, he calls his Calvinist critics' theory of imputed atonement into question, making an argument against it the major part of his enterprise.

Dunlavy unequivocally states that the first and radical ground of salvation is Jesus Christ, the crucified man, as he is preached in the Gospel (pt. 1, chap. 7, p. 66): "he is the true and only access to the Father" (pt. 1, chap. 7, p. 71). With this he meets the charges of his critics that the Shakers have relativitized the soteriological centrality of Jesus. Yet Dunlavy insists that however essential to the project of salvation Christ Jesus may be, he is not a substitute for the necessity of personal atonement for sin; rather he has become the model for such personal atonement.

> That Christ sustains the glorious character of redeemer and mediator between God and man is not to be disputed, and that he is the true and only medium of access to the Father is also true. But that he was our surety to God to pay in our room that debt in which we had failed, so as to release us from the payment, is quite another matter, unsupported in the Scriptures. (Pt. 1, chap. 7, p. 71)
> For there is no prospect in anyone being a partaker

with Christ in his salvation and glory, unless he first partake with him in his sufferings and death, unless he embrace the same faith of Christ to do the will of God, walking as he walked. (Pt. 1, chap. 7, p. 77)

As the model of salvation, Jesus died to "the nature of sin in himself" (pt. 1, chap. 10, p. 130), by which Dunlavy means the disorder of the sexual nature. Believers, then, are baptized into the death of Christ, "our leader and our example...that we might have fellowship with him in his sufferings and in his reward" (pt. 1, chap. 8, p. 94). For Dunlavy, salvation is the laboring process of following Christ manifested in Jesus through the bondage of the flesh and toward the liberation of the spirit — by way of celibacy. Furthermore, he brings the discussion of exemplaristic christology toward a more characteristically Shaker pneumatological expression by saying that it is in virtue of his divine anointing with God's Spirit, and his mandate to extend that anointing to his followers, that Jesus is the Christ.

And if we consider Christ as the advocate with the Father; whether we use the word ADVOCATE...to call to, or retain the Greek word Paraclete, to exhort, or comfort, it amounts to the same thing, he is given to the people to exhort, call and encourage them to come to God, in full confidence of his being as good as he had promised. Thus he is the mediator between God and man, an advocate with the Father calling them to come to God, and an exhorter and comforter with the people, encouraging them to come, showing them that the way is open making intercession for them. (Pt. 1, chap. 7, p. 76)

Salvation in the Gospel of the Church of Christ/ Ecclesiological Themes

The link between Dunlavy's exemplaristic christology and his ecclesiology is an implied pneumatology which becomes more explicit in his discussion of the Church of Christ as the only source of salvation.

> When Jesus was anointed with the Spirit, he alone was the only anointed priest of the Gospel, the only true habitation of God on earth until he made his sacrifice, and then his disciples were anointed with the same Spirit and became one with him: for he breathed on them, and said receive ye the Holy Ghost. Howbeit they were not fully commissioned or qualified to minister the Gospel to the people, until he had ascended to the Father and returned in the gift of the Holy Ghost, on the day of Pentecost. They were then fully empowered, according to the work of that day, to preach repentance and the remission of sins in his name, and to do all that work in the spiritual house. They were then one with Christ and with the Father, according to the work of that day: and these in their proper order and power are the true body of Christ, and the true Christ, having received the same anointing of the Father, as Jesus Himself. (Pt. 2, chap. 2, p. 218)

Because Dunlavy chooses not to discuss any other dramatic or extraordinary instance of this anointing than that of Jesus, his pneumatic christology becomes simply the foreword to the fuller expression of that christic anointing which is the Church. By celebrating the Church as the continuation of the anointing of Jesus as the Christ, Dunlavy has more than managed to safeguard Shakerism's essential faith. Moreover, he has intensified the keynote of all their theology: the primacy of the Holy Spirit. For Shakerism all things originate in the Spirit, are manifested in and by the Spirit, and ultimately return to the Spirit.

> As it was the anointing of the Holy Ghost that constituted Jesus the Anointed, or the Christ, which is the same, so the Church being anointed with the same, they were constituted the Anointed, the Christ. And the same authority, power, and office, ascribed to and possessed by the Church...received that anointing in its fullness which constituted Jesus the Christ, but the Christ collectively. (Pt. 2, chap. 2, p. 219)

The fundamental issue, therefore, is Spirit. This is the economic orientation of God toward the world for salvation. For its salvific labor, Spirit must employ an agent, that is anoint a servant, who, by receptivity to the Spirit, becomes its historical embodiment. The first instance of such Spirit embodiment was in Jesus, duly designated as Christ, the Anointed. His soteriological task was to extend that anointing to a greater body, no longer a single person, but many persons. This corporate person, the Church, was as truly and uniquely Christ as was Jesus. "Thus the true Church of Christ is very Christ, and possesses all the power of Christ as a Savior and Judge" (pt. 2, chap. 2, p. 219). By employing many biblical, and particularly Pauline, allusions, Dunlavy stresses over and over again the union of Christ, indeed the identity of Christ, with Church. He himself adds the emphasis to this classic passage from 1 Corinthians: "For as the body is one...*so also is Christ. For by one Spirit we are all baptized into one body*" (1 Cor 12:12-14; pt. 2, chap. 2, p. 219).

On pneumatic grounds, Dunlavy has established an identity between corporate christology and ecclesiology, just as, on the same pneumatic grounds, an identity was made between the charismatic anointing of Jesus and his disciples. Furthermore, he has established the essential necessity for the manifest, visible, physical expression of the Spirit, since Christ is always the embodiment of God's grace. Therefore, as Dunlavy says, people "cannot be initiated into union and fellowship with Christ, except in union with his body the Church" (pt. 2, chap. 2, p. 222), concluding that

> "wherever the true Church of Christ is, there is the true Christ of God."...And wherever a true Church of Christ is found, having regained the communion and unity of the Spirit...there is Christ in his second appearing. (Pt. 2, chap. 2, p. 219)

Salvation in the Gospel of the Church of Christ's Second Appearing/Eschatological Themes

In Christ's Second Appearing, the full revelation of God's decree of redemption is ultimately shown. This is the most liberal season of the Gospel because it is the last. This phase of evangelization "is already commenced" to call everyone to salvation and final judgment. In this age of eschatological fruitfulness the preaching of the Gospel, which has ever been the task of Christ, "will have its full effect" for "God will have his house filled, and no man will be left to perish without first having a fair opportunity to escape" (pt. 1, chap. 12, p. 193).

It is imperative to Dunlavy that this time which introduces a new dispensation be recognized. What dawns in this moment is "a new degree of light for the great work of redemption and what belongs to us is to be ready and obedient to his proposals...without being overly anxious about those which are not yet made known" (pt. 1, chap. 13, p. 195). In his analogy of gradual enlightenment, Dunlavy reiterates the Shakers' sense of unfoldment and understanding of history as the context of revelation. Indeed history is revelation: "to keep up with the time is what is required, and no more" (pt. 1, chap.

13, p. 196). This calls for a historical congruence, "fulfilling the duties as [time] passes along" (pt. 1, chap. 13, p. 196). The duty of this final age is to respond in freedom to the liberal gift of loving salvation willed by God. Accordingly, the task of this age is to seek the true Church in which Christ's Second Appearing is manifested, because only there is the Gospel of salvation truly known and proclaimed. Only there can the ministers of eschatological salvation be found.

> It is only in this living temple, the Church, that a sinner can find the new eschatological priesthood gathered for the ministry of forgiving sin.
>
> Thus believers in Christ are (not now a legal or ceremonial) but a holy priesthood. Not that each one of them is an appointed ministering priest; but the true priests of God are all among them, Jesus Christ being the high priest; and separated from them, there is no access to God for salvation. (Pt. 2, chap. 1, p. 214)

Dunlavy concedes therefore that God does elect certain persons in the economy of salvation to "execute certain labors in carrying on the work of redemption for the whole" (pt. 1, chap. 2, p. 159). In fact, it is this servant community with its ordered ministry which is the true Church, the embodiment of Christ's Second Appearing: the elect, who are finally to compose the Church of God in its happy and glorified state, in whom the decrees are to receive their special and final accomplishment (pt. 1, chap. 10, p. 157).

> Every duty or work necessary for the edification of the whole, must be done by some one or more; and every man is not capable to fitting every place. It is therefore no injury to the whole that God should elect...helpers of the faith of others. (Pt. 1, chap. 11, p. 159)

The true intention of God's election is to gather an eschatological community for the final ministry of salvation, who will
be its sign and living expression to the world.

> Accordingly we have the united testimony of the
> apostles in their writing, that Christ with his whole
> salvation dwells in his Church on earth; the Church
> is his peculiar people, a people for a possession or
> acquisition...that is, his temple or house wherein to
> offer sacrifice, make confession, and offer praise;
> therein are his priests to receive the offerings and
> make atonement; this same Church is his kingdom,
> the people, the members of which show forth the
> praise of him who has called them out of darkness
> into the light. These are the inhabitants of the
> kingdom of God, the kingdom of heaven on earth...
> the same heaven of which we are the citizens. (Pt.
> 2, chap. 2, p. 230)

Eschatological Ecclesiology/The True Church of Christ's Second Appearing

Union: The Sign of the True Church of Christ's Second Appearing

But now the question arises, "How are we to know the true
Church of Christ, and where shall we find them?" (pt. 2. chap. 3,
p. 235). The urgency of the question lies in the conviction that

> no faith, in whole or in part, separate from the one
> faith of the one body, the Church, can furnish and
> maintain sufficient motive to overcome sin, root and
> branch, because as long as anyone has hope or expec-
> tation that salvation possibly be found without the full
> cross, his faith is inadequate...no one member can live
> disconnected with the body. (Pt. 2, chap. 3, p. 235)

This relationship of salvation and union with the Church is a radical one. Indeed one must become the Church, for no one can "have the truth of the Church, mentally, while separate from the body," because the truth and substance would be lacking, "for want of union" (pt. 2, chap. 3, p. 236). This rich notion of union implies a profound and lifelong relationship to Christ, head and members, whereby one progressively travels out of the disposition, attitudes, and behaviors of sinfulness to salvation by a life of celibacy and community of goods. By exercising those free choices which turn one from exclusive selfishness in relationship to persons and things, one is restored to union with God and consequently to right relation to all else. But this transformation is impossible outside of the community designed for such renewal. One must be in union to learn union, and union can only be effected by the Spirit who is the source and power of union: Christ in the Second Appearing. Participating in the experience of manifest union, found in the only true Church, is the only way to salvation.

> Take away visible union of the member with the body, and the member must perish: for there can be no visible union extant, so as to support life, without a visible [sic]. The knowledge, therefore, of the true Church, and an open profession of the one faith are indispensable in attaining to final salvation, and full redemption. (Pt. 2, chap. 3, p. 236)

Having established the urgency for discovering the true Church of Christ's Second Appearing in the union of Believers, Dunlavy offers his readers its two clearest identifying features: its visible union in temporal things and its eschatological celibacy.

Manifestation of Union: Joint Interest
That "inimitable love and union prevail in the church of Christ, are manifested in a joint inheritance in all things tem-

poral as well as spiritual" (pt. 2, chap. 6, p. 265). The most indisputable evidence that Christ is with the Church is the living witness of love. For Dunlavy there are two correlations which follow from this fundamental reality: this love "must be satisfactorily manifested," and the concrete manifestation is union in all things (pt. 2, chap. 6, p. 266).

> But let it be granted that love is not known by intuitive knowledge; that the gift and sensation, or internal affection of love is not visible, or in the abstract, to the natural man, it can nevertheless be discovered in its operations; for as faith without works is dead being alone, so love without effects is a contradiction in terms. (Pt. 2, chap. 6, p. 266)

The immediate production of Christian love is the union of Believers, a point which Dunlavy supports with many Johannine references. "This union is of a different nature, separate and distinct from all the union" which exists in the world, because it is not the work of human hands. Rather it is the fruit of the one eschatological Spirit manifest in Christ's Second Appearing who realizes the unity of the Spirit in the bond of peace (pt. 2, chap. 6, p. 267). Neither is this union an abstract theological concept, but one effecting and manifesting a thoroughly renovated attitude in all the matters of concrete existence. "The world have no such union, neither can have," notes Dunlavy, "because they are governed by a different principle, incapable of producing it" — namely, the lust which separates and divides (pt. 2, chap. 6, p. 273). But the Spirit drains Believers out of the flesh and into that love which is the matrix of Gospel union, and which expresses itself in one body and enjoyment of "the mutual benefits of one consecrated and united interest and inheritance in all good things, whether temporal or spiritual" (pt. 2, chap. 6, p. 268).

The principle on which Believers are thus united is "no

other than the present operation of the Spirit of the one and only true God" (pt. 2, chap. 6, p. 270), concretely expressed in the form of "joint interest." This union in all things temporal as well as spiritual proves the Shakers to be "of God and in the Spirit of Christ" (pt. 2, chap. 6, p. 271), and is one of the pillars of Shakerism. Such "joint interest" implies that for covenanted members all property, possessions, and inheritance are freely and permanently ceded to the Society in return for the new inheritance of life in the union of Christ's Second Appearing. "It cannot be supported by any cause separate and distinct from the Spirit of Christ dwelling and acting in the people thus united" (pt. 2, chap. 6, p. 272). Dunlavy makes clear, however, that although "they only possess in common with their brethren, and claim no private property," no one is required to cede one's resources to the community "contrary to their own faith and best understanding." Rather joint interest is only the practice of those mature in their commitment: "until their faith is thus ripe for a united interest, believers are admitted to a full privilege in things spiritual, their separate interest notwithstanding" (pt. 2, chap. 6, p. 273).

If joint interest is the manifestation of the radical and all encompassing union of which Dunlavy speaks, it is clearly the fruit of a wholly regenerated nature effected only by the power and presence of the eschatological Spirit of Christ, for

> no human wisdom—no philosophy—no philanthropy—no degree of order of godliness, short of crucifying the flesh with its affections and lusts, each one denying himself, taking up his cross, renouncing the old generation and following Christ in the regeneration, can ever lay a proper foundation for this union. (Pt. 2, chap. 6, p. 269)

Condition for Union: Celibacy

The second indisputable sign of the true Church Dunlavy

offers to those who search for its eschatological salvation is celibacy. If union is the effect of the presence of Christ's Second Appearing, and union in all things temporal as well as spiritual its undeniable sign, then celibacy is the fundamental condition for such union. Since, Dunlavy argues, "the love of God unites but the lust of the flesh separates and divides" (pt. 2, chap. 6, p. 268), then it is clear that union can only be realized by those who have suffered the sacrificial transformation from fleshly life to spiritual life. Observing that for the spirit to be saved the destruction of the flesh must be made to God, Dunlavy describes the living sacrifice of self offered by the Believer who would come into the mystery of union. Alluding to the rites of the Old Testament he says:

> Let us now inquire how these sacrifices will apply to those which men have to offer when they believe the Gospel in the presence of the Gospel priest, or minister of Christ. He lays his hands on the head of the beast to be sacrificed, which is his own carnal nature, and there confesses his sins, robes the beast that it may be burnt on the altar of God; that is, having confessed his sins, he set himself, soul and body, to resist the practice and nature of evil, and thus to crucify the carnal mind that it may die forever...thus denying himself and taking up his cross, he follows Christ, not doing his own but the will of the Father in heaven. Thus the man gives himself up wholly a living sacrifice for the destruction of the flesh, that the spirit may be saved. There must be a whole surrender. (Pt. 1, chap. 9, p. 100)

Dunlavy does some refining of his apparent antagonism toward the flesh, modifying his typically Shaker vehemence about sex by saying that

> evil is not originally or primarily in the order of the flesh or in the corresponding union between the male and female, but is that nature...received in and by the fall, consisting in a spirit of disobedience to God, and a subversion of his order and appointments. (Pt. 2, chap. 7, pp. 281-282)

The distortion of the passions or sexual appetite then can only be rehabilitated by the discipline of celibacy. But the intensity of Dunlavy's conviction is only made clear in light of his eschatological point of view. Since the fundamental disorder constituting the fall is the subversion of the spirit to the flesh, it is the explicit intent of eschatological salvation to invert this disorder, that is, to bring the flesh into submission to the spirit by the regenerative life of celibacy. The issue is not how to channel, discipline, or consecrate sex to serve a higher principle, but how to move out of its domain entirely to the spiritual plane.

Therefore, not even Christian marriage, however religiously understood, is appropriate to the new age, since the eschaton is by definition the end of fleshly existence. In an allusion to the Gospel prophecy concerning the "abomination of desolation" that will stand in the holy place at Christ's Second Appearing (Matt. 24:15), Dunlavy argues that it is marriage: "to introduce marriage, therefore, or natural generation into the Church of Christ, is to put it where it ought not to be" (pt. 2, chap. 7, p. 279). Honorable and innocent in its own order, "without abuse" marriage has nothing evil in it; "but it does not belong to the order of Christ" (pt. 2, chap. 7, p. 281).

Since marriage perpetuates the systems, habits, structures, and mentality of the world, it is precisely the principal convention which supports the life of the old fleshly order. Because it is not perceived by Dunlavy as a Gospel relation, it is an inappropriate way to order relationships in the true Church of Christ. Rather, celibacy is the distinctly eschatological mode of Gospel relation which demonstrates the newness of life in the Spirit and as such, it is in defense of a radical profession of faith. Dunlavy says, "if Christianity must not be professed in that order or to that degree, that it will condemn the world, it cannot exist on the earth, for Christ is not of the world" (pt. 2, chap. 9, p. 303).

> A fundamental error among those who profess the Christian name, is not to distinguish, properly and radically, between Christ and Adam, or the old creation and the new, and between Christ and Moses, or the Law and the Gospel. ...But the Scriptures make it evident, that the order of Christ is not the order of the old creation, in any of its different forms, insomuch that those who follow Christ are no more of this world. (Pt. 2, chap. 7, p. 277)

The most infallible mark of eschatological salvation, therefore, is the dramatic renovation caused by reorienting the fundamental instincts of possession and generation. This transformation is evidenced in the two indisputable characteristics of the true Church of Christ: its joint interest, or community of goods, and celibacy. These two signs, according to Dunlavy, are the unmistakable proof that the Spirit of Christ is truly present among a people realizing that union which is the authentic seal of the true Church.

> Finally, whatever work, under the name Christianity, does not in its progress, give power over all sin and the darkness which leads to it, so as to produce a people who are saved in the present tense, falls short of being the true gospel...This is the sweeping rule of Christ and his apostles, which puts a period eventually, to all the contentious debates, about who is a Christian and who is not. (Pt. 2, chap. 4, p. 251)

As was the intention of God's eschatological decree, the Second Appearing of Christ has more than restored human nature to its prelapsarian state. The eschatological Spirit has brought humanity to the resurrection.

Consequence of Union: Resurrection

The renovation of Believers effected by Christ's Second Appearing is, Dunlavy contends, the resurrection. This new state of existence is a transformed relationship within the most fundamental and dialectic structure of reality: the flesh and the spirit.

> For what can mean these new heavens and new earth, but a new state and order of things, both in outward things, and in things relating to the Spirit. (Pt. 2, chap. 6, p. 274)

What is at issue in Dunlavy's sense of the resurrection is not a reanimation of the flesh, but its annihilation as the principle and motive of life, since "flesh and blood cannot inherit the kingdom of God."

> And the Scripture makes not provision for any qualification of that unequivocal expression; for neither is there any doctrine in revelation, nor any principle in natural reason, philosophy or morals, to teach us that matter can, by method or degree of modification, be transformed into spirit; all such conceptions, therefore, are at best vague and groundless. (Pt. 3, chap. 1, p. 333)

Dunlavy is aware that

> the foregoing doctrine bears hard against the children of this world, whose only dependence is the

flesh, who trust in it for their existence and continued succession here, and finished happiness in heaven. For, cut off the flesh and the world is ruined; its children are enervated; they have no longer any source or existence, no longer any comfort or lively spring of action or pursuit, in this stage of action; and their grand concentration, hope and prospect of perfected happiness (most of them) in the next world, is the resurrection and reanimation of the flesh, or natural body; so that their great confidence is in the flesh, without which they have no hope. (Pt. 2, chap. 10, p. 319)

Yet it is precisely away from natural, fleshly existence that Believers are called in the progress of the resurrection because "the flesh is not to be redeemed from its loss, purified and saved, but to be crucified" (pt. 2, chap. 10, pp. 317-318). Humanity's attachment to life in and of flesh has arrested their development toward the Spirit. People are so identified with bodily life, its exigencies and orientations, that their vision of the life to which they are called by the eschatological Gospel is obstructed, and they misperceive the more radical possibilities of their own being. Dunlavy contends, therefore, that the death of the flesh by the cross of celibacy frees men and women to realize their higher mode of being in the Spirit.

But the truth may be illustrated in this particular by a man in Christ. He is said to be a new creature; not because there is any change in the identity of his existence; he is the same person as before, having the same soul and body. The change is not physical; he has new objects and pursuits, is converted from the flesh to the Spirit, from the old order of things in Adam, to the new order in Christ, having renounced and put off the old man with his deeds,

> which are corrupt according to the deceitful lusts,
> and put on the new man, who after God, is created
> in righteousness and true holiness. So when Christ
> shall possess that kingdom on earth which is
> promised, and every individual in it shall be thus
> renewed, such a happy change in spirit will be pro-
> duced, and as the effect thereof, in outward econ-
> omy, as is fitly represented by new heavens and a
> new earth. (Pt. 2, chap. 6, p. 274)

The theme of the new heavens and new earth recapitulates
much of Dunlavy's thought and points to the consequence of
the new life in the Spirit born of the death of the flesh. This
new state of affairs is the resurrection not understood in the
physical sense, but in a spiritual sense which changes the very
soul of the Believer.

> To be in the resurrection, to rise from the dead and
> to be accounted worthy, are one and the same
> thing...which could not be truly of any resurrection
> of the body, literally: But is strictly applicable to
> that moral or spiritual change which is effected in
> the soul by becoming one with Christ in the Spirit,
> so passing from death to life. ...The resurrection is
> stated as the medium whereby they become chil-
> dren of God, which is confessedly no other than
> receiving Christ and being alive in him. (Pt. 2,
> chap. 8, p. 289)

The Second Appearance of Christ inaugurates the new Age
of the Spirit which marks the surpassing of the flesh as a vehicle
for divine disclosure. The flesh, in Christ's First Appearing, was
the very symbol and manifestation of God's saving power, since
in that prior phase of revelation, Christ was known in the body

of Jesus. But Dunlavy contends that revelation has progressed to reveal Christ now, in this eschatological phase, as Spirit: "Head of the new spiritual creation" (pt. 2, chap. 10, p. 319).

> That which is of the Spirit is Spirit; they, therefore, who are born of the Spirit, or are regenerated into Christ who is a quickening spirit, are spiritual and inherit spiritual bodies of incorruption and immortality. (Pt. 3, chap. 5, p. 376)

Dunlavy's conclusions concerning the eschatological resurrection differ from the orthodox Christian faith in several ways which highlight his distinctly Shaker perspective. He insists that it is the death of the flesh. Therefore, resurrection does not imply the rising of the flesh of the body, but rather its ultimate annihilation; as such, it is a radically pneumatological term, describing the recreation of the human spirit in the Christ Spirit. It is not a state to be realized after the death of the body in an afterlife, but rather after the death of the flesh, particularly in its generative and possessive instinct, in this life. Ultimately, resurrection is a progressive state of being, in which one gradually moves into higher degrees of union with the Christ Spirit.

> It is vain to argue that these happy effects are to take place at some future period, for the apostle brings the matter right down to the present tense, to take effect now and henceforth, as the foundation work of future increase and glory. (Pt. 2, chap. 5, p. 260)

Such eschatological union with Christ in the resurrection is known by those who comprise the new Spiritual Body and

> reigns at this instant among the believers who have the faith of the second appearing of Christ...and it

is the effect of the Spirit of Christ, in the Gospel,
and the necessary product of that Spirit, without
which there can be no true Church." (Pt. 2, chap.
6, p. 275)

In the *Manifesto*, we find an expression of the ecclesiological eschatology prevalent in nineteenth-century Shakerism.
Rather than focusing on the eschatological significance of
Ann Lee, as did Benjamin Seth Youngs, Dunlavy developed a
pneumatological ecclesiology as the way to perceive Christ's
Second Appearing. Against the background of his evangelical
soteriology with its emphasis on the eschatological Gospel,
Dunlavy described the Millennial Church as the only one
wherein the true Gospel of salvation for the new age could be
found. Only Christ and the anointed of Christ can minister
the salvation of the eschaton; therefore it is imperative to recognize the presence of Christ in the Church deputized to for-
give sin and render salvation. The two indisputable signs of
the presence of Christ in the true Church are community of
goods and celibacy. Where Believers have been transformed
from the demands of the flesh to the freedom of the Spirit,
there is the Second Appearing of Christ.

Most particularly, Dunlavy establishes an intricate series of
correlations and identities between God and Christ, Christ
and the Church, the Church and the eschatological state of
the resurrection. The mode of linkage for his complex theological vision is the motif of "union." By consistently working
through this notion in the *Manifesto*, he has developed a rich
representation of the Shaker eschaton as the coming of the
Christ Spirit in the true Church of Shakers. In the simplest
and most radical terms, Dunlavy claims that it is the very
union of Believers which is Christ's Second Appearing.

The faith and participation of the second appearance of Christ are necessary to keep the unity of the
Spirit in the bond of peace.

It is therefore indispensibly necessary, that they
who are able to keep the true order of God should
possess the faith, and actually partake of Christ in
his second appearing. (Pt. 2, chap. 7, pp. 277-278)

Dunlavy's contribution to nineteenth-century Shaker eschatology is a refinement of the ecclesiology of the Society; he con-
centrates on its explicitly pneumatological foundations and
communitarian structure. In this way he has drawn a portrait of
the Second Appearing of Christ as the union of Believers.

Thus we have performed what was proposed, to
show what are the distinguishing characteristics of
the Church, or body, of Christ, by which they can be
known and distinguished from all other people —
They are found to be a people in the possession of
that gospel which giveth them power over all sin, so
that in the progress of the work they cease to commit
sin, or do any iniquity — a people living in the exercise of such love and union as no other people can
imitate, being the product of no other cause, no
other spirit than that of which they are possessed —
the Spirit of God. (Pt. 2, chap. 10, p. 325)

GREEN'S MILLENNIAL CHURCH:
THE SECOND APPEARING OF CHRIST AS
THE DAWN OF THE MILLENNIUM

Apologist of Shakerism

Calvin Green had the unusual distinction of being born a Shaker. Just before his birth at Hancock, Massachusetts, in 1780, his pregnant mother was converted by Ann Lee herself, and the child was named for one of the illustrious original Shakers, Elder Calvin Harlow. Growing up in the early Society, Green wholly imbibed its spirit. His clarity of thought and expressiveness in both the spoken and written word contributed to his great missionary success on behalf of the Society. Green was among those responsible for the Savory, Massachusetts, and Sodus Bay, New York, communities and was active in the evangelization of Vermont. His literary talent also served his efforts to communicate an understanding of Shaker faith to the outside world.

The most avid chronicler ever of Shaker history, Green wrote *A Biographical Account of the Life, Character, and Ministry of Father Joseph Meacham, the Primary Leader in Establishing the United Order of the Millennial Church*, published in 1827, and his own *Biographic Memoir*. Begun in 1861 but never published, his memoir is the most comprehensive work by any Believer in the genre of autobiography, comprising three volumes of 795 manuscript pages. (It is now in the Shaker library at Sabbathday Lake, Maine.) He also collaborated with Seth Youngs Wells on other publishing projects, among them *A Brief Exposition of the Established Principles, and Regulations of the United Society of Believers Called Shakers* (1830), reprinted and reedited several times till 1895. Furthermore, Green was responsible for the 1856 revision of the *Testimony of Christ's Second Appearing* (Youngs). It is understandable why his writing is credited with greater influence in the Society than either of his predecessors, Youngs or Dunlavy. As one Shaker scholar writes,

> It may be argued, and convincingly so, that Elder Calvin, like Elder Benjamin lacked the formal theological education which had been Elder John Dunlavy's, but it is the former two, not the latter, whose work was not only looked upon as definitive, but was most read and quoted both among Believers and by the world.[39]

Toward a Shaker Millennium

Green's most celebrated work is a major contribution to the development of nineteenth-century Shaker eschatology called *A Summary View of the Millennial Church, or United Society of Believers, (Commonly Called Shakers.) Comprising the Rise, Progress and Practical Order of the Society; Together with General Principles of Their Faith and Testimony.* This work, too, was co-authored with Seth Youngs Wells. Published in 1823, it was reedited in 1848 to include an elaboration of the Church history section. The two editions reflect changes within Shakerism in several interesting ways. The earlier one reflects the defensive attitude prevalent in the early society and expends energy answering charges against the character of Mother Ann and the first Elders. The later one, printed during the period of communal revival known as Mother Ann's Work, reflects some of the spiritualist concerns of that period as well as highlighting the greater assurance Shakers had achieved in relation to the world.

The change in the Shakers' religious awareness during this phase is mirrored in different statements from the Preface to the first and second editions. The original reads "not a single principle of faith ever advanced by Mother Ann and the first Elders, of which we have any knowledge, but is still maintained by the Society, without any variation whatsoever" (p. x). This was replaced in the second edition to say:

> As to the real substance of the gospel of salvation, it
> was fully revealed to the first witnesses of Christ's
> Second Appearing; but as the work of salvation
> advances, the light becomes more clear, and the
> truth appears more plain. (P. iv)

The light and truth of which Green speaks refers to the growing understanding of Christ's Second Appearing. As Meacham, Youngs, and Dunlavy had each contributed to an explicitly ecclesiological reading of the Society's eschatology, so Green will add to the reflection by developing more fully what he considers to be the exemplaristic features of the Millennial Church. In this way he advances the Shakers' understanding of their eschatological purpose by turning them toward the world as witnesses to the effects of life lived in the eschatological Christ Spirit. No longer on the defensive about the peculiarities of their faith, the Shakers, through Green's voice, present themselves as heralds and models of the millennium now dawning in the world.

> The present age of the world is an age of wonders.
> The most extraordinary changes, revolutions and
> remarkable events are rapidly rolling on through the
> physical, political, moral and religious world, that
> were ever known on earth. These premises, we
> believe, will generally be admitted. It appears to be
> the prevailing sentiment and expectation among
> nearly all ranks and orders of people, that something
> wonderful is about to take place, that there will be
> such a revolution of public sentiment, and such a
> reformation will be effected in the various branches
> of human economy as never has been exhibited in
> the world since the creation of man.
> These expectations are evidently effected by the
> operations of Divine Providence upon the hearts of

the people, and are manifestly the precursors and signals of coming events. These events can be truly understood in no other light than as allusions to the period of Christ's Second Coming. (*Millennial Church*, 1848 Introductory Remarks, p. 1)

Green's work, like Youngs' and Dunlavy's, is a comprehensive statement of the faith of the United Society of Believers. But in order to focus on the particular contribution he makes to the Shaker understanding of Christ's Second Appearing, those sections of the *Millennial Church* will be cited which repeat the insights of the previously treated Shaker writers, and I will concentrate on the last part of his book where he develops his particular proposition on the millennial and pneumatological character of the Shaker Church. With the exception of two passages from the introduction to the second edition, the original 1823 text will be used.

The major theologians of early-nineteenth-century Shakerism evolved an ecclesiological language to make their eschatological statements: Youngs with a christological accent, Dunlavy more consistently ecclesiological with an accent on communitarianism. Green's work differs from his predecessors' in two significant ways. First, he advances the Believers' millennial eschatology by accenting the ecclesiological pneumatology at the heart of Shakerism: it is the work of the Christ Spirit in the Church which absorbs Green. Furthermore, while the two former writers were preoccupied with the Church's self-understanding, Green is now more interested in the relationship of the Church to the world — an issue that will engage later nineteenth-century Shakerism. With Green, the Society exhibits greater security and self-assurance, indeed, even a daring confidence that the course it has charted is to become the way of the world.

Calvin Green believed the Shakers offered the world a millennial blueprint for the regenerated social order. But even more, he was convinced that they offered access to the source of reformation: the rebirth of the human soul in the Christ Spirit. Therefore, Green exposes an eschatological pneumatology as the mystical foundation of the transfigured society, the living model of which was the Millennial Church. The Shakers' vivid belief in the availability of the Christ Spirit to transform the sinful structures of the world gave them enormous energy for creating and sustaining the exemplaristic societies of the Shaker Order. In fact, they began to see themselves not so much as set apart from the irredeemable world, but rather as set before the world as the model and inspiration of its own redemption. The Shakers, therefore, began to turn toward the world, holding out both the challenge and the promise that the United Society embodied the form of the new human society.

In this posture the Shakers were aligned with many other advocates of social reform, since much of the enthusiasm of the Second Great Awakening with its notably eschatological strain was channeled into various humanitarian movements. Revivals wed reform in areas as diverse as temperance, Sabbath observance, world peace, vice, women's rights, slavery, the conditions of penal institutions, and educational innovations.[40] But the revivalists were often postmillennialists, who assumed that the age of peace and justice would precede Christ's Second Appearing. Therefore their approach to social reform was incremental and ameliorative, patiently and hopefully correcting or rectifying the abuses of the old order, rather than waiting passively for the catastrophe which would inaugurate the new. However much men and women were enlisted to prepare the world for Christ's advent, the preparations brought changes in continuity with the past.

The Shakers, on the other hand, nearly alone of all American millennialists, claimed the Second Appearing had already occurred. They also believed that human history as a whole would improve as reforms were introduced, until at last the reign of peace and justice would be fully present. For them, the Advent of Christ was both an event in the past and a progressive unfolding of the Christ Spirit in the present, oriented toward an endless and universal realization. Unlike other social reformers who actively labored to improve the old world, the Shakers believed the present world with all its structures and conventions had come to an end. Therefore they engaged themselves in modeling the eschatological societies of the new age. Their highly distinctive craftsmanship and folk art created a culture which showcased the revolutionary gender and racial equality celebrated and fostered within their societies. Not only was there absolute equality between men and women in leadership and governance, but only the Shakers included both Blacks and Jews within their settlements. Moreover they protested slavery, war, and the range of social disorders plaguing the nation, offering not simply impassioned words, but an alternative way of life believed to model those right relations which would bring heaven to earth.[41]

In an exceptional way, Calvin Green advanced Shakerism's eschatological thought to the frontier of dialogue and relationship with the progressive secular movements of his day. By developing a sense of the broad panorama of the Spirit's eschatological designs, Green helped move Believers from an introspective and defensive posture to a dialogic one, thereby opening them to a more expansive understanding of Christ's Second Appearing and the exemplaristic function of the Millennial Church in its regard. Indeed, it was by exploring the specifically millennial situation of the Church and the world that Green brought a more highly developed eschatological pneumatology to light, for he was convinced that

> the events relating to Christ's Second Appearance,
> of which we are more particularly to treat in this
> volume, are rapidly progressing towards their

accomplishment, in many and various ways. (1848
Introductory Remarks, p. 2)

The Millennial Church

Features of the Millennium

Green considers "The Second Appearing of Christ" by enumerating
the several facets of the eschatological event, which, he insists, can
only be understood by those who are in the work. He observes that
the great dawning of new light in the social and political realm is
seen by many to be the inauguration of the millennium itself, in the

> societies for the abolition of slavery, missionary and
> bible societies, and humane and benevolent soci-
> eties of every description, together with the exten-
> sive and general diffusion of principles of civil and
> religious liberty. (Pt. 5, chap. 1, p. 200)

But he further observes that, apart from the Shakers, there has
been no corresponding revolution of the Christian religion in
this millennial age, either in essential faith or in practice.

> As the latter day of glory has been the theme of
> patriarchs and prophets, of poets and philosophers,
> of almost every age and as it has been held up to the
> view of mankind by the promises of God, ever since
> the fall of man, and most pointedly confirmed by
> Jesus Christ and his inspired apostles: it is certainly
> rational, as well as scriptural, to believe that it will
> produce by far the greatest revelation that the world
> ever yet witnessed. (Pt. 5, chap. 1, p. 200)

Therefore, Green isolates what he considers to be those radically new elements of Christianity in its eschatological phase,

revealed in the particular features of the Second Coming. He coherently delineates the fourfold nature of Christ's Second Appearing as pneumatic, gradual, revealed in the female, and radically regenerative, and subsequently explores its concrete manifestations as they are known in the seven moral principles of the Millennial Church. Green's unique insight into the eschatology of Shakerism will be disclosed in the explication of his program. By intensifying the pneumatological character of the Second Appearing, he was able to present it as a dramatically progressive event of which the Millennial Church was the first instance — and even more, the essential paradigm of its universal realization. In this way, he offers a description of Christ's Second Appearing as the dawn of the millennium.

Christ's Second Appearing: In the Spirit

As one alleging to stand in the revelation of Christ's Second Appearing, Green claims a warrant to describe its authentic features. He begins by establishing its essentially pneumatological ground, noting that "the second coming of Christ, [is] not the appearance of the same personal Being, but a manifestation of the same Spirit. This [is] illustrated by various similitudes, which also points out the increasing work of his kingdom" (pt. 5, chap. 2, title). Here Green states the essential Shaker understanding of christology:

> As God is a Spirit, so his work, pertaining to the restoration of fallen man, is a spiritual work. And as the first appearing of Christ, to take upon himself human nature, and declare his mission, was in the flesh; so his second appearing, for the redemption of his people, must be in the Spirit.
>
> The word of Christ is derived from the Greek word which signifies Anointed. Jesus being anointed with that Divine Spirit which proceeded from God, and which contained the elements of

> eternal life, was constituted the Christ of God; that
> is, the anointed of God. Wherever that Divine
> Spirit exists, there is Christ. (Pt. 5, chap. 2, p. 201)

As we have seen with Youngs and Dunlavy, the eschatological Spirit-christology of the Shakers redefines the meaning of
the body. It no longer has any reference to flesh, as it did in
relation to Christ's First Appearing in the body of Jesus. Now
the term body refers to an entirely New Creation which has
no fleshy ties or qualities: the corporate body of the new
Church, "his true and living body" (pt. 5, chap. 2, p. 202). It is
the mission of the Christ Spirit to quicken and anoint a body
for salvation — first in one, and through that one to the many.
Therefore, Green concurs with his colleagues that the logical
consequence of Spirit-christology is a Spirit-ecclesiology,
where the anointing is to be found in the Millennial Church
for the world's salvation, in the dispensation of the fullness of
time (pt. 5, chap. 2, p. 202). The Spirit, therefore, is the
ground of the millennium, and although he elaborates other
features at greater length, it will be seen that each of them in
turn is at root pneumatological.

Christ's Second Appearing: In Progress
The next feature of Christ's Second Appearing is its progressive character: "the second manifestation of Christ [is] not
instantly universal, but gradual and progressive, like the rising
of the sun" (pt. 5, chap. 3, title). Green addresses the common
assumption that the *parousia* will be a sudden, public event of
universal realization. This expectation is supported by the
often quoted prooftext: "They shall see the son of man coming
in the clouds of Heaven, with power and great glory" (Matt.
24:30). But Green appeals for a more subtle understanding of
the prophecy, aided by the insights of those who claim to
stand in its fulfillment. The Shakers held that the eschatologi-

cal "cloud" in question is "a figure used to express a multitude" (pt. 5, chap. 3, p. 207). That multitude was none other than the great numbers of men and women who had had the experience of the new birth and had come to live in the real presence of Christ's Second Appearing. The *parousia*, then, is a social and corporate event whose first instance was the Millennial Church, but whose influence would gradually extend to the world.

Second, Green repeats "as Christ, the anointed of God, is a Spirit, and can only be seen and known in the spirit; therefore, his kingdom must be spiritual and divine; not natural and sensual" (pt. 5, chap. 3, p. 207). The appearance of Christ, then, must be in the spirits of persons who have received the one same anointing, and not in a particular, physical body of a personal being. If the latter were the case, the event could not be, as it is destined to be, universal, omnipresent, or transtemporal, but infinite, local, and relative — not formally different from Christ's First Appearing and therefore not really eschatological at all.

> But if we consider the Christ as the elemental spirit of eternal life, difficulty is at once removed; because upon this principle, that Spirit can appear in many places at the same time, however distant or differently situated. (Pt. 5, chap. 3, p. 208)

For Green, the things relating to Christ's Second Coming and the finishing mystery of God, must be of a spiritual, corporate, and progressively universal nature. Calling into question the literalism with which most Christians read the millennial prophecies, he insists that

> the ideas formed in the mind of man, concerning the coming of Christ in the natural clouds, and appearing visible to the natural eye, are merely nat-

> ural conceptions.... It is true that, in the progress of
> his work, "every eye shall see him"...but they will
> see him with the eyes of the soul, not of the body.
> (Pt. 5, chap. 2, p. 208)

Therefore he calls for an awakening of eschatological consciousness with its new perspectives, suggesting a more appropriate way of envisioning the dim realities coming to light in
the dawn of the millennial day.

> The light of the millennial day is as gradual and
> various, in its commencement and progress, as the
> light of the natural day: and, like this, cannot possi-
> bly take place throughout the world at once, any
> more than the light of sun can be seen at once over
> the face of the whole earth. It appears to be the pre-
> vailing opinion among those who are looking for
> the millennium that the preparation for that day is
> to be finished over the whole world first; and that
> the second coming of Christ is to take place in a
> similar manner, and become at once universal. This
> idea is wholly inconsistent with reason, and has no
> foundation in truth. (Pt. 5, chap. 3, p. 211)

To direct the vision of those who seek the millennium as the
sign of Christ's Second Appearing, Green points to many "prov-
idential events which are evidently preparatory to the introduction of this new era to the world" (pt. 5, chap. 3, p. 211).
Among these he notes increasing religious tolerance; intensified
peace advocacy; the variety of liberal social and political initiatives, most significantly the Abolitionist movement; and ongoing religious revivals (pt. 5, chap. 3, pp. 211ff.).

These events herald the approaching millennium, calling
sleepers to wakefulness. But to be actually in the millennium,

one must take up the eschatological work of the new day — by which Green means becoming a Shaker.

> Some seem to be aware that these events are preparatory to the millennium, and view them as evident signs of the coming of Christ, while they are utterly unconscious that the preparation and the real work of the day, are both in actual progression, at the same time, agreeable to the similitude already noticed: the work of rising from spiritual sleep, of being convinced of the need of a Savior, and of lifting up the head and looking for redemption in Christ's Second Coming, are all very different from receiving and walking in him, and being in the real work of the kingdom; yet all these are necessary, and pertain to the work of the millennial day. The forementioned events are evident preparations and actual signs of the approach of that day to an extensive increase, which, in a limited degree, has already commenced. (Pt. 5, chap. 3, p. 212).

The second feature of Christ's Second Appearing, then, is its progressive nature, witnessed in its stages of preparation in the world in various social movements of moral reform, and in its actual, however initial, realization in the Millennial Church. In a more profound way, however, the progressive feature of the Second Appearing is a function of its more fundamental pneumatological nature, since it is precisely the appearing of Christ as Spirit which is gradually manifesting itself in and to the whole world.

Christ's Second Appearing: In the Female

The third feature of Christ's Second Appearing is "the manifestation of Christ in the Female," which Green must reconcile with the patriarchal disposition of mainstream

Christianity. Calling to mind the foremothers of salvation —
Miriam, Deborah, Esther — Green asks the disconcerting
question whether it debases the pride of fallen man to be saved
through the instrumentality of a woman. Furthermore, he
posits resistance to such an idea as an expression of the primordial disorder between the sexes which is the very root of
sin. Indeed, it is to heal this fundamental sexual disorder — in
its psychological, physical, and spiritual dimensions — which
is the purpose of the redemptive, eschatological "anointing."
Therefore, it was as necessary for this anointing to be experienced in the order of the female as it was in the order of the
male, because it is in their reconciled and renovated sexuality
that human persons realize their true spiritual destiny.

> Since then, Christ must appear in every female,
> as well as in every male, before they can be saved;
> and since that Divine Spirit has appeared in one
> man, whom God has chosen as the Captain of our
> salvation, and an example of righteousness to all
> men; is it not reasonable and consistent that the
> same anointing power (which is Christ) should also
> appear in a woman, and distinguish her as a leader,
> and an example of righteousness to all women?
> It may be asked, How can Christ appear in a
> woman? With the same propriety we might ask, how
> can Christ appear in man? Christ is a Spirit: "The
> Lord is the Spirit." In that Spirit is contained the
> only power of salvation. If Christ could not appear in
> a man, then no man could be saved; so also, if Christ
> could not appear in a woman, then no woman could
> be saved. Christ first appeared in Jesus of Nazareth,
> by which he was constituted the head of the new and
> spiritual creation of God. The Spirit of Christ was in
> the primitive church; and the Spirit of Christ is also
> in every one of his true and faithful followers. The

> Spirit of Christ is the same, whether revealed in man,
> woman or child. (Pt. 5, chap. 4, p. 216)

Once again Green moves toward the fundamental pneumatology behind the particularly female character of Christ's Second Appearing and in so doing makes two affirmations. First, that salvation requires the very presence of the Christ Spirit "to appear" in a person — that is, demonstrably to anoint and effect the radical transformation of each woman or man. Second, since men and women are the manifestation in the natural world of the bipolar nature of Christ in the spiritual world, it is necessary that the Spirit of salvation ordained for the female come from that dimension and economic relation of Christ. Therefore Green, like Youngs, will also argue that the first instance of this millennial innovation happened through the instrumentality of Ann Lee, who was the female form of Christ's Second Appearing. She was

> a chosen vessel, occupied as an instrument, by the
> Spirit of Christ, the Lord from Heaven, in which
> the second appearance of that Divine Spirit was
> ushered into the world. It is the Spirit which has
> constituted her immortal part the second pillar in
> the new and spiritual creation; it is the Spirit which
> is the image and likeness of the Eternal Mother, and
> which is, in reality, the true Bride of the Lamb, and
> first Mother of all the children of Christ. The apos-
> tles saith, "We preach Christ the Power of God and
> the Wisdom of God." But the Spirit of Wisdom in
> Christ, could not be manifested in her true charac-
> ter on earth, as the Mother Spirit in the work of
> regeneration, until she was revealed in the female,
> as a Mother in Christ. (Pt. 5, chap. 4, p. 219)

Here again, Green reiterates the pneumatological significance of this feature: it is to reveal the "Spirit of Wisdom" as the "Mother Spirit" that the Second Appearing is accomplished in a woman. But it must be noted that Green is not equating eschatological salvation with the redemption of woman; rather, the redemption of woman by Christ's Second Appearing in the female establishes the conditions by which the ultimate redemption of the race may be achieved, namely, the new spiritual union of the sexes.

> This spiritual union between male and female, in the body and in the head of the church, is that which the apostle calls a great mystery. And indeed it is a great mystery to the lost children of men, who seem to have no conception of any other union between the male and female, than that which is natural, according to the order to the flesh. Nor do they seem to know any other design in the creation of the female, nor any other essential use for her than that of carnal enjoyment in a sexual union, and the production of offspring through that medium. But the work of Christ, being a spiritual work, the union must therefore be spiritual; and it is most impossible for souls to come into this work, and enjoy this union, unless the Spirit of Christ become their life.
>
> As the true church of Christ, which is his body, is composed of male and female, as its members, and as there must be a correspondent spiritual union between the male and female, to render the church complete, as a spiritual body; so it is essentially necessary that such a spiritual union should exist in the head of that body, which is Christ; otherwise there could be no source from which such a correspondent, spiritual union could flow to the body. (Pt. 5, chap. 4, p. 216)

Green's pneumatology has a subtlety which reveals the radical influence that the bipolar sexual paradigm had on all things Shaker — even to the relative gender of the Holy Spirit:

> It is proper here, that in all languages, the term Holy Ghost is the same as Holy Spirit, and is generally expressed by a substantive in the neuter gender, which, of itself implies neither male nor female. The application of masculine or feminine terms to the Holy Spirit must depend on its relative manifestations, and its operation in the line of male or female. (Pt. 5, chap. 4, p. 218)

On this pneumatological note Green reiterates the basic theme of his eschatological pneumatology, reminding the reader, "we worship neither man nor woman but we honor and obey the Spirit of Christ, whether revealed in man, woman or child" (pt. 5, chap. 4, p. 215). Therefore, as the feature of progress simply modified the more fundamentally pneumatological character of Christ's Second Appearing, so will the feature of the female. For what is actually being affirmed here is the primacy and centrality of the Holy Spirit as the ultimate subject of the eschaton whose life is at once the source, the means, and the goal of Christ's Second Appearing.

> And as this Spirit is Christ, and whether it be revealed in male or female for salvation, it can never be separated from Christ; therefore it is by this Spirit of Christ only, that salvation and final redemption can be wrought in any soul. (Pt. 5, chap. 4, p. 219)

Christ's Second Appearing: In the New Birth

The fourth and final feature of Christ's Second Appearing is its relationship to "Spiritual Regeneration and the New Birth." As we have seen, Shakerism's openness to the reality of woman introduces feminine metaphors and processes into theological discourse. Green continues to build on the female feature he has just outlined in several ways. He uses it to clarify the eschatological nature of the new birth by distinguishing between the relation of Christians to God in the First and Second Appearings of Christ. The beginning work of the First Appearing succeeded in bringing men and women into relation to God by means of adoption; in the Second Appearing, by the new birth, Believers are truly the offspring of God, accomplished by "the manifestation of Christ...in the order of the female, as the Mother Spirit, to bear souls to God" (pt. 5, chap. 5, p. 234).

Anticipating by some 150 years the issues fundamental to certain lines of the feminist critique and revision of christology, Green asks:

> If spiritual regeneration and the new birth, is the work of the father only, then the female is entirely excluded from any part in it; consequently no woman can ever enter the Kingdom of Heaven. How then is the regeneration to be perfected? and how are souls to be brought to the birth? (Pt. 5, chap. 5, p. 234)

He answers the question by saying, "This great spiritual work has now commenced," in the revelation of Christ in the female, in whom the spiritual labors of the new birth have begun.

But the feminine analogy is not meant to discount the importance of Christ Jesus in relation to the new birth; on the contrary, he was its first instance. Since Jesus, too, was born into a fallen nature he "necessarily had a progressive travel out of it" (pt. 5, chap. 5, p. 228). Therefore the work in question "first began in Jesus Christ; and no one was ever born out of the flesh, into the kingdom of Heaven before him" (pt. 5, chap. 5, p. 225).

And by yielding obedience to his heavenly Parents, he overcame the power of that death which reigned in the fallen nature of man, and was thus formed into the very nature of eternal life, the elements of which he had received from his Eternal Parents. Thus he was "the first begotten from the dead, and the first-born among many brethren." (Pt. 5, chap. 5, p. 228)

Jesus, newly born, was the beginning of a new and eternal creation of God. Since he was the first to travel in regeneration, he was the first to teach it. And what was the mystery of the new birth? Simply this: to enter into regeneration one must "become entirely dead to generation" (pt. 5, chap. 5, p. 228). Hence, the coming to life, or new birth, of spiritual men and women is by an inversion of the mode of natural birth. As it is by natural, sexual generation that the "kingdoms of the world have been peopled," so it is by spiritual, celibate regeneration "that the Kingdom of Heaven is to be peopled" (pt. 5, chap. 5, p. 229).

But the work of generation, being corrupted by the fall, must be put away, and cease in man, before the work of regeneration can have any salutary effect upon the soul: for souls must be born out of the nature of the flesh, in order to be born into the nature of the Spirit. (Pt. 5, chap. 5, p. 229)

In effect Green has made an equation between celibacy and the new birth, or, more clearly, celibacy is the life at once subsequent to and concomitant with the new birth. Regeneration is the translation to the spiritual plane of the power of generation, the fruit of which is not the birth of another, as in the natural sexual process, but the birth of one's own eternal soul.

Green develops an interesting notion of "soul" as the eschatological issue of the new birth noting it as "the real acting principle in man," which must be "waked up to see and feel [its] real situation in the world of spirits" (pt. 5, chap. 5, p. 227). Because the veil of the flesh obstructs an authentic view of the dimensions of the spiritual world, one must "travel out of the life of nature, by regeneration, and be born into a heavenly and eternal life" (pt. 5, chap. 5, p. 227). This travail of labor is a gradual — even lifelong — process:

> As the natural conception, or planting the seed of natural life, the birth of the natural offspring, are operations entirely distinct from each other; and as the travail of generation commences with the former, and is completed in the latter; so is the planting of the seed of eternal life in the soul; and so is the travail of the regeneration and the spiritual birth, which are truly prefigured by the natural. (Pt. 5, chap. 5, p. 229)

But if one does not undergo this new birth, one remains in the state of nature throughout existence, for "unless he can be born into the heavenly life, he never becomes a living being in that world" (pt. 5, chap. 5, p. 227). Furthermore, the new birth of this eternal soul occurs in consequence of the new sexual relationship of men and women to one another in the Spirit, as witnessed in the Millennial Church. Green suggests that the celibate union or spiritual marriage of Shakers in the United Society causes the spiritual conception which issues forth in the new birth of one's everlasting soul. Such is the new situation of men and women in relation to each other, and of each person to his or her own sexual — now translated into spiritual — nature.

> The true foundation being thus laid, in both the male and the female, the work of God proceeds by a

> corresponding spiritual union and relation between
> them, through which souls are regenerated, and born
> into the everlasting Kingdom of Christ. And without
> this correspondence, the work of the new creation
> could not proceed, any more than the work of the old
> creation could go on without a natural correspon-
> dence between the male and female. Hence it
> appears evident, that the work of regeneration and
> the new birth could not be accomplished until the
> second appearing of Christ. (Pt. 5, chap. 5, p. 230)

In Green's metaphor, the eschatological life of the Spirit,
quickened in the Second Appearing of Christ in the female,
gestates in the Millennial Church and comes to term progressively, swelling the world with its promise of rebirth. For
Green, as for Meacham and Youngs before him, the regeneration begun among Believers had universal import and intent.
The Shakers were the witnesses and exemplars of the new life
of the millennium.

> So all souls who are partakers of the work of this
> great day, will be nourished by the spiritual ele-
> ments of eternal life, and will grow into the very
> nature of Christ, and bring forth the precious fruits
> of the gospel...and the cheering spring of Christ's
> second appearing is now made manifest, and will
> extend from clime to clime, and from shore to
> shore, until "all the ends of the earth shall see the
> salvation of the Lord," and all shall have an oppor-
> tunity to come into its work, and enjoy its blessings,
> to their eternal glory; or to reject it to their ever-
> lasting destruction. (Pt. 5, chap. 5, p. 235)

These then are the features of Christ's Second Appearing: it
is a spiritual event occasioned by the Spirit; it dawns progressively, first in the Millennial Church and from there its light

begins to illumine the whole world; it has begun in the female line and occasions a radically new spiritual relationship between the sexes; it is experienced in the new birth of celibacy.

Principles of the Millennium

The Second Appearing of Christ, Green contends, has inaugurated the millennium, or new creation. Its center is the Millennial Church from which radiates the power and presence of the Christ Spirit to influence the progressive transformation of the world, and within which Believers live according to the new mandates of the Spirit. Thus Shakers traveled progressively into the life of regeneration by the practice of "the seven moral principles of the Church of Christ" which fashioned and informed their millennial life-style. These values, drawn from the life of Jesus, directed the practical and external life of the christic community which had become the living reality of the reign of the Spirit now begun on earth. Enacted, they were the substance of the millennial witness which Believers offered the world. Because certain of the seven principles, said to be constitutive of the dawning millennium, are uniquely Shaker in their expression of Christian life, these will be given more attention.

The first two principles, namely "Duty of God" and "Duty to Man," are not essentially eschatological, but refer to the twofold great commandment taught by Christ in the First Appearing: the love of God and neighbor. The third principle, however, "Separation from the World," is more clearly millennial since it is a value intended to keep the children of God in relationship to the Kingdom of Christ. The world, as the Shakers saw it, is generated by the flesh, so they committed themselves to stay free of complicity and compromise in its regard. Civil and political offices, party connections, and political strife were renounced, because Believers had pledged allegiance to Christ's Kingdom and not the kingdom of the world.

Christ's Kingdom and Government can never be established on the earth, among any people whatsoever, without a separation from the world; not indeed a separation from the natural creation, which is good in its order, nor from any thing which is virtuous in it, commendable, or useful to his people but a separation from the lies, vanities, contaminating principles and wicked practices of fallen men, under the reigning influence of a depraved human nature, and from all those things in which the great bulk of mankind seek their own honor and glory instead of the honor and glory of God. (Pt. 6, chap. 2, p. 261)

The fourth eschatological principle is "Practical Peace" or nonviolence. "Indeed," says Green, "this heavenly principle so clearly characterizes the Spirit and Kingdom of Christ, that the violation of it seems evidently a violation of every Divine attribute, and of every Christian virtue" (pt. 6, chap. 2, p. 262).

Christ's Kingdom is a Kingdom of peace; hence his subjects must be peaceable and harmless people. "My Kingdom is not of this world," Jesus said; "If my Kingdom were of this world, then my servants would fight." And because his Kingdom is not of this world, those who are truly his servants will not fight. (Pt. 6, chap. 2, p. 262)

"The peaceable religion of Jesus Christ" was founded upon his messianic inheritance which is peace and was maintained by the Church so long as it remained faithful to the Christ Spirit. The Shakers believed that war and violence are the hallmark of the anti-Christian spirit, manifestations of the law of death reigning in fallen nature. For them the "Christian warrior" is an incongruity arising out of infidelity to the Spirit.

> But it is vain for the advocates of war to call themselves
> Christians, or to claim any relation to Christ, for they
> have no part in him. They are subjects of the prince of
> war and not of the prince of peace. (Pt. 6, chap. 2, p. 262)

The fifth millennial principle, "Simplicity of Language," is
the practical operation of the virtue of honesty and simplicity in
all one's communications, since language is expressive of the
heart. This principle forbids swearing and oath-taking, as well as
profanity, and enjoins speech stripped of those terms and titles
like "Miss," "Mr.," "Madam" which speak of worldly vanity.
"Sister" and "Brother" are the words of right relation and identity in the redeemed human community of the Millennial
Church. In effect, language itself must promote union.

The sixth principle, the "Right Use of Property," is rooted not
in some value of economic efficiency, but, as Dunlavy has shown,
in a millennial christology and ecclesiology. If true Believers are
united in the Christ Spirit this oneness includes all they possess,

> for he that has devoted himself to Christ, soul, body
> and spirit, can by no means withhold his prop-
> erty.... This oneness is the fruit of the gospel, and it
> can be obtained in no other way than by obedience
> to the gospel. The very nature and design of the
> gospel is to lead souls into this oneness, that they
> may possess one faith, enjoy one hope, and be able
> "to keep the unity of the spirit in the bond of
> peace." This unity of the Spirit leads to a oneness in
> all things, both spiritual and temporal, while the
> nature of selfishness tends only to scatter and
> divide. (Pt. 6, chap. 2, p. 269)

This principle enables the life of the new millennial family in
"united interest," in which the community of goods supplies every-

one's needs. Green underscores the eschatological intent of such a principle, which has within it the promise of the millennial society.

> The primitive church at Jerusalem, was also founded on a united interest. Thus, they divested themselves of all selfishness, and like a band of disinterested brethren and sisters, lived in love and harmony, and all fared alike. These amiable examples were designed as a pattern for christians: and had all who have since professed that name, been led by the true spirit of the gospel, and carefully conformed to this pattern, what an amiable and harmonious band of christian nations might, long ere this day have existed upon earth! (Pt. 6, chap. 2, p. 272)

Naturally enough, the most lengthy and systematic consideration is given the last and most eschatological Shaker principle: "A Virgin Life." Green argues that a people of virgin character must build and design the Church of the Latter Day. Summarizing several eschatological themes drawn from the Pauline Scriptures Green notes:

> But after the apostle's permissions and indulgences to the Corinthians, whom he declares to be "carnal," he points them to a future day in which all these indulgences must cease; when carnal gratifications, separate possessions and whatever else among Christians pertains to the customs and manners of this selfish world, must be done away with in the Church of Christ, and a more inward and spiritual work be wrought in the soul, and a new order of things succeed in the Christ. (Pt. 6, chap. 2, p. 281)

It is clear that Shaker faith perceives these eschatological signs as realities of their own historical moment and not some other-worldly situation. Even the apocalyptic features of the Johannine Revelation speak of their experience: they are the virgins who follow the Lamb, first fruits of the millennium.

> In this vision of John, is a prophetic display of the true character of the work of God on earth, in the great millennial day of Christ, which is, as it were, but just commenced. And these virgin characters, above described, are the subjects of it, and none will finally be able to stand the test of this great day, without becoming the subjects of this work and attaining to this character. (Pt. 6, chap. 2, p. 283)

The ultimate effect of regeneration in the Spirit, therefore, is a radical congruity of the individual to the virgin character of Christ. In fact the crux of the millennial work in question is precisely the choice of celibacy which is the mark of the Christ Spirit in the body and soul of the Believer.

In these seven moral principles Green has presented the Shaker model for the millennium. He claims that the Millennial Church, which these principles inform, is the first instance and herald of the new situation effected by the Second Coming of Christ. More exactly, these principles, embodied in the lives of Believers, are the manifestation of the transforming power of the Christ Spirit being poured out upon all flesh — first upon the Shakers, and gradually, by virtue of their witness, upon the whole world.

Context of the Millennium: Resurrection and Judgment
Having described the features and principles of the millennium, Green explores its context in two familiar eschatological notions which the Shakers have thoroughly redefined: resurrection and judgment. His remarks, in regard to these, further illustrate the pneumatological accent which he brings to the ecclesiological definition of Christ's Second Appearing.

A brief review of his perspective concludes this study of *The Millennial Church.*

As Green attempted to demonstrate the pneumatological features and principles of the millennium inaugurated in the Shaker Church, he further attempts to demonstrate the pneumatological character of its fundamental context: that victory of the divine Spirit which is the resurrection of the human spirit. Green situates Shaker understanding of the resurrection in the basic theological presupposition that "God is a Spirit," and "needs no natural body to complete his glory" (pt. 6, chap. 1, pp. 304-305). Nor does the human soul need a natural body to complete its happiness; indeed "in its present state, it is considered as a clog to the soul" (pt. 6, chap. 5, p. 305).

> No transformation whatever can change matter into spirit. ...And tho the living spirit may be enclosed in a body of flesh; yet they cannot be so blended together as to become one in essence. (Pt. 6, chap. 5, p. 304)

The human person must leave off the material body in order to achieve a new state of transparency, subtlety, and freedom known by the angels. Green therefore stresses the interim character of the fleshly body, in which the soul is tempered as it grows to maturity. Liberated from it, souls would "be able to feel and sensibly realize the due reward of their deeds" (pt. 6, chap. 5, p. 305).

> The resurrection, in its fullness, is the highest state of glory ever expected by the saints. But according to the doctrine of a carnal resurrection, the highest state of glory to be obtained by the righteous cannot be realized short of raising up that dead and disorganized matter which once constituted the soul's earthly tabernacle. And if the soul must again be confined in this, and clogged with it, in order to be made perfect in glory, it must be because this dead matter, which

was originally composed of the elements of the natural world, is of a nature superior to the soul, which is composed of the elements of the spiritual world; how else could it possibly increase the glory of the soul by being reunited with it? For it is obvious that in this case, the body must be first in view, and therefore must forever eclipse the glory of the soul. But this absurd doctrine would, if true, wholly reverse the established order of God's creation, in which the earthly part was formed as a mere temporary shadow, to represent that spiritual and eternal substance, which was to succeed. (Pt. 6, chap. 5, p. 305)

Green concludes his reflection on the resurrection by saying:

Thus we may see that the true resurrection consists in the rising of the spiritual part of man from the terrestrial elements, into which it has been sown by generation, to the celestial and heavenly body, endowed with immortality and eternal life, and thus it becomes an everlasting inhabitant of the celestial world; and thus it is that "this corruptible puts on incorruption, and this mortal puts on immortality." This glorious work of the resurrection has commenced, and will continue with increasing power and progress, until all souls shall have experienced its effects, either by coming forth into the resurrection of life, or to the resurrection of damnation. (Pt. 6, chap. 5, p. 313)

Likewise, Green's pneumatological orientation requires a Shaker clarification of the Day of Judgment. For him, this eschatological reality is

inseparately connected with the Resurrection; and tho the belief in both is probably as extensive and universal as the profession of the christian; yet mankind appear to be as much in the dark with respect to the former as the latter. (Pt. 6, chap. 6, p. 313)

The question of the last judgment is a critical eschatological issue, for it portends the consummation of salvation history and the return of the Lord in glory to reckon with earth's people. However, as Green notes, this apocalyptic interpretation is in conflict with the popular belief that "the final and everlasting fate of the soul is decided at the hour of death" (pt. 6, chap. 6, p. 314). In answer to this conflict between a personal and general judgment, Green says:

> But we view the day of judgment in a very different light from all this. We view it as a work already commenced; a work which we ourselves have seen and felt, and can therefore testify from our own experience, that it is a work which, tho unseen by the natural man, is real and substantial; and tho gradual and progressive in its operations, it is certain and effectual; and will continue to increase in power, till a full and final separation be made between good and evil. This work will be accomplished, both by the order and course of God's providence, and by the operations of the Spirit of Christ in his chosen witnesses. (Pt. 6, chap. 6, p. 314)

Shakers, therefore, consider the Day of Judgment a work in progress which will continue its influence until "all souls shall have seen and felt its purifying effects" (pt. 6, chap. 6, p. 319).

> But this day of judgment is yet in its beginning;...while the unseen, tho powerful agent, shall increase and grow, like a mountain of righteousness, it shall fill the whole earth. This work, tho powerful and effective in

its operations, will at the same time, be so apparently slow in its progress, and so much out of sight of the natural man, that those who, through impenitence and hardness of heart, chuse [sic] to put far away the evil day, will be so blinded by willful unbelief, that they will not be aware of the danger to which they are exposed, until, like the inhabitants of the old world, they shall be finally overwhelmed in the deluge of destruction which it will occasion. (Pt. 6, chap. 6, p. 317)

Calvin Green's *Millennial Church* provides the last systematic portrait of Shaker eschatology produced in the nineteenth century. In it he has elaborated upon the ecclesiological definition of Christ's Second Appearing formulated by Meacham, Youngs, and Dunlavy by adding an explicitly pneumatological accent while exploring the features of the Millennial Church, its moral principles, and its more radical context as the community of the resurrection. Green's entire logic in *The Millennial Church* rests in his conviction that the Second Appearing of Christ is the eschatological outpouring of the Spirit progressively transforming the world according to the millennial values upheld by the Shakers. As such they are the first instance of the millennium which has dawned with Christ's Second Appearing.

As the last systematician of Shakerism, Green made at least two enduring contributions to its theological tradition. First, he further clarified the Shaker insight which linked eschatology and pneumatology, developing a richer understanding of the work and effects of the Spirit in the Millennial Church and in the world; second, by defining more clearly the exemplaristic role of the Millennial Church with regard to the advancing millennium, Green helped prepare subsequent Shakers to adopt a more dialogic posture toward the world whose transformation they believed their witness to serve.

CONCLUSION

This chapter has taken us through the major theological works of Shakerism in which the four writers moved the Shakers beyond a christological to an ecclesiological definition for Christ's Second Appearing. Meacham's seminal work describing the Second Appearing "in a people" was further elaborated by Youngs, who explored its feminine christological foundations in the "Church born of woman," then by Dunlavy who explored its communitarian nature in the "union of Believers," and lastly, by Green who explored its pneumatological and exemplaristic character in relation to the world in the "dawning millennium."

This development of eschatological understanding from a preoccupation with the person of Mother Ann to a deliberate concentration on the Millennial Church as the locus of Christ's Second Appearing was linked to several assertions which underlie Shaker belief. The first assertion was eschatological: the Second Appearing of Christ introduced an essentially new revelation. While there were continuities with the previous dispensations of salvation, it is really the discontinuities which are of consequence for Shakerism since the innovation formed the eschatological substance of their faith. What then was the novelty which distinguished Christ in the Second Appearing from the First, thereby advancing, complementing, and completing the christological event? The innovation was in the very nature of Christ, who in this ultimate phase of redemption was no longer a singular person, as originally, but eschatologically was a corporate person — a community. Therefore, ecclesiology was the eschatological form of christology for Shakerism, since the new revelation of Christ for salvation was no longer in a person, but in a people.

But this eschatological innovation regarding christology which led the Shakers to an ecclesiological understanding of

Christ's Second Appearing was, more fundamentally, associated with a pneumatological assumption. The Second Appearing of Christ could be a corporate person, the Millennial Church, precisely because the eschatological Christ was in reality not a person at all, but a power: that Christ-making power of divine anointing — divinity itself outpoured on humanity in the Holy Spirit. Claiming an eschatological revelation of Christ as Spirit, Shakers could formulate a christology that was ecclesiological by way of pneumatology and vice versa since it was precisely the Spirit indwelling in its fullness in the Millennial Church which constituted it the Christ of the Second Appearing.

Therefore, these writers, though offering an apparently ecclesiological depiction of Christ's Second Appearing, nevertheless progressively oriented the Shakers toward their most influential and fundamental source of theological insight, namely their own unique eschatological pneumatology: the outpouring of the Spirit as the true revelation borne by Christ's Second Appearing.

It is this pneumatology, beyond its christological and ecclesiological expressions, which would preoccupy later Shaker writers, and, as we shall see, becomes the final radical term of Shaker eschatology.

NOTES

1. Stephen Marini, *Radical Sects of Revolutionary New England* (Cambridge: Harvard University Press, 1982), pp. 136-137.

2. Calvin Green, *Biographical Account of the Life, Character, and Ministry of Father Joseph Meacham* (Sabbathday Lake manuscript, 1827), gives the date "Feb 11, 1742 (old style)," chap. 1, sec. 1.

3. See William G. McLoughlin, *Revivals, Awakenings, and Reform: An Essay on Religion and Social Change in America, 1607-1977*. (Chicago: University of Chicago Press, 1978), pp. 18-23.

4. Edward Deming Andrews, *The People Called Shakers: A Search for the Perfect Society* (New York: Dover Publishing, 1953), pp. 54-55.

5. Marini, *Radical Sects*, pp. 40-59.

6. In his *Biographical Account*, Green does not mention this delegation, stating rather that the revivalists chose Meacham and two others for the mission (see chap. 1, sec. 12).

7. May 19, 1780, was called the "Dark Day" in New England, an apocalyptic reference to the natural event of daylong darkness occasioned by the aftereffect of a great forest fire (see Marini, *Radical Sects*, pp. 47, 78, 88; and Andrews, *People Called Shakers*, p. 21).

8. Bishop and Wells, *Testimonies* (1816), p. 220.

9. Shakerism underwent a critical phase without membership growth and with significant internal unrest during Whittaker's leadership. His letter to his family at the end of Meacham's *Concise Statement* reveals him to be a mystical but rather eccentric religionist who nevertheless held the course of the early Society until Meacham could steer it securely toward the future. See Garrett, *Spirit Possession and Popular Religion*, pp. 195-222.

10. Andrews, *People Called Shakers*, p. 55.

11. Lucy Wright was born in Pittsfield, Massachusetts, February 5, 1760. Exceptionally intelligent and strong willed, Wright had been attached to Mother Ann from the beginning, and after the death of Meacham, she would guide the destinies of the Shakers for over twenty-five years.

12. There are many precedents for the covenant practice in American Church history, particularly among the Congregationalists and Freewill Baptists. See Marini, *Radical Sects*, pp. 130ff.; and Andrews, *People Called Shakers*, p. 56.

13. Robley Whitson, ed., *The Shaker Way: Two Centuries of Spiritual Reflection* (New York: Paulist Press, 1983), p. 17.

14. See Andrews, *The Gift to Be Simple: Songs, Dances and Rituals of the American Shakers* (New York: Dover Publishing, 1962).

15. As Whitson and others have noted, the Shakers from earliest times, beginning with Joseph Meacham, exhibited a commitment to the notions of progress and spiritual growth. Although Father Joseph gave the first clear orientation to the whole tradition, he was always explicitly open to the next "new light" to be revealed in the Spirit. For this reason Meacham refused to allow any printed publication, either of the rules and regulations of the Society, or of its song or other forms used in worship. He insisted instead that these be handwritten so that they could always be changed, adapted to developing conditions, and ultimately, if need be, abolished altogether to be replaced by a new light. He would not even refer to the governing precepts as "rules" or "regulations" but preferred to call them "Waymarks" (Whitson, *The Shaker Way*, p. 18).

16. Marini, *Radical Sects*, pp. 138-139.

17. This notion of "progressive unfoldment" is essential to Shakerism and informs every aspect of its religious awareness, as is seen repeatedly throughout its theological history.

18. Because of the brevity of the *Statement* and the absence of pagination in the original publication, no page references are given here.

19. For some reason, Meacham repeats the "water to the ancles" metaphor, ascribing it to both the first and the second dispensations.

20. Calvin Green, "Father's Word Respecting the Millennium or Work of Christ's Second Appearing," *Biographical Account*, chap. 4, sec. 8.

21. From the autobiography of Issachar Bates, as quoted in Andrews, *People Called Shakers*, p. 72.

22. The other leaders in the revival included Matthew Houston, David Purviance, Robert Marshall, and John Thompson. See Richard McNemar, *The Kentucky Revival* (Cincinnati: John W. Browne Press, 1807); Rhodes Thompson, *Voices from Cane Ridge* (Bethany, WV: Bethany Press, 1954); Catherine Cleveland, *The Great Revival in the West* (Gloucester, MA: Peter Smith, 1959).

23. From the "Last Will and Testament of the Springfield Presbytery," quoted in Andrews, *People Called Shakers*, p. 72.

24. The story of the Western mission is chronicled in Issachar Bates' autobiography and Benjamin Seth Youngs' journal. These are in manuscript form and not available in the

ordinary sources of Shaker literature. I have relied on chapter 5 of Andrews, where he quotes extensively from these works.

25. Quoted in Andrews, *People Called Shakers*, pp. 75-76.

26. Barton Stone was enthusiastic at first, but later became a bitter detractor of the Believers. See John Dunlavy's "Letter to Barton Stone" at the end of *Manifesto*.

27. Quoted in Andrews, *People Called Shakers*, p. 76.

28. In all, fifteen societies were founded in the West — in Ohio, Kentucky, Tennessee, North Carolina, and western Pennsylvania.

29. As quoted in Andrews, *People Called Shakers*, pp. 96-97.

30. Ibid., p. 95.

31. Mother Ann's Work is the extraordinary revival which swept through the Shaker society itself during the 1830s. Its significance for Shakerism's understanding of Christ's Second Appearing will be discussed in Chapter 4 of the present work.

32. "Joint parentage" is the paradigmatic substitute for the Trinity in Shaker usage. It is an unfaithfulness to this existential analogy of sexual nature and relationship which Youngs blames for the radical deficiencies of conventional Christian theology, which he says are "evident from their doctrine of three distinct personalities in the Deity, all in the masculine gender: First the Father, second the Son, and third the Holy Ghost, He proceeding from Father and Son, everlasting, without the attribute of either Mother or Daughter. To complete their heterogenous system they

unite two distinct and contrary natures in the Son of God — and finally look for the mystery of God to be finished in the odd number of three males" (pt. 7, chap. 7, sec. 47).

33. The first edition will be cited here, except where the microfiche type was more legible in the second.

34. Numerous studies of Shakerism as an example of nineteenth-century communitarianism are cited in the bibliography.

35. John Chandler, "The Communitarian Quest for Perfection," in *A Miscellany of American Christianity*, ed. Stuart Henry (Durham, NC: Duke University Press, 1963), pp. 75ff.

36. See Charles Nordhoff, *The Communistic Societies of the United States* (1875; reprint, New York: Schocken Books, 1965).

37. Shaker Joe Bishop, cited in Andrews, *People Called Shakers*, p. 47.

38. John Humphrey Noyes, *History of American Socialisms* (New York: Hillary House Publishers, 1961), pp. 141-142, 191-192.

39. See Theodore Johnson's introduction to Green's *Biographical Account of the Life, Character, and Ministry of Father Joseph Meacham* in *Shaker Quarterly*, 10:1 (Spring 1970), p. 20.

40. Winthrop S. Hudson, *Religion in America*, 3rd ed. (New York: Charles Scribner's Sons, 1981), p. 199.

41. Mark Holloway, *Heavens on Earth: Utopian Communities in America, 1680-1880* (London: Turnstile Press, 1951), p. 78.

4 The Maturity of Shaker Eschatology: The Second Appearing of Christ as the Universality of the Christ Spirit

The second half of the nineteenth century marks the third and last significant period of development of Shaker faith in Christ's Second Appearing. This period presents the greatest challenge to the theological researcher for many reasons. Unlike the two earlier phases studied, later Shakerism has no major theological voice or document to articulate clearly the eschatology of Believers. Rather, there are a variety of minor voices, often in discord, located in a plethora of minor texts which suggest rather than state an eschatological revision.

In our reading of these materials, the theological innovation is proposed by Shaker progressives among whom we perceive a movement toward a comprehensive pneumatology. While this thesis seems to be clearly supported in the surveyed documents of this period, both the method and argument developed to present the thesis are the researcher's own constructions. Therefore, the conclusions reached here must be more tentative than in previous chapters where, in many cases, the theological documents spoke for themselves. Nevertheless, familiarity with the wide range of later Shaker theological discourse leads one to formulate the following perspective as one possible way of understanding Shakerism's ultimate movement toward a comprehensive pneumatology.

In an effort to bring simplicity and clarity to the complexity and frequent vagueness of late Shaker eschatology, three principles will be developed derived from the various recurring themes in the literature: spiritualism, universalism, and progressivism. These three principles serve as tools for the analysis and interpretation of the texts; they also serve as the structuring device of the chapter. In light of them, I hope to demonstrate how Shakerism's millennial faith was dramatically changed in the late nineteenth century, particularly by the community progressives, and became essentially pneumatological.[1] In this process reformist Shakers seem to have effectively blurred — if not erased — the unique, qualifying boundaries earlier Believers had provided for the eschatological event, first in the person of Ann Lee, and then in the community of the Millennial Church. In place of these, the various writers suggest a new understanding of Christ's Second Appearing — now in wholly pneumatological terms — as essentially spiritual, universal, and eternally progressing toward its fullness.

The theological literature of later nineteenth-century Shakerism is markedly different from the previous varieties. As already noted, the later nineteenth century produced no theological landmarks or systematic expressions of the developments of Shaker faith. Instead, a number of religious commentators elaborated and speculated on a variety of issues germane to Shakerism. Aurelia Mace, Frederick Evans, George Lomas, Giles Avery, Daniel Fraser, Harvey Eads, Catherine Allen, Alonzo Hollister, Henry C. Blinn, Antoinette Doolittle, and Oliver Hampton, among others, produced essays, pamphlets, and minor publications intended mainly as representations of Shaker faith to the world. But for the most part, their contributions offer no particular advance on the great antebellum Shaker books treated in the previous chapter. For our purposes, the interesting evidence of postwar development occurs in Shaker periodical literature.

Toward the end of the century, the Society published a journal, largely under the editorship of progressives, which served as a news medium among the various communities, and as a mode of address to the world. In fact it became their primary vehicle for theological inquiry and reflection, though the idiom was journalistic. The publication went through various name changes under several editors during its twenty-eight year history:

The Shaker (1871-1872), George Lomas
Shaker and Shakeress Monthly (1873-1875), F. W. Evans and Antoinette Doolittle
The Shaker (1876-1877), George A. Lomas
The Shaker Manifesto (1878-1882), George A. Lomas
The Manifesto (1883-1899), Henry C. Blinn.

Since the journals span the period of the almost thirty years which marked a dramatic change in Shakerism's self-awareness, they offer insight into the evolution of Shaker religious thought, particularly regarding eschatology.

However, the journals pose several critical problems for the researcher, since the theological material found in original articles, editorials, diary fragments, letters, and reprinted Shaker publications is difficult to isolate in a format that includes community news, book notices, agricultural and household information, advertisements for Shaker goods, obituaries, music, poetry, and pious reflections. Furthermore, a clear designation of the source or authorship of these pieces is often unavailable since, "in accordance with Shaker custom, personal names are generally avoided even in the indexes."[2] Therefore, when quoting from these journals, collectively called The Manifesto, whatever particular information is available for any given piece will be cited.[3] In addition to the journals, several works of the early twentieth century by Anna White will also be considered: Motherhood of God (1903), Present Day Shakerism (1906?), and Shakerism: Its Meaning and Message (1904), which she co-authored with Leila Sarah Taylor. With these publications, the formal theological work of Shakerism comes to an end.

These sources will be the basis of inquiry into the eschatology which was proposed by certain Shakers of this period and which offered a significantly different understanding of Christ's Second

Appearing. Before turning to these works, a brief review of the social situation of late-nineteenth-century Shakers is in order, since it provides the background and impetus for much of their eschatological revision.

THE CONTEXT FOR THE REVISION OF SHAKER ESCHATOLOGY

Post-Civil War Decline

In order to understand the background against which later Shakers reformulated their understanding of Christ's Second Appearing, it is necessary to note the process of membership decline which began in the West in the 1830s and became ubiquitous and irreversible after the Civil War. Several commentators have attempted to account for the phenomenon, pointing to rapid urbanization, industrialization, and the social dislocations of the war as primary causes. Others have suggested the waning communitarian impulse in America at large, and the failure of the postwar revivals to provide Shaker converts as they had previously. Still others looked within the United Society for clues, noting on the one hand their demanding perfectionism, excessive spiritualism, and the inflated christology of Ann Lee; and on the other, the burdensome management of vast community lands and other resources which fell to the dwindling corps of younger, able-bodied Shakers. Also noted is the critical disproportion between the numbers of unconverted young members and the community leaders needed to provide for their spiriutal formation if they were to sign the Shaker covenant on reaching adulthood.[4]

Whatever the constellation of reasons, the postbellum period was critical for the Shakers, who saw their numbers plummet as quickly as they had risen a few decades earlier. About fifty years before the Civil War, the Society had approximately a thousand adherents; ten years before the war the number had grown to approximately six thousand, with Believers flourishing in eighteen societies from Maine to Kentucky in a total of fifty-eight families. Fifty years later, after gradual atrophy, there were again only a thousand members, from which time the pattern of decline became irreversible.[5] The first society to close was in Tyringham, Massachusetts, in 1875. Between 1897 and 1920 all but six societies folded; by 1961 (and to the present) only the communities at Canterbury, New Hampshire, and Sabbathday Lake, Maine, remain.[6] Therefore, the eschatological questions of the last things, of end-time, of the millennium, and the ultimate meaning of Christ's Second Appearing, took on particular poignancy for this people who believed themselves to be the vanguard and witnesses of the eschaton.

The failure to add as many new members as in former decades and the steady departure of covenanted Believers in the second half of the nineteenth century undermined their previous eschatological consensus and was the critical context in which they revised their sense of Christ's Second Appearing. In effect there emerged two essentially different diagnoses and cures for the manifest decline of the Society. On the one hand were the conservatives, or introversionists, like Harvey Eads who blamed a growing laxity and worldliness for Shaker ills and prescribed withdrawal and reentrenchment in communal values.[7] On the other hand were the revisionists who proposed a new phase of the Shaker testimony, now more aligned with those reformist movements laboring for the transformation of the world.

The Shaker journal from these years is alive with discussion and controversy concerning the meaning of such decline. In the gathering of all the various voices, there was, by the close of the century, a mounting sense among some Shakers that if the Societies did not progress into a significant renewal "it will only be a question whether the old will come into the new increase or become extinct" (F. W. Evans, "The Future of Shakerism," *Elder Frederick W. Evans*, Pittsfield [MA], 1893, p. 114). Elder

Henry Blinn called for such an internal renewal among the Shakers in 1883, asking the Society:

> Are we asleep? Have we fallen into a lethargic state, dreamily passing away our days, waiting for some form of electric shock to arouse us to more active duty? . . . We need a revival, a revival of truthfulness and honesty, and a living kindness for poor humanity. We need a school for prophets from which men and women can graduate as saviors and redeemers. Preachers of the testimony of Jesus Christ, which is the sure word of prophecy, and the only effectual door of hope. (*Manifesto* 13.3 [1883], pp. 66-67)

But a decade later, Arthur W. Dowe, a Shaker missionary and leader of an urban communal experiment in San Francisco, offered this indictment:

> Since the present generation of Believers have never been through a great revival and reformation of spiritual power, their own experience does not fit them for the tremendous issues now before the world. In all the great questions of the coming age, the majority of Believers have no practical knowledge and consequently little practical sympathy. So to disturb their quiet sleep and rest and their dreams of security would be of very little use, and would only provoke needless discussion and friction...when a people become fixed and immovable...God is accustomed to raise up a new people and the former is left to wax old and decay away. (Letter of Arthur W. Dowe, leader of San Francisco, CA, urban community, *Manifesto* 24.7 [1894], pp. 157-158)

If the undeniable pattern of diminishment provoked pessimism among some Believers, it also provoked the characteristic spirit of Shaker optimism among others, particularly those progressives whose eschatological revison is of interest here. To these, decline was seen as heralding a greater rebirth of spiritual life in the world at large, in which Shakers were to play a critical and essential role. Indeed, these Believers would insist that the new spiritual life of the larger world, seen as evidence of the ever increasing eschaton, might require their own near extinction. From this liberal perspective a reinterpretation of Shakerism's role in the eschatological designs of God would emerge, orienting their vision all the more in the direction of pneumatology.

Shakers were reminded by an anonymous voice that they "must remember that the dawning of only the second of the seven cycles of progress in the Church of the Millennium" was opening upon them (*Shaker and Shakeress*, Social Gathering, August 19, 1873, p. 4). This notion of "seven cycles" was an allusion to an obscure revelation made by Father Joseph Meacham and noted in Calvin Green's biography of him:

> His revelation of the future state of the church was far seeing. He said that he saw by revelation a perfect church completed on earth and he labored with all of his powers to gain and establish its system and order as far as possible. But after having done all he was able, he then found that but one general order, that is the united system, as a foundation had been gained, and further predicted that it would take seven general and distinct travels of believers to bring to maturity that perfect church order which he then saw by revelation would ultimately be accomplished.
>
> By general travels was understood the periods from one general opening of the gospel to another, including all the degrees and changes in each one. (Green, *Biographical Account*, chap. 2, sec. 7, p. 39)

Change and travel from one form to another offered promise as well as threat, and in this more optimistic light, decline was seen as a form of spiritual evolution. This was the perspective of later Shakers like Anna White and Leila Taylor, who attempted to recast the crisis of diminishment in a more hopeful context. They recalled that earlier in the century, in 1827, Brother Daniel Merton had received this prophecy during a visit to Union Village, Ohio:

> After great and peaceful growth, then change and decline — when annihilation seems inevitable, the church will rise again to a higher culmination of glory...till a child in its mother's arms can count the remnant, [then]:
>
> A new opening of the Gospel, a far grander and more universal revelation of these and other sacred truths will come. The faithful remnant shall become the germ of a new, far-reaching life and the glory of the latter days shall outshine the brightest that went before. (White and Taylor, *Shakerism: Its Meaning and Message,* pp. 369-370)

This promising perspective on the unexpected, though undeniable, phenomenon of diminishment was shared by several influential Believers from the middle to the close of the nineteenth century and gave them a new viewpoint from which to examine the emerging features of a more pneumatological expression of their eschatology. Therefore, they looked at a world in rapid transition for the clues to a new understanding of their faith in Christ's Second Appearing. What they saw corroborated and provided a broader context for their own long-held convictions, particularly that the Second Appearing of Christ begun in the Millennial Church was destined eventually to encompass the whole world.

Later Shakers believed they were witnessing this further

eschatological unfoldment of the Christ Spirit particularly in developments which this researcher classifies as spiritualist, universalist, and progressivist in nature. These three principles, evidenced in the social, and sometimes religious, movements they inspired in America, parallel three essentially Shaker principles witnessed in the eschatological revisions they inspired in the Millennial Church. These principles also provide the backdrop and the impetus for postwar developments in relation to which Shaker eschatology assumes its final pneumatological form. Upon brief examination of each one as it was manifested in the larger society, and then particularly within the United Society, there emerges a basis for the further evolution of the term "Christ's Second Appearing."

INFLUENCES OF AMERICAN CULTURE ON LATER SHAKER ESCHATOLOGY

Spiritualism

The notion of spiritualism has a twofold meaning. Primarily, and most often in this discussion, it refers to the view that sees the spirit as the prime element of reality; second, and of lesser significance to the perspective at issue, it refers to a belief that spirits of the dead, and the spirit world in general, communicate with the living. Such a spiritualist principle was prevalent in nineteenth-century American religious life and had a significant effect on the eschatology of later Shakerism. As an organized movement, spiritualism had its origins in that famous "Burned-Over District" of upper New York State. In 1847, a Methodist minister's two young daughters, Kate and Margaret Fox, began to hear "rappings" in their recently purchased old house. By devising a simple code they became the first of many mediums who made contact with the spirit world. With the support of devotees, such as Horace Greeley of the *New York*

Tribune, séances and spiritualist societies became commonplace around the country, as did more popular and entertaining forms of spiritualism: mesmerism, fortune-telling, magic, and various roadshow events.[8]

However, spiritualism retained its particularly religious character and appealed to a wide range of groups — Universalists, Swedenborgians, liberals, communitarians, and reformers among them. And while never giving rise to a particular religious sect as such, spiritualism became an influential and pervasive form of theological liberalism which left its mark on American religion in general and Shakerism in particular. Two earlier nineteenth-century phenomena demonstrate the double influence the spiritualist principle would have on later Shakerism, orienting it toward its final radical pneumatology: "Mother Ann's Work," and the failure of Millerite Adventism.

Mother Ann's Work

While Believers always had an affinity to the spirit world, during the nineteenth century this orientation significantly asserted itself within the Society and lasted almost twenty years in its intensity. In 1837, a decade prior to the "rappings" heard by the Fox sisters, a remarkable spiritualist phenomenon swept the various Shaker communities. Known as Mother Ann's Work, and alternately called the New Era or Mother Ann's Second Appearing, this powerful and protracted period of internal renewal paralleled in time and place the dramatic revivals and spiritualist phenomena sweeping American society.[9] The Shaker revival had no preachers, neither was it instigated by the leadership of the community, however much it was welcomed and supported by them. As with the Fox phenomenon, it began unexpectedly among some adolescent girls at the Niskeyuna community. The children suddenly began to shake and whirl, moving into trance states from which they announced revelations about a new season of the Spirit for Believers. Recently departed Shaker and sometimes other spirits began communicating with the elder members inducing revival, insisting upon renewal. Like wild fire, the Work spread to the other societies, as far west as North Union, deeply engaging all the membership in its nearly twenty-year duration.

The manifestations of Mother Ann's Work were highly enthusiastic and charismatic, like most revivalist phenomena. But its particularly striking feature was spiritualism: through the medium of certain Believers who became "instruments" for the Spirit and spirits, extraordinary gifts and messages from Holy Mother Wisdom, Mother Ann, and the departed elders, from angels and souls of the illustrious dead were delivered to the community for its spiritual guidance, growth, and progress. During one of his visits to a Shaker community, John Humphrey Noyes witnessed the influence of Mother Ann's Work among the Shakers and remembered it this way:

> At one of the meetings, after a due amount of marching and dancing, by which all the members had got pretty well excited, two or three sisters commenced whirling, which they continued to do for some time, and then stopped suddenly and revealed to us that Mother Ann was present at the meeting, and that she had brought a dozen baskets of spiritual fruit for her children; upon which the Elder invited them to go forth to the baskets in the center of the floor, and help themselves. Accordingly they all stepped forth and went through the various motions of taking fruit and eating it. You will wonder if I helped myself to the fruit, like the rest. No; I had not faith enough to see the baskets at the scene; but in truth, I was so affected by the general gravity and the solemn faces I saw around me, that it was impossible for me to laugh.

> Other things as well as fruit were sometimes sent as presents, such as golden spectacles. These heavenly

ornaments came in the same way as the fruit, and just as much could be seen of them. The first presents of this kind that were received during my residence there, came as follows: a sister whirled for some time; then stopped and informed the Eldress as usual that Mother Ann had sent a messenger with presents for some of her most faithful children. She then went through the action of handing the articles to the Eldress, at the same time mentioning what they were, and for whom. As near as I can remember, there was a pair of golden spectacles, a large eye-glass with a chain, and a casket of love for the Elder to distribute. The Eldress went through the act of putting the spectacles and chain upon the individuals they were intended for; and the Elder in like manner opened the casket and threw out the love by the handfuls, which all the members stretched out their hands to receive, and then pressed them to their bosom. All this appeared to me very childish, and I could not help so expressing myself to the Elder, at the first opportunity that offered. He replied, "that this was what he labored for, viz., to be a simpler Shaker."[11]

Whatever its complex and elusive cause, the purpose to which the Elders put Mother Ann's Work is more clear. Without doubt Mother Ann's Second Appearing was timely, since the charismatic era of the founders was past, and the Society had begun to suffer the loss of original inspiration consequent on its enormous and rapid growth. Therefore the ministry welcomed and supported the intervention of the Work to renew and reform the Society toward the second century of its life.

This spiritualist phase of later nineteenth-century Shakerism is significant because it influenced the trend toward Shakerism's diminishment, and also the pneumatological direction of

Shaker eschatology. Regarding the issue of numerical decline, Mother Ann's Work had an ambivalent effect. The protracted event was so engrossing and extraordinary that worship in the Society was closed to the outside world for several years during its peak; this served only to isolate the Shakers further from the larger American culture, which was on the verge of tremendous social transformation. Furthermore, the spiritualism which was the essence of the revival tended toward an otherworldly preoccupation, and succeeded for a while in imposing a burdensome perfectionist ideal on the Society.

But more positively, Mother Ann's Work provided the much-needed renewal of Shaker life for a generation who had begun to question its relevance. The spiritualist phenomena — whether prophecy, song, image, or dance — put them in touch once again with the living presence of the founders, renewing the motives needed to sustain the discipline and separation from the world which they considered essential to their unique millennial witness. By introducing a variety of innovations in ritual and custom and by engaging the attention and commitment of all Believers, Mother Ann's Work forestalled for a few decades the crisis of decline, and while it revitalized for a time the perfectionist ethos of the society, it also released the powerful spiritual energies which would become the driving force behind the progressive revision of their identity and mission. The celebrated and controversial liberal, Elder Frederick Evans, later noted its long-term effects by insisting that "the followers of Ann Lee are also undoubted spiritualists — believers in spiritual manifestations, the immortality of the human soul, the intercommunication between the visible and invisible worlds" (F. W. Evans, *Shaker* 1.3 [March 1871], p. 20). This unique variety of spiritualism would contribute to bringing Shakerism beyond its own original eschatology to an explicitly pneumatological understanding of Christ's Second Appearing.[12]

The Failure of Millerite Adventism

While Mother Ann's Work demonstrated Shaker spiritualism with regard to the spirit world, another contemporary phenomenon, though not in itself spiritualist, afforded Shakerism a way to affirm the first sense of the principle in question (the spirit as the primary element of reality) — namely, Millerite Adventism. As already noted, hope for Christ's Second Appearing had always been a feature of revivalistic preaching in America, and in the 1830s and 1840s this desire greatly increased again in the Burned-Over District of upper New York State. Whether a reflection of the enormous optimism and perfectionist temperament of the American people, or a compensation for the sense of social insecurity, the expectation for the imminent return of Christ to inaugurate the new world was great.

William Miller (1782-1849) became a key personality in the Adventist excitement of this period, since he calculated and preached the date of the *parousia* to be sometime during 1843, failing which he reassigned that date to October 22, 1844. On that occasion Adventists expected the literal reappearance of Christ in the flesh, the assent of the saints into heaven, and the judgment of the wicked. The popularity and fervor of the movement quickly made it interdenominational, with perhaps as many as 50,000 adherents. But when Christ did not return in the flesh at the appointed time, the movement tragically collapsed in disillusionment.[13] It was from among these disheartened Millerites that the Shakers received their last influx of several hundred new members, whose addition swelled their ranks to nearly six thousand as Believers marked the centenary of the Millennial Church around 1847.

An interesting observation can be made concerning Shaker eschatology in light of Millerism, which illumines our spiritualist thesis. The Millerites and the Shakers differed on the manner of Christ's Second Appearing: for the former, it was in the flesh; for the latter, in the Spirit. Given the extraordinary attention paid to the Adventists' expectation in the religious world of America generally, those who held a spiritual notion of Christ's Second Appearing no doubt felt vindicated by the non-occurrence of the advent of Christ in the flesh. Such a supposed eschatological misperception could only serve to reinforce the pneumatological construction the Shakers put on their millennial faith, which was then reinforced in turn by the ingathering of numerous Millerite converts who came to the United Society during the spiritual phase of Mother Ann's Work.

These two events, therefore — Mother Ann's Work and the failure of Millerite Adventism — point to the influence which the spiritualist principle had on antebellum Shakerism. This spiritualist orientation, magnified in the religious culture at large in more formal movements, would be an important factor in the Shakers' subsequent revision of their eschatological faith, since it provided the impetus and direction toward its ultimate pneumatological form.

Universalism

The second principle to affect the revision of late Shaker eschatology was universalism, a belief in the essential unity of humankind. This orientation was, in many ways, inherent to Shakerism, and became most prominent in nineteenth-century American religion at large. As a theological principle in the wider religious sphere, universalism affirmed that God's salvific purpose extended to every member of the human race. The logic of Wesley's Gospel of "grace to all" was amplified by universalists such as the British Methodist James Relly (1720-ca. 1780), who insisted that Christ's sacrifice won redemption not only for the elect but for everyone.[14] On this conviction one of Relly's English converts, John Murray (1741-1815) founded the Universalist Church in the United States in 1779. But the real prophet of the movement was Hosea Ballou (1771-1852), whose *Treatise on the Atonement* (1805) bore resemblance to Shakerism's own interpretation of redemption, which as we have seen, rejected substitutionary atonement in favor of an exemplaristic model, and opened wide the portals of salvation. On the basis of this theological conviction the Universalist Church, which began as a sect, grew steadily throughout the nineteenth century to become a significant though small denomination, boasting several major educational institutions, Tufts College among them (1852). The church's lasting achievement was the influence of its universalist theory of salvation, which won broad acceptance among liberals and among more traditionally conservative revivalists alike, and which echoed Shakerism's own growing universalist orientations. In the words of one Shaker:

> For in spite of all drawbacks the blessed attraction of the love of the Infinite Father and Mother is an eternal and persistent energy and activity, and so, sooner or later, we shall all be saved. (Oliver Hampton, "Necessity of Expansion," *Manifesto* 18.3 [1888], p. 57)

Another brand of universalism, more cultural than theological, was also prevalent at the time. Radical changes in the intellectual climate of America were introduced by the new sciences of psychology, sociology, and evolutionism, and the newly developing critical study of both the Bible and comparative religions. These developments posed serious problems for the churches, challenging as they did the previous assumptions about, and modes of understanding, the Christian faith. Within Protestantism at large there arose a variety of responses to the crises posed by the new scientific world view, creating a broad spectrum of Christian options from left to right, which included Evangelical Liberalism, scientific modernism, conservatism, and dispensationalism. The new intellectual environment also bred a variety of more radical religious orientations which moved outside the parameters of traditional Christianity, among them the quest for a "religion of humanity," Christian Science, theosophy, and a fascination with esoteric Eastern wisdom, as well as various unity movements which sought to integrate many elements of the new religious consciousness.[15]

Intellectual progressivists that they were, liberal Shakers welcomed these developments which extended their religious horizons to new frontiers, particularly with regard to Eastern spirituality. As new modes of communication and information made more of the world accessible to them, progressive Shakers began to explore the global significance of their millennial faith. In consequence, this universalist orientation contributed to the dramatic recasting of their eschatological vision.

> Universality is the watchword of the age. If "God hath made of one blood all the nations of the earth," then shall mankind eventually become one brotherhood. The easy communication between the countries of the globe makes it possible. The exchange not only in the commodities necessary to physical life, but in thoughts, ideas, and religious experiences, seem to be the moulding or leavening process. Intelligence grows apace, and the barriers of narrow sectarianism, and the monopoly of God and heaven, must give way to the broader ideas of enlightened reason and soul expansion. God is love, and when man grows to divinity of character he too will be loved, and will enlarge the sphere of his activities. (Editorial item, *Manifesto* 24.12 [1894], p. 279)

Progressivism

The third important principle to influence the reformation of Shaker eschatology was progressivism — a belief in humankind's ability to develop gradually to a higher, better, and more advanced state of existence. This characteristically American notion of progress was embodied in the various religious and secular movements of reform which particularly dominated the latter half of the nineteenth century. Numerous and broad-ranging initiatives for social transformation greatly encouraged liberal Believers and reinforced their fundamental conviction that the millennium of which they were heralds was at last being manifested in the world.

The Shakers had always claimed that the Second Appearing of Christ was happening progressively, beginning with the messianic motherhood of Ann Lee, and gradually being realized within the new ecclesial family she bore; so too would the social millennium subsequent to the return of Christ be gradually and progressively realized. The Shakers acknowledged and celebrated the conception of the New Creation in the larger world, believing that their eschatological witness had helped to sow the exemplaristic seeds of the eschatological harvest growing up before them. Eldress Antoinette Doolittle spoke for the Society when she said, "We watch with profound interest every endeavor — whether by visible or invisible agencies — to reform and elevate the race to which we belong" (*Shaker and Shakeress*, 5.1, p. 138).

Like various American social reformers, from Charles Finney to the advocates of the Social Gospel, Shaker progressives had their own vision of the eschatological reformation which the advancing millennium would achieve. It was a concrete, this-worldly, historical vision, a "work of the present," in Anna White's words. Indeed, liberal Shakers had been awaiting the evidence of just such wide-scale social transformation to corroborate their premillennial faith. They regarded all manner of humanitarian progress with sympathy and solidarity and were quick to give moral support to every earnest endeavor. Therefore, during the later nineteenth century, many Shaker minds lent their insight and encouragement to the millennial hopes of the nation and encouraged the Believers' uniquely exemplaristic role in furthering its realization. As *Manifesto* editor, Henry Blinn reminded the Society,

> Those who anticipate the millennium of God's love
> on earth, must be actively engaged in the preparatory
> stages, or the fullness can never be realized. (Blinn,
> "Millennium," *Manifesto* 20.9 [1890], pp. 206-207)

"That it will come: that it is now coming to those who have
eyes to see and ears to hear; and that it has already come to many"
was constantly repeated in their writing (ibid.). Their optimism
mirrored that of the society around them, as they witnessed an
acceleration of intellectual development, scientific breakthrough,
and social transformation unparalleled in history. It seemed that if
such great progress could be achieved in America in such short
time, how far behind could the rest of humanity be from the realization of the millennium? So these Shakers looked eagerly for the
discernible features of its fuller appearing.

> When the whole race of mankind comes into the
> new earth and the heavens — the millennium — the
> resurrection, "war will cease to the ends of the earth,"
> and men will cease to do evil and learn to do well,
> the generative resurrected into a spiritual sexual rela-
> tion, above the animal, propagative plane. The back
> brain will go up into the intellectual, and the intel-
> lectual will go up into the spiritual brain region.
> Private property acquisitiveness will be raised into
> pure communion, where each one can seek another's
> wealth and not their own, without becoming a "prey"
> to a wolfish pack of self-seekers. And the war force
> and power will be "turned, as the battle to the gate"
> against war itself, on the selfish plane. (F. W. Evans,
> *Manifesto*, 20.9 [1890], pp. 195-197)

William Bushness further celebrated the power of the Spirit to effect a new social order noting the progressive nature of this millennial work already prefigured in the Millennial Church.

> Judged by these, in the progress of this eternal day, the apostolic age of ages, the nations shall yet be impelled to convert their instruments of destruction into implements of peace; not only to abandon all efforts to acquire fame by conquest and slaughter, but also to change all the customs of servitude, whether of man to man, or woman to man; all the distinctions of wealth, all the marks of honor that arise not from the indwelling of the spirit of love and exact justice in the soul; and to employ the abundant resources which the earth contains for the highest welfare of all its children. This is the universal prophecy that has come hymning its joyous melody all along the ages, uplifting many a heart that seemed over-whelmed by the accumulated evils of its own times. (William Bushness, "The Day of Christ," *Shaker* 6.5 [1876], p. 36)

Shaker journals are full of such commentaries, correspondence, and outcries on a range of issues being debated at the time: the equality of women, capitalism, revolution, labor, monopolies, commerce, Native Americans, race relations, war, capital punishment, socialism, and a host of other social concerns. As the only American communitarian society to boast of multiracial and ethnic integration, the Shakers had been a significant voice in the abolitionist movement.[16] As a pacifist church they were represented among the leaders of the American peace movement, forming their own and supporting other peace societies intended to influence personal and political attitudes toward war as a means for settling international disputes. The commitment to social transformation, so characteristic of the progressive wing of the Society, was nevertheless very much linked to the Shaker gospel of celibacy, now reinterpreted as a social ethic.

> The cause of social purity is very near our hearts. May God give us a voice of thunder and a glance of lightning, to protest at all times and in all places against the demon worshipped in so many households under the holy name of love! But when we come to the provision made for raging passions, the lust-license granted in the government of war, when we know of disease and rot that pollute the citizens, young and old, who in military ranks become butchers; we, in sackcloths and ashes, send up its plea for strength and wisdom to meet such deplorable conditions. And oh, the many social wrongs, the cankering love of gold that is eating out the heart of the nations, the constantly increasing power of the gigantic trust which, like the angel of the apocalyptic vision, standing with one foot on land and one on sea, swears that though freedom has been, it shall be no more! We cannot forget that in all the sacred writings of the people of the past and present, no greater anathemas are pronounced than against those who gather field to field, and the cries of whose oppressed laborers rise to the ear of the Lord God of Sabbath.
>
> The woman question, being answered today in letters of fire that whoso runneth may read, has always been an ever present one with us. Our founder, Mother Ann Lee, spoke out boldly for the God given right of woman to the common right of humanity. (Eldress Anna White, "Voices from Mt. Lebanon," paper delivered at the Universalist peace meeting, 1899, p. 7)

As they beheld the implementation of many of their most cherished values, the Shakers intensified the conviction that their eschatological principles "carried out today would make a paradise of this world" (Abraham Perkins, *Shaker* 7.1 [1877], pp. 6-7). Interestingly, the controversial Elder Frederick Evans, an ex-Owenite and chief spokesman for the revisionists, would rank their progressive social principles even before their religious beliefs:

> It is more than one hundred years since the founders of the Shaker Church, arriving in America, preached the good news of a present salvation from sin, and consequently from the punishments of sin through a life of self-denial, similar to that lived by Jesus, and which saved Jesus. *Purity, Peace, Equality* and *Unworldly ambitions* ranked first, a most worthy attainment. For the possession of these, any and every necessary self-denial was endured. Closely allied to these, but secondary in importance were theological beliefs, which, however unorthodox and heretical at the time, have since become the popular beliefs of the millions...("Hell" the torment of conscience; a non-physical resurrection; equality of the sexes; God Father and Mother; anti-slavery; communism; anti-war.)...There have been no forward movements yet made by the Church nor State but were anticipated and longed for by the little, obscure people, called Shakers. We would welcome more progress, particularly in the churches; we would welcome the relinquishment of the unstable hope, dreamed of in the *atonement* doctrine, and the substitution of the real life of Christ, which will save, and make us *at-one-ment* with Christ. We look for this consummation with positive certainty, and welcome

its dawning from any circumstance and from every quarter. The Shakers have very much to gain before they assert their proficiency as a Christian people; but they have thus far been in the van of all the righteous demonstrations that have reformed Church and State for the better; and yet stand ready to welcome more, and an eternal increase of morality, justice and true religion. These forward movements have been made at the expense of proneness to selfish considerations; and extreme self-denial in the foundation of the Shaker life and Church. (Frederick Evans, "Welcome Progress," *Shaker Manifesto* 11.12 [1881], pp. 274-275)

But, unanimously, the Shakers considered that their primary contribution and commitment to progressive reformism was to maintain their exemplaristic communities, which they believed offered the light and power for the social transformation at work in the world. Their long and dearly cherished value of "eternal progression" toward perfection, fusing with the broader cultural ethos of social progress, became a powerful principle which exerted its influence on the revision of Shaker eschatology underway at this time.

Spiritualism, universalism, and progressivism had exceptional influence on late-nineteenth-century Shaker eschatology for two reasons. First, all three notions were constitutive of Shaker faith, being present and nuancing the expression of Shaker theology throughout its development. Second, these three elements characterized the religious and intellectual concerns of the contemporary American culture, thereby providing Shakerism with a broader context and motivation for recasting its eschatological faith. The later Shakers undertook their work of radical theological revision not in isolation from the events and movements of the world, but now in consequence of, and in dialogue with, them. And as I will venture to demonstrate, these Shakers began to fashion an explicitly pneumatological language to describe their ultimate vision of Christ's Second Appearing.

THE REVISION OF SHAKER ESCHATOLOGY

Alethian Shakerism

Although no one Believer wrote the final treatise or tract on Shaker eschatology as such, several progressive Believers of the late nineteenth century took up the task of theological reorientation, calling themselves "Alethians," or followers of truth. Under the leadership of Elder Alonzo Hollister, Sister Aurelia Mace, and Eldress Anna White, the United Society of Alethians, as they now preferred the Shakers to be called, began a new religious venture: to reinterpret Shakerism's millennial eschatology in light of its new cultural and religious situation, while at the same time providing necessary theological rationale for the community's diminishment. With their guidance, the Society began to deal with the absolutist character of their former millennial claims, tempering the exclusive and definitive language of the old formulation in light of the new truth's being discovered in the world and in other religious traditions. Alethians earnestly sought whatever spiritual truth might advance their theological task, adopting an unusual openness to the world. In this new attitude, the Alethians discarded their former eschatological language and risked adopting a more dynamic grammar and syntax which might communicate a new awareness of the millennial mystery in progress. This development can be seen at work, particularly in a critical reading of the *Manifesto* throughout its three-decade history, and in some Shaker publications thereafter.

The three principles recently outlined — spiritualism, universalism, and progressivism — had a significant effect on the work of theological revision, altering the eschatological expressions of late Shakerism. The Alethian influence clearly expands and moves the Shakers beyond their initial eschatological formulations, toward more plastic christological and ecclesiological categories. With this new flexibility, their eschatology took a pneumatological form, speaking of the Spirit, universal and omnipresent, as endlessly unfolding its purpose in history. Therefore, by suggesting a developmental construction for late Shaker theology, it is possible to trace the notion of Christ's Second Appearing beyond the category of christology (particularly under the influence of spiritualism); beyond ecclesiology (particularly under the influence of universalism); and ultimately, even beyond eschatology (particularly under the influence of progressivism), to a thoroughly pneumatological, universal, and progressive notion of Christ's Second Appearing.

Beyond Christology

As we have seen, the earliest formulations of Shaker eschatology spoke of the Appearings in christological categories, in relationship to Jesus of Nazareth and Ann Lee. But by the late nineteenth century, christological language became more pneumatic, dynamic, and cosmic, as the remarks of Shaker Jessie Evans illustrate:

> He who walked the streets of the material Jerusalem is no more, the Christ that reigns today in the spiritual Jerusalem, the Christ that is ever cognizant of the needs, the sins of the world that "God so loved" is an omnipresence. His spirit inclines as two or three meet touching anything we would ask. In our human thoughtlessness we, too, like James and John, may ask for an end, but Christ will teach us

that the means only are for us; we may desire an
effect, but it springs from its corresponding cause.
   The life which Jesus lived is a life of processes. Was
ever intimation given by him of a goal, a resting place
for his workmen? The eternal knows no boundary
lines, and recognizes neither time nor space. (Jessie
Evans, "We Are Able," *Manifesto,* 29.11, p. 165)

The progressive ethos felt in this and other Shaker writings
of the period had always been Shakerism's, yet Alethian
Believers sensed an acceleration and diffusion of the processes
of revelation, with the Spirit overreaching the boundaries of all
former christological definition. Indeed, it is the Spirit, time
and time again, which becomes the ultimate term of late Shaker
theological discourse, rendering their carefully crafted, earlier
christology a mere modifier to their more fundamental and now
fully developed pneumatology. With this, the particularity and
uniqueness of God's revelation in Christ Jesus or Christ Ann
becomes subordinate to the anointing Spirit's inexorable movement toward humanity. In his essay, "Universality of the Christ
Spirit," Elder George Lomas expressed this new perception:

   Christ may be in millions, at one and the same
   time....What is Christ? It is a power, emanating from
   God to humanity; and transmissible from us, to other
   apostles of the same life. Upon whom this emanation
   rests, to them is given power to rise superior to themselves, and to become sons and daughters of
   God....Christ is a saving power, not a person....Let
   us manifest the salvation of this power to others, by
   impartation. As the disciples became Christs and did
   impart the power of salvation over every human
   weakness; so, in this era of the new creation, let the
   name "Christ in us" be exercised. (George Lomas,
   Shaker and Shakeress 4.2 [1874], pp. 89-90)

This reformulation of christological awareness, particularly under the impulse of spiritualism, significantly altered late Shaker eschatology. No longer was the ultimate appearing of Christ seen as particularized in a given time or place, in history or space, but primarily as an interior personal event, that is, a radical transformation of the human being in the anointing Spirit. Therefore the traditional notion of eschaton as the time or place of Christ's Second Appearing becomes *eschatos:* a thoroughly pneumatic being as Christ's ultimate Appearing.[17] Lomas clarifies further:

> We can never grow in truth, until we perceive that it is as really in our power to become Christs as it was the province of Jesus. And then there will be no...uncertainty regarding this important principle. Then will Daniel Christ, Anne Christ and _____ Christ attached to other Christian or Jewish names, declare the power intended by Jesus Christ. (George Lomas, *Shaker and Shakeress* 4.2 [1874], pp. 89-90)

Beyond Ecclesiology

Past christology, the dynamic principles at work in late Shakerism brought its understanding of Christ's Second Appearing beyond ecclesiology also. As we have seen, the earliest eschatological christology of Christ's particular appearing in Mother Ann gradually and deliberately evolved into an eschatological ecclesiology of the Millennial Church. Such a development was the direct consequence of the fundamental pneumatological orientations of their original Shaker faith, which held that the Christ Spirit was poured upon and pervaded all Believers, drawing them into a unified corporate body. Likewise, late Shakerism's eschatological christology, which envisioned Christ universally appearing in all who sought the truth of the Spirit, logically pointed to an analogous ecclesiological notion of union of the expanded universal body of believers. Thus, Catherine Allen could hope that

> through Deific impulse the better life in man will be quickened till all realize the essential unity of the race, and gradually merge into one great family of nations, speaking one tongue, having one Bible and one religion, all written in the simple words: "Love one another." ("The Millennium," *Manifesto*, 24.12 [1894], p. 275)

Particularly under the influence of the universalist principle, these later Shakers recast their original ecclesiological term of "union" in a greater context than simply its reference to the United Society. The principle of union was now seen to reach beyond the Church to the world, marking a change in their traditional perspectives. No longer did they perceive the Millennial Church as the single, spiritual center of union for everyone, everywhere. Salvation was now understood to be available wherever the quest for unity gathered men and women in a transcendent purpose. In consequence of this change of view, much of the antagonism between Church and world felt by former and conservative Shakers dissipated. With this boundary and line of demarcation blurred, the Shakers more willingly affirmed Christ's omnipresence in the Spirit. From this new perspective, progressive Shakers saw that their eschatological task was not to gather the world into the Millennial Church, but to be heralds and witnesses to Christ's advancing presence everywhere, while offering a model for the Spirit's discovery and a pattern for living in it.

In this ecclesiological mindshift, Believers affirmed the one Christ Spirit as the universal ground of all truth, essentially unified and unchanging in its essence, which, followed to its source, would lead Believers into communion with others who shared its life. Therefore, as Shaker communities diminished, they sought communion with non-Shakers with whom they felt spiritual affinity, convinced that "whatever the future may have in store for the Shaker Institution, Shaker principles are imperishable, and are finding wider and firmer acceptance continually" (Walter Shepherd, *Manifesto,* 24.11 [1894], p. 260). Therefore, ecclesiology moved toward universality as the former Shaker theme of union was expanded to include the whole Christian world.

Before the ultimate unity of humanity could be achieved, however, the Shakers realized that the disunity of the body of Christ had to be rectified since the Christ Spirit was the bond of union. For partnership in this enterprise of unification, the Shakers turned to the other Christian churches, and as if to transfer their own quest for ecclesial union onto the larger bodies of faith, they urged

> a united opinion as to what constitutes genuine Christianity; and so to take action upon the subject as to have but one grand Church, one united brotherhood of faith and life. (George Lomas, *Shaker Manifesto,* 10.9 [1880], pp. 203-204)

Elder Lomas called for a "conference for a union of the now divided churches," to ask the fundamental question, "How did Christ live?" This, he argued, is the key which would "unlock the bar to complete union." He took this ecumenical initiative in the name of the United Society, "with unbounded confidence...that...this scheme will be consummated: a united Christ family" (ibid.).

The movement toward reconciliation with other Christian churches helped the Shakers revise their understanding of the role they played in religious history, and led them to believe that "there are bonds of union far more important than doctrinal divisions" (*Shaker Manifesto,* 11.2 [1881], p. 41). This new attitude underscored the rather dramatic evolution from extreme ecclesial sectarianism and separateness of the previous century to a posture of open dialogue achieved by progressive Shakers. Their own traditional suspicion of any fixed expressions of faith made the Shakers critical of the various creeds and dogmas which maintained divisions between Christians, and which they saw to "shroud the truth of faith in mystery and inconsistency" (Giles Avery, "Soul Travel," *Shaker Manifesto,* 11.12 [1881], pp. 268-270). In their opinion, to focus on creed at all was futile, for the desired union of Christians was rooted not in theory but in practice, that is, in the lived faith of believers. Theology or doctrine was not a "reliable basis for unification of the human family in religion" (ibid.); what was necessary was profound and integral conversion of persons, comprehending all aspects of their lives.

> We propose the burning of all so-called Christian theologies, and substituting the simple, faultless life of Christ as a guide — this is all the theology needed. (Anonymous, "What Is Truth?" *Shaker* 2.7 [1872], p. 49)

Wherever this existential and eschatological spirituality was alive in the present, there, progressives claimed, was Shakerism, regardless of other ecclesiastical identifications.

> If such souls can be found among Shakers, Quakers, Methodists, Baptists, Episcopalians, Presbyterians, Catholics, or any other of the multitudinous cognomens of those professing religion, or those making no religion profession, such reality are Shakers of worldly elements, principles and institutions; they are the laboring agents whom God hath declared...should shake the world and its old heavens of pleasure in unrighteousness.
>
> When names, and sects, and parties shall have passed away, true Shakers will be found to possess a

kingdom eternal, while the world, and its elements will be burned up by fire of truth. (Giles Avery, "The Shaker Problem," *Manifesto*, 15.3 [1885], pp. 51-53)

This development to embrace the "anonymous Shaker" into the expanded union of the universal Christ Spirit was followed to its inevitable conclusion: opening the eschatological panorama to non-Christians, as well. As Anna White suggests:

We built the temple of our faith 132 years ago, making its four corner stones Purity, Peace, Justice and Love, but they were quarried from one rock and that rock is Christ. We recognize many shrines under the roof of the great world cathedral of the All-Mother, All-Father, God. (*Present Day Shakerism*, p. 1)

Exploring those non-Christian shrines for deeper coincidences with the Millennial Church led the Alethian Shakers to conclude that the eschatological Christ Spirit whom they at one time believed to be uniquely revealed in and by them alone was in actuality the manifesting principle of every authentic disclosure of truth.

No greater truth, whether enunciated by Confucius, Buddha, Zoroaster, or Jesus, will ever be lost. The grandeur and stability of moral principles outlive all forms, ceremonies and traditions. ("Religious Sentiment," *Shaker Manifesto*, 11.5 [1881], pp. 102-103)

Therefore, the ultimate goal of the millennial dynamism went beyond the union of Churches to the union of religions in a new corporate body of spiritual truth.

Buddhism is at present attracting great attention from scholars and liberal thinkers because of its literature, language, and antiquity, and the influence these are supposed to have exercised upon the growth of human ideas and conduct....

Whenever...the divine germ (in man) is allowed to freely expand in its own native element, it always asserts the same general principles of purity, gentleness, humility, self-sacrifice, patient willingness to serve, serenity, rectitude, harmony, and enlightened intelligence, whether in Jesus, Ann, Buddha, Plato, or any who look to them as teachers. (Alonzo Hollister, "Writing on the Sky," *Manifesto*, 13.5 [1883], pp. 97-100)

Toward the end of the nineteenth century, with their self-understanding set in a more ecumenical and pluralistic context, Giles Avery could confidently engage the Shakers in the dialogue meant to "forecast and inaugurate that grand reconciliation, mutual acceptance and harmony, which is believed may be the basis of the religion of the future":

While Shakers understand that truth is an eternal reality, and that all phases of its manifestations are necessary, and living stones in its glorious temple, they do not believe that any formulated opinions of mere human conception, anchored at the dock of creed has claimed the heavenly Argosy of Divine Truth, with all her cargo of revelations, within the finite harbor of human attainments. She is out upon the boundless ocean of God's wisdom and love; and, though she may often come to human port, with her cargo, will never be chained to the dock of any finished Venice on a human strand. (Giles B. Avery, Letter to Stephen P. Andrews, *Shaker Manifesto*, 12.8 [1882], pp. 193-195)

At last, the notion of eschatological "union" originally revealed as the ultimate presence of Christ in the Millennial Church was seen as being progressively realized in the world effecting a new spiritual synthesis, first among Christians, then among other religionists, toward the ultimate union of humanity in the Spirit.

Beyond Eschatology

The eschatological intention of the Christ Spirit had always been union, as the Shakers faithfully repeated for over a century and a half — a union originally for Believers, then for all people of faith, and now revealed to and for the whole world in the eschatological union of humanity. This perception of the expanding context of revelation, with its widening field of address, was the fruit of the Shaker's long-held commitment to progressive unfoldment. The enduring progressivist impulse always turned the Shakers toward the future, orienting their expectation toward new revelation and greater expression of truth.

> If all revelation were in the past, it shows poor design in placing the eyes in the fore part of the head, or giving the feet the direction they have. The physical, mental, and spiritual vision, prophecy [sic] forward, onward, upward.
>
> True prophecy is a science, by which the higher intelligences reveal to faith what experience will record in the book of knowledge. (*Shaker* 2.5 [1872], pp. 34-35)

The idea of eternal progression, in concert with the principles of spiritualism and universality, had its most dramatic effect on later Shaker eschatology by subverting the very theological notion of an ultimate eschaton. Shakerism's eschaton was to be a gradual ascent of humankind toward a unifying religious vision, which Giles Avery described this way:

> Oneness of faith refers prominently to the principle
> of an ever-increasing revelation of the truth of God
> in Christ's Church, manifest through the quickening
> spirit — Christ. And as truth is eternal, there will be
> a oneness of faith in all souls who have traveled, or
> progressed to the same degree of light and Christian
> baptism. ...Those who have learned the same lessons
> in Christ's school. (Giles Avery, "Oneness of Faith,"
> Shaker 2.4 [1872], pp. 26-27)

While truth is considered eternal and unchanging, its unfoldment to human beings necessitates a gradual disclosure and continuous adaption of form to serve the revelation process within
history. In view of this, Oliver Hampton added that

> forms are evanescent and changeable, but principles
> are eternal and unchangeable. Every discrete unfold-
> ment of higher truth to finite man requires a new form
> to express itself in. This is because it is some little dif-
> ferent from anything which preceded it ("Necessity of
> Expansion," Manifesto 18.3 [1888], p. 57)

The late Shaker ethos of universal progress toward the Spirit
had its leavening effects not only on Shaker theology, episte-
mology, and anthropology, but on Shaker cosmology as well.
The eschatological dynamism of eternal progression gave rise to
a sense of not simply human but even cosmic ascension, with
the whole universe returning to its divine source. The Shakers
envisioned the eternal progress of the many worlds to higher
modes of existence, being in their travel refined, perfected, and
divinized. Oliver Hampton described the universe as "the divine
manifestation and...image of the Godhead bodily" (Manifesto
14.9 [1884], pp. 193-194); and "the house of our Father and
Mother, and all progressive manifestations are the results of

their influence and presence" ("Hampton Logic," *Shaker* 1.11 [1871], pp. 84-85).

> One of the laws of the universe of finite beings and things is progress — improvement — evolution (i.e.) rolling out or unfolding from lower to higher degrees of perfection. Between the finite spirit of man and the infinite spirit of the All Good there is an eternal attraction. ...Through the above named attraction, resurrection is possible. For in spite of all drawbacks the blessed attraction of love of the Infinite Father and Mother is an eternal and persistent energy and activity, and so, sooner or later, we shall all be saved. (Oliver Hampton, "Necessity of Expansion," *Manifesto* 18.3 [1888], p. 57)

Late-nineteenth-century Shakers came to believe that Christ's Second Appearing, revealed in and to them, was in fact always and everywhere revealing, in different forms, under different names, the one truth of the Christ Spirit: purity, peace, unity, and love. They seem to see themselves as one dramatic instance of the universally emerging eschaton. The new eschaton which was dawning was the acceleration and inevitable progress of the Spirit's unfolding fullness. The Shakers concluded, therefore, that the age of the Spirit, that millennium subsequent to Christ's Second Appearing, was progressively emerging and ultimately unending. By the threshold of the twentieth century, progressive Shakerism seemed to have outgrown the very presupposition of Christian eschatology: that there would indeed be an end.

> Our most satisfactory view is that there seems to be an unending category of individualized intelligences extending endlessly and infinitely higher and lower, and all located along line of everlasting evolu-

tion and progress to higher conditions of perfection toward which they will forever and ever approach, but never reach....

We do not know and cannot conceive of any end of this that would be satisfactory to the party and therefore do not believe there is an end. (William Bushell, *Shaker Manifesto* 8.1 [1878], p. 2)

In this brief, cursory survey of liberal voices of late Shakerism, drawn particularly from the journal entries of the *Manifesto*, there is discovered a dramatic change in the notion of Christ's Second Appearing from the original formulation of millennial faith. Driven by the acceleration of its own inherent spiritualist, universalist, and progressivist orientations, late Shaker eschatology appeared to be dramatically rerouted toward new theological horizons. The spiritualism of late Shakerism moved Believers beyond Christ to the Spirit; universalism moved them beyond ecclesiology toward a worldwide religious community; their commitment to the truth of eternal progression ultimately moved them even beyond eschatology toward a progressive and universal pneumatology. These dynamisms were successful in dramatically altering the Shaker notion of eschatology — that is, the expectation of an ultimate spiritual transformation of humankind and the world by either a definitive change or a definitive ending.

Depending on the perspective drawn from this study, one of two conclusions can be reached. Late-nineteenth-century Shakers may have moved beyond their own unique expression of eschatology either because they perceived that "eschatology" as such had come to an end in the radical presence of the universally emerging Spirit; or because eschatology itself, as the process of spiritual transformation, is eternal and therefore unending. In either case, an important shift in awareness seems to have happened which brought the Shakers beyond the category of eschatology to thoroughgoing pneumatology, since in either perspective, what dominates the theological horizon is Spirit — universally, progressively, and eternally drawing the world toward heaven.

CONCLUSION

The Eschatological Harvest

The metaphor so often used by late Shaker writers to express the pneumatic, universal, and progressive character of their revised eschatology was the various expressions of "the harvest." This image, suggestive of an ongoing labor of gathering that which has come to fruition, took the place of the traditional eschatological notion of "the end," and enabled the Shakers to develop a more evolutionary eschatological category to complement their universal millennial pneumatology. In Giles Avery's words, "That theology alone is Christian which teaches 'The Harvest of the World'" (*Shaker* 7.10, [September 1877], p. 73).

> The millennial age, or thousand years' reign of the saints, upon earth, with Christ, is the harvest age of the race, in which time, be it longer or shorter, the Everlasting Gospel will be preached to every creature, and all souls will enter the judgment — a new probation for their final order. It is the transition period of the race, from their natural life, to the spiritual. (Alonzo Hollister, "The Harvest Period," *Shaker and Shakeress* 5.9 [September 1875], p. 68)

In this metaphor of the eschatological harvest, Shakers imagined a process of tremendous spiritual transition of the human community, moving from one evolutionary phase to another, as persons emerged from an absorption and preoccupation with materiality toward an increasing spirituality.

> Were man merely animal, no doubt all his long-
> ings and aspirations would be satisfied with a fullness
> of the pleasures of an animal life; but human history
> presents the fact, that in all ages, among all classes of
> human beings, from the wildest natives to the most
> refined and enlightened of our race, there is an intu-
> ition reaching beyond the shores of time, to realms of
> pleasure higher than the sensual. An angel nature,
> born for spirit life, in heavenly spheres, crops out,
> and yearns for its native Eden; and heaven, of some
> ideal character, above earth's provisions, in all ages,
> has been the deer's vision; the poet's song; the sooth-
> sayer's amulet; the resting place for the weary; the
> sufferer's panacea, and the pilgrim's home.
>
> For every field sown, there is an harvest.
> Generation is the sowing of the world, regeneration
> the new birth into the kingdom of heaven; the resur-
> rection; are synonymously the elements of this heav-
> enly order, and this order is the harvest of the world.
> (Avery, "Christianity Is the End of the World,"
> *Shaker* 7.10 [September 1877], p. 73)

The late-nineteenth-century Shakers witnessed what they considered to be the process of harvest in the various millennial and reform movements, a process which dramatized for them the great eschatological labor of the Christ Spirit effecting the spiritual ripening of the race.

> In the movements of events, the trend of thought
> and reformatory action in the world at large, Shakers
> see the approach of a RIPENING OF HUMANITY to
> higher and nobler development. For the benefit of

the many whose life of self-denial and spiritual activ-
ity would mean satisfaction and completeness, they
send out thought waves of attracting power, to draw
men and women, honest, true-hearted, desiring
purity, strength and brotherhood, the attainment of
self-control, contentment and spiritual happiness,
those willing to work for soul-development, for the
good of others, for the uplifting of humanity. (Anna
White, *Present Day Shakerism*, p. 31)

The Shakers widened their vision of "harvesters," therefore,
to include all and any who labored for the spiritual life of the
world. However, it must be underscored that in Shakerism's
eschatological end one still sees its beginning. Beneath the various theological transformations of this period which modified
Shaker belief in many ways, one conviction was unchanged: in
the eschatological harvest, celibacy was the state of ultimate
spiritual ripeness, and the virgin life or kingdom-of-heaven
order was still humanity's ultimate fruit. The process-image of
ripening and harvest, therefore, remained bound to that seminal
commitment of the Millennial Church to celibacy. For
Believers, celibacy was the way of birth into the eschatological
Christ Spirit and remained the way of ultimate mystical regeneration for everyone everywhere. Its value as the abiding eschatological orientation of the Shakers was never questioned, even
though celibacy proved to be a formidable deterrent to membership and a significant reason for the community's decline.
Nevertheless, the Shakers persisted in their claim that celibacy
— that kingdom state — was constitutive of the eschatological
age of harvest.

The pre-eminent work Christ came on earth to inaugurate, was to institute the kingdom-of-heaven order
— the harvest of the world. This work would have
been necessary for the perfect evolution of human-

ity's soul life, had mankind never sinned. (Avery, *Shaker* 7.10 [September 1877], p. 74)

After more than a century of experience and reflection, the Believers developed a fuller pneumatological context for the life of celibacy which they understood to be the essential work of the millennial harvest. It was not seen simply as the rectification required by a disordered libido; rather, celibacy was perceived as the inevitable and predestined state by which creation evolved from flesh toward spirit. The Shakers would claim that the highest impulse of life was not toward material increase on the natural plane but a radical augmentation and development of the human spirit: "to enlarge interiorly, expand and articulate the 'life of the Spirit'" (John Kenworthy, "Marriage," in *Alethianism or Shakerism: The Truth of Eternal Life Lived Here and Now*, ed. Alonzo G. Hollister [Mt. Lebanon, NY, 1892-1899], p. 25).

> Perfectly attained by every human being, this ideal would mean the extinction of the present race of animal men certainly. But is that a loss, weighed against the gain of perfected human souls? Those who despair, imagining that such souls become extinct at the death of their bodies, may also rightly despair of everything in life. (Ibid.)

Celibacy, then, is the pneumatological labor of "soul-development," an eschatological work by which the whole race is called into the Christ Spirit. Thus, regeneration — always identified as the end of generation — was seen by late Shakers as a divided humanity's struggle to evolve to the next unifying, reconciling, and sanctifying stage of being. The alienating practices of the unredeemed (i.e., noncelibates) such as "private families, private property and private residences" were to the Shakers anachronisms which threatened human survival (Giles Avery,

"Christianity Is the End of the World," *Shaker* 7.10 [1877], p. 74). The conventional biological family required "isolation of interests and resistance for its existence" (ibid.). Such a conventional model of human community and organization could only maintain and perpetuate the present status of the race; it could not of its own design effect the movement to the next, higher level of spiritual union essential for humanity's eschatological development. Late Shakers insisted that though "the family relation is a great primal necessity...and the seedfield of the human race," it is not the priority of the eschatological age of harvest. They constantly reiterated their plea that humanity go beyond the particular tribal concerns of family, society, and nation, to a universal consciousness that sought not mere self-preservation, but a new mode of creative bonding and interdependence to establish a new unified world order, whatever the cost. "Besides these, there is no true way for men and women to live upon this planet" (ibid.).

By the twentieth century, the eschatological faith of the Millennial Church had achieved its own final season of harvest, with all of its seminal concerns having blossomed and then ripened into a fruitful vision of Christian faith. There would be little further development of theological awareness recorded for future generations. What remained was an invincible hope and a lucid witness concerning the Christ Spirit believed to be mysteriously appearing as humanity more profoundly realized its sacred and essential union. In the development of Shaker theological understanding, the meaning of Christ's Second Appearing had moved beyond the projections of eschatology to pneumatology, the realized presence of an eternally revealing mystery which Shakerism would ever herald: the all pervasive, all inclusive Spirit.

NOTES

1. For a discussion of the controversy between Shaker revisionists and introversionists, see John McKelvie Whitworth, *God's Blueprints: A Sociological Study of Three Utopian Sects* (Boston: Routledge and Kegan Paul, 1975), pp. 54-64.

2. Mary L. Richmond, compiler and annotator, *Shaker Literature: A Bibliography* (Hancock, MA: Shaker Community, 1977), Vol. 1, p. 139.

3. Although the AMS Press reprinted the entirety of the *Manifesto* in 1973, my gratitude is to the Sabbathday Lake Shakers who made their microfiche of it available to me. For a good annotation to the various editions of the journal, see pp. 138-142 of Richmond, *Shaker Literature.*

4. For a summary of the factors influencing the decline of the order, see Andrews, *People Called Shakers,* pp. 224-240; and Whitson, *The Shaker Way,* pp. 21-22. See also Priscilla J. Brewer, *Shaker Communities, Shaker Lives* (Hanover, NH: University Press of New England, 1986), pp. 178-205.

5. Andrews, *People Called Shakers,* p. 224.

6. For a broad statistical analysis of the Shakers, see the collection of demographic data compiled by Brewer, *Shaker Communities,* pp. 207-238.

7. Whitworth, *God's Blueprints,* p. 60.

8. Sidney Ahlstrom, *A Religious History of the American People* (New Haven: Yale University Press, 1972), p. 489.

9. For an account of the various revivals and religious movements in the region at this time, see Whitney Cross, *Burned
Over District: The Social and Intellectual History of Enthusiastic
Religion in Western New York* (New York: Harper and Row,
1950).

10. For a fuller description of Mother Ann's Work, see Andrews,
People Called Shakers, chap. 4, and the reference to his
sources, p. 296. See also Brewer, *Shaker Communities*, pp.
115-139.

11. John Humphrey Noyes, *History of American Socialisms* (New
York: Hillary House Publishers, 1961), pp. 611-612.

12. The temptation to explore Mother Ann's Work more fully
must be resisted, since such a study is beyond the primary
concern of this book and fraught with methodological diffi-
culties. The surviving evidence consists of a profusion of
prophecies, inspired songs, dances, drawings, and rituals,
much probably still in manuscript form. There are very few
publications from this period which treat of Mother Ann's
Work directly (see Paulina Bates, Ebenezer Bishop, David
Rich Lamson, and Philemon Stewart in Richmond, *Shaker
Literature*). Even most of the published material, largely spiritualist prophecies and songs, was subsequently rejected as
inauthentic by the Ministry. Only much later, at the turn of
the century, did a few Shakers, particularly Henry Blinn,
Frederick Evans, and Anna White, attempt to consider the
significance of "Mother Ann's Second Appearing."

13. See *The Disappointed: Millerism and Millenarianism in the
Nineteenth Century*, ed. Ronald L. Numbers and Jonathan
M. Butler (Bloomington: Indiana University Press, 1987).

14. Ahlstrom, *Religious History*, p. 482.

15. Winthrop S. Hudson, *Religion in America,* 3rd ed. (New York: Charles Scribner's Sons, 1981), pp. 286ff.

16. The Philadelphia Shakers were an interracial community of twenty or more members under the leadership of the noted Black Shaker Mother Rebecca Cox Jackson. See Jean Humez, ed., *Gifts of Power: The Writings of Rebecca Jackson, Black Visionary, Shaker Eldress* (Amherst: University of Massachusetts Press, 1981); Richard E. Williams, *Called and Chosen: The Story of Mother Rebecca Jackson and the Philadelphia Shakers* (Metuchen, NJ: Scarecrow Press, 1981).

17. Patrick Regan, "Pneumatological and Eschatological Aspects of Liturgical Celebration," *Worship* 57 (1977); p. 347.

Conclusion

The expectation of the Second Coming of Christ has lingered in the Christian imagination for centuries, surfacing from time to time with great drama and vehemence. Down through the ages, from the apostolic and patristic eras to the medieval and Reformation period, and even to the evangelization of the New World up to the present day, there has been a great procession of millennialists whose major religious preoccupation has been how, where, and when Christ would come again. But to the Shakers, the Second Appearing of Christ had already commenced; it had begun in and through the messianic ministry of a woman: Ann Lee.

In this Shaker conviction, Christian history witnessed one of the most radical expressions of eschatological faith: two hundred years of belief that Christ had actually come again and fulfilled the millennial promises long ago made to believers — to pour out the Spirit upon all flesh. As such, the Shaker phenomenon was a unique instance of Christian faith and remains an accessible environment in which to explore the nature and implications of a truly realized eschatology.

The earliest phase of Shakerism was defined by a christological description of the Second Appearing, since the initial focus of the Shakers' eschatological faith was the very charismatic Ann Lee, who led them into the presence of Christ through her gospel of transformative celibacy: One must give up sexual generation in order to experience the spiritual regeneration — indeed, the very life of the resurrection — made available by

Christ's Second Appearing. At this stage, the Shakers struggled with a way to express the uniqueness which characterized their eschatological claim: the Second Appearing of Christ in and by a woman — a christological novelty, to be sure.

The *Testimonies* tradition recorded the Shakers' attempts to articulate their original eschatological understanding in the voices of particular Believers who spoke about their spiritual rebirth through the ministry of Mother Ann. Indeed this maternal labor to bring forth souls through regeneration was the exclusive messianic task of Mother Ann which, Shakers claimed, established her anointing as the first instance and agent of Christ's Second Appearing. This foundational christological kerygma, drawn from the testimonies of the earliest Believers, oriented and directed subsequent attempts at formulating and then reformulating Shaker eschatology.

After the death of Mother Ann, as we have seen, the Believers entered a new period of their religious life. In her absence, the focus of concern shifted to the spiritual children whom she had brought into the faith of Christ's Second Appearing. At this phase, the Shakers very clearly perceived themselves to be a unique body of salvation — a Church — with a historic mission to proclaim the presence and reality of the *parousia* and the real and present availability of the resurrection in this life. Consequently the language of their eschatological expression became more ecclesiological.

As the numbers of Believers grew, they were drawn into communities. Mother's successor, Father Joseph Meacham, made his own lasting contribution to Shakerism and American religion by gathering the faithful into what he called "Gospel Order": communistic groups of highly disciplined celibate families who shared "one joint interest in all things spiritual and temporal." Through this engrossing labor, he reoriented Shaker eschatology decisively toward ecclesiology, though with a new communitarian element. His only written legacy to the Believers, *A Concise Statement*, shifted the locus of the Second Appearing from

Mother Ann, whom he never mentions, to "a people." With this document, Meacham became the pioneer of Shaker theology in general and of their eschatology in particular, establishing the direction and guiding the course of subsequent Shaker writers.

The first attempt to articulate a coherent and systematic expression of Shaker eschatological faith was the work of Benjamin Seth Youngs, whose *Testimony of Christ's Second Appearing* united primitive christological eschatology with the emerging ecclesiological one by means of the notion of the Second Appearing as the Church born of the eschatological, indeed christological, woman — Ann Lee. His theological construction was supported by an intricate and characteristically Shaker set of correspondences — in the human order, the bipolarity of male and female; in the messianic order, that of Christ in Jesus and Ann; and in the divine order, that of God as Father and Mother, both and at once. In each case the poles are somehow united, and the fruit of the union, fully revealed in the eschatological age, is the Shaker Church, that new society of salvation realized in the spiritual union of its members in celibacy, members who corporately are Christ in the Second Appearing. John Dunlavy specified this ecclesiological description more exactly in the *Manifesto*, where he underscored the communitarian nature of the Church as the true manifestation of Christ's Second Appearing. It is precisely in the union of Believers — in their joint interest or community of goods predicated on celibacy — that one encounters the true Church established by the Christ of the Second Appearing. This Christ is not Ann Lee (Dunlavy, like Meacham, never mentions her name), neither is it the historical Jesus; it is the eschatological Christ Spirit who alone has the power to effect that union of Believers which is the manifestation of the Second Appearing.

The last significant work of this ecclesiological period was Calvin Green's *Millennial Church*. In it Green examined more specifically the pneumatological features of the eschatological community, which he considered the first instance and essential paradigm of the millennium advancing in the world. Against the backdrop of the many movements of moral reform, Green explored the progress of the eschatological Christ Spirit which was transforming the social order. By enlarging the field of operation of the Christ Spirit beyond the Millennial Church to the world, Green adjusted the Society's focus from narrowly ecclesiological concerns to more explicitly pneumatological ones. In this, he prepared the Shakers for their final eschatological revision, as they came to witness Christ's Second Appearing as the dawn of the millennium.

The last phase of Shaker eschatology had no particular voice to articulate the consensus of the Believers' faith, but a sounding of many voices, with the interesting and innovative discourse offered by the progressive wing of Shakerism. Since there was really no single coherent representative of Shaker eschatology at the end, my interpretation of the various writings of the later nineteenth century has been more speculative than my earlier exposition. What I perceived was a movement away from christological and ecclesiological definitions of Christ's Second Appearing, a reorientation occasioned by the challenge of the apparent emergence of the millennium in the world alongside their own unexpected but undeniable decline. Led by the Alethian revisionists, the Shakers moved toward a more radically pneumatological understanding of Christ's Second Appearing, no longer seeing it as confined to the Millennial Church, but everywhere and always advancing. As such, it was interpreted as essentially a spiritual event, progressive and universal, which paradoxically would grow as the Shakers diminished. This new understanding brought them beyond all the previous formulations of their eschatological faith, which had defined them as a unique Church and a particular species of Christianity. Indeed, it prepared them for their decision, in the twentieth century, to declare the end of the season of the Shaker testimony.[1]

This study concludes that the eschatology of Shaker

Christianity was always a pneumatology, even at its source in the mystical experience and charismatic anointing of Ann Lee. At every phase of the Shakers' efforts to articulate their understanding of Christ's Second Appearing, I have pointed to the implicit or explicit pneumatology at the heart of every expression. Furthermore, we have watched it emerge from each ancillary definition — whether christological or ecclesiological — until it stood alone as the sole guiding concept of Shakerism's eschatological faith. However, in standing alone, pneumatology brought eschatology to an end, since the ultimate goal of Christian hope had been reached with the realized presence of the Christ Spirit.

Hope is the very stuff of eschatology. It yearns for a fulfillment of sorts — some final, ultimate realization of divine purpose and human destiny. In Shakerism the last disclosure of divine mystery is linked to the outpouring of the Spirit, the power which transforms earth into heaven, which brings men and women home to union with God. When the eschatological secret is discovered, there is in some way an ending. In the case of the Shakers, pneumatology is the end of eschatology, since their hope, they claimed, had led them into the living presence of the Spirit — therefore, past the eschaton. Finally, this pneumatology became the end of the Shakers themselves, who, having followed the path of radical eschatological faith, had reached and surpassed their goal: union in the Christ Spirit.

I came to this study with certain questions about realized eschatological faith. Shakerism answered these in an entirely new configuration of Christianity — an exposition of variant forms of belief and alternative expressions of religious life informed by their radical pneumatology. Originally I asked, When the last things are put first in Christian living rather than in theological formulation, what are the actual effects on the believer, the community of the Church, the society? Shakerism said that for the believer, there is a new sense of spiritual possibility occasioned by the nearness of the Spirit. The human person is seen as perfectible, here and now, because the real source of sin and also its cure have been revealed. Since sex is sin and celibacy is redemption, sexuality and spirituality are linked in such a way as to alter dramatically the normal course of human life. In this renovation, woman particularly experiences a new valuation, since she is seen to play such a significant role in the eschatological designs of the Spirit. Because in this last dispensation she is redeemed from her ancient stigma regarding the fall of man, there can finally be a new relation between the sexes — no longer a physical but now a spiritual union in celibacy establishes the new patterns of human family making.[2]

The effects of realized eschatology on the Church seem to render it, according to Shakerism, the enduring manifestation and promulgation of this renovated relationship of men and women made possible by celibacy. The Church celebrates and supports this new union most dramatically by being a gathered body bonded by a perpetual covenant to share all things in common. Furthermore, Church structure, with its separate but parallel polity and ministry for males and females, supports this new union in the Spirit manifested among persons.

The broader social effects of radical eschatological faith, Shaker style, derive from the long-standing witness to spiritual values by a dedicated counterculture, which offers the world more than challenging ideas about what life could be. It offers a living example of what life actually is, under certain conditions, particularly with regard to the perennial social problems of racial, sexual, and economic injustice, violence, and the right use of natural resources.

I also asked the Shakers, What recessive attributes of Christian faith come to the fore in this new eschatological situation? Their tradition replied, "The Spirit" — the Spirit manifested in charisms and ecstasy, in Shaker song and dance, and in a new religious consciousness and culture which constituted a radically pneumatic mode of life. The stress on pneumatology brought about a new formulation of anthropology, christology, and theology, based on the eschatological numerology of two: What comes to the fore is the second sex — woman; the Second Appearing of Christ — Ann; the second revelation of God — Mother. Therefore, the binary — the essential polarity of all union — is seen more clearly than in the orthodox formulae of one and three.

In consequence, the unaccompanied "one" is diminished, particularly in the male mode. In Shakerism, it is not good for the man to be alone, therefore the traditional male dominance in Christian symbol and practice yields to a new mode of union, though, ironically, not without the elimination of marriage as a way of Christian relation. With the diminishment of the Father God and Christ Jesus as sole objects of faith, the Bible, their source of revelation, also is relativized. Since the Christ Spirit is present, the sacraments recede; dogma and creed are also jettisoned as the Spirit opens new eschatological revelation to the community.

I also asked about the new language and symbols of radical eschatological pneumatology. In Shakerism I discovered plain speech interrupted by ecstasy — a coupling language drawing opposition into union by the rediscovery of polarities. Their pneumatic language was spoken into matter to bring to expression a new order of reality in architecture and artifact. Past traditional sacramentality, they moved toward new ways of perceiving the sacred, in which the liturgy was the work of making visible the harmony, order, and perfection of the heavenly world brought into their midst by the Spirit.

Last, I wondered what was the new configuration of belief occasioned by a radical eschatology? The Shaker spiritual quest is not for a restoration of all that is prelapsarian, but for the truly eschatological, the absolutely novel: a life drawn from the vision and power and promise of the resurrection. The Shakers leave with us a bold and faithful witness to a dramatic form of radical eschatological Christianity — or must one hesitate here and say, rather, a radical pneumatology? And then, in orthodox terms, how really Christian? However theologians may classify

Shakerism as an expression of human faith, its witness causes us to wonder just how long a people can sustain the desire and the labor for heaven on earth, the very life of resurrection here and now. The Shakers endured for over two hundred years, and the vestiges and relics of their once vibrant witness recall that there is, in the congruence of the human spirit with the divine Spirit, a desire, and more importantly a capacity, from time to time and from age to age, for a splendid epiphany of the mostly hidden, often merely suggested, glory and goodness of which men and women are capable, if they be reborn in the Christ Spirit.

NOTES

1. In a controversial decision contested by the Sabbathday Lake Community, the Shaker Ministry at Canterbury, New Hampshire, "closed" the Shaker covenant in 1958.

2. For a fascinating study of the symbolic significance of celibacy for the equality and unity of the sexes and integral liberation for women, see Sally L. Kitch, *Chaste Liberation: Celibacy and Female Cultural Status* (Chicago: University of Illinois Press, 1989).

Appendix: Profile of the *Testimonies*

Thomas Swain's article, "The Evolving Expressions of the Religious and Theological Experiences of a Community: A Comparative Study of the Shaker *Testimonies*,"[1] is the first effort at the form and literary criticism of the *Testimonies* material so necessary as a foundation for Shaker studies. What follows is a synopsis of his descriptions of the various texts as they represent different periods of Shaker development.

The four texts (1816, 1827, 1845?, 1888) were produced by Shakers for Shakers; two were also directed at general readership by the world's people. Each had an explanatory preface, "Introduction," or notes "To the Reader," which helped in gaining the *Sitz im Leben* for the individual document. The texts did not reflect the ideas of one author; they were a compilation from many individual members of the Society. There was an editor for each of the volumes who used the original materials of the various contributors and on occasion made editorial comments when there was a deviation from the original.

In addition to the obvious changes the original material underwent during three-quarters of a century, there are the complex sociopsychological factors involved in the writing process which must be considered. The *Testimonies* material always involves three voices: the speaker, the recounter, and the redactor. The speaker was usually Ann Lee or one of the Elders; the recounter was the person telling the story (e.g., Jemima Blanchard); the redactor was the editor of the recounter's recollections (e.g., Youngs, Grosvenor, or Avery). Out of these historical, literary, and sociopsychological factors there emerged four very distinct editions of the early testimony material. A brief description of these follows:

1816 *Testimonies of the Life, Character, Revelations and Doctrines of Our Ever Blessed Mother Ann Lee, and the Elders with Her* was published at Hancock for Believers who had never met or heard Ann Lee and the first Shaker leaders. The basis of the text was "Mother's Sayings" collected by Elder Rufus Bishop and Seth Wells several years earlier. Since the number of original witnesses to the birth of Shakerism was declining, there was a concern to gather their testimonies for future generations. Green and Wells compiled this material into a kind of biography with additional material about her charismatic powers. There was, for several years, a growing feeling in leading minds "that a Memoir of our blessed Mother Ann's wise instructions & virtuous examples should be written, while many were yet living who were personally acquainted with her."[2]

1827 *Testimonies Concerning the Character and Ministry of Mother Ann Lee and the First Witnesses of the Gospel of Christ's Second Appearing* was printed in Albany. Since the 1816 edition was for Shakers only, this compilation by Seth Youngs Wells was the earliest one available. Unlike the other, this collection simply offered independent testimonies of particular witnesses, with no attempt to integrate them into a biographical account. The concern of the 1827 *Testimonies* is not so much to instruct Believers as to dispel the accusations of unbelievers concerning Mother Ann.

1845? Manuscripts of Roxalana Grosvenor entitled *Sayings of Mother Ann and the First Elders* and *Incidents Related by Jemima Blanchard of Her Experience and Intercourse with Mother Ann and Our First Parents.* These editions were gathered during the highly charismatic and spiritualistic phase of Shakerism, from the late 1830s to late 1850s. They, too, were meant only for Believers and, therefore, never were published.

1888 *Testimonies of the Life, Character, Revelations, and Doctrines of Mother Ann Lee* was called a second edition of the 1816 publication. It was slightly revised and edited by Giles Avery and evidences the various changes of perspective the Shakers underwent concerning their understanding of Mother Ann's person and revelation.

NOTES

1. *Shaker Quarterly* 12.1, 2 (Spring/Summer, 1972).

2. Green, *Biographic Memoir of the Life and Experience of Calvin Green* (Sabbathday Lake manuscript, 1861).

Bibliography

WORKS BY THE SHAKERS

Avery, Giles Bushnell. "The Living Christ." *Shaker Manifesto* 10 (January 1880): 2-9.

———. *Sketches of "Shakers and Shakerism": Synopsis of Theology of the United Society of Believers in Christ's Second Appearing*. Albany: Weed, Parsons, 1883.

———. *Spiritual Life*. Canterbury, NH: Published at Shaker Village, 1888.

Barker, Mildred R. "Our Mother in the New Creation." *Shaker Quarterly* 1 (Spring 1961): 10-15.

Bear, Henry B. *Scientific Demonstration of Theology, Prophecy and Revelation*. Preston, OH: 1869.

Bishop, Rufus, and Seth Youngs Wells. *A Circular Epistle. The Ministry of Elders of the Church, to All Those Living and Faithful Witnesses of the Truth, Whose Early Faith in the Gospel Gave Them the Privilege of a Personal Acquaintance with Our Blessed Mother and Elders*. Hancock, MA: J. Talcott and J. Deming, 1816.

———, eds. *Testimonies of the Life, Character, Revelations and Doctrines of Our Ever Blessed Mother Ann Lee, and the Elders with Her; through whom the Word of Eternal Life* was Opened in this Day of Christ's Second Appearing: Collected from Living Witnesses, by Order of the Ministry in Union with the Church. Hancock, MA: J. Talcott and J. Deming, 1816.

————, eds. Testimonies of the Life, Character, Revelations and Doctrines of Mother Ann Lee, and the Elders with Her, Through Whom the Word of Eternal Life was Opened in this Day, of Christ's Second Appearing, Collected from Living Witnesses in Union with the Church... Second Edition. Albany, NY: Weed, Parsons & Co., 1888.

Blinn, Henry C. Advent of the Christ in Man and in Woman. East Canterbury, NH, 1896.

————. The Life and Gospel Experience of Mother Ann Lee. 1882. 2nd ed., East Canterbury, NH: Shakers, 1901.

Bostwick, C. W. "Work as a Mode of Worship." Shaker Manifesto 11 (February 1881): 29-30.

Brown, Thomas. An Account of the People Called Shakers: Their Faith, Doctrines and Practice, Exemplified in the Life, Conversations, and Experience of the Author During the Time He Belonged to the Society. To Which is Affixed a History of Their Rise and Progress to the Present Day. Troy, NY: Parker and Bliss, 1812.

Constitution or the Covenant of the United Society of Believers Called Shakers in the United States of America. Louisville, KY: Printed by John P. Morton and Company, 1883.

Dunlavy, John. The Manifesto; or, A Declaration of the Doctrines and Practice of the Church of Christ. New York: E. O. Jenkins, 1847. (Originally published Pleasant Hill, KY: P. Bertrand, 1818.)

Eads, Harvey L. *Condition of Society: And Its Only Hope, in Obeying the Everlasting Gospel, as Now Developing among Believers in Christ's Second Appearing.* Union Village, OH: Day Star Office, 1847.

————. "Shaker Novitiate Covenant." *Shaker Manifesto* 8 (June 1878): 136-137.

————. *Shaker Sermons: Scripto-Rational. Containing the Substance of Shaker Theology. Together with Replies and Criticism Logically and Clearly Set Forth.* Watervliet, NY: Shakers, 1879.

————. *Shaker Theology.* Watervliet, NY: Shakers, 1884.

————. *Types of Christ, and Manner of His Second Appearing.* South Union, KY: 1878.

Evans, Frederick W. *Ann Lee (Founder of the Shakers), A Biography with Memoirs of William Lee, James Whittaker, J. Hocknell, J. Meacham, and Lucy Wright; Also a Compendium of the Origin, History, Principles, Rules and Regulations, Government, and Doctrines of the United Society of Believers in Christ's Second Appearing.* 4th ed. London: J. Burns, 1858; Mt. Lebanon, NY: F. W. Evans, 1871.

————. *Autobiography of a Shaker, and Revelation of the Apocalypse.* Mt. Lebanon, NY: F. W. Evans; Albany: C. Van Benthuysen and Sons, 1869.

————. *Celibacy, from the Shaker Standpoint.* New York: Davis and Kent, 1866.

————. *Christ.* Mt. Lebanon, NY, 1883.

————. *The Conditions of Peace.* Mt. Lebanon, NY, 1890.

————. *Elder Frederick W. Evans.* Pittsfield, MA, 1893.

————. *Resurrection.* Mt. Lebanon, NY, 1890.

————. *Shaker Russian Correspondence, Between Count Leo Tolstoi and Elder F. W. Evans* (February 15 and March 6, 1891). Mt. Lebanon, NY, 1891.

————. *Shakers: Compendium of the Origin, History, Principles, Rules and Regulations, Government and Doctrines of the United Society of Believers in Christ's Second Appearing. With Biographies of Ann Lee, Wm. Lee, Jas. Whittaker, J. Hocknell, J. Meacham and Lucy Wright.* New York: D. Appleton and Company, 1859.

Fraser, Daniel. *The Divinity of Humanity: The Cornerstone of the Temple of the Future.* Boston: Rand, Avery, 1874.

Green, Calvin. *Biographical Account of the Life, Character, and Ministry of Father Joseph Meacham, the Primary Leader in Establishing the United Order of the Millennial Church.* 1827. Sabbathday Lake Library manuscript. See also Theodore Johnson.

————. *Biographic Memoir of the Life and Experience of Calvin Green.* Sabbathday Lake Library manuscript, 1861.

Green, Calvin, and Seth Y. Wells. *A Brief Exposition of the Established Principles, and Regulations of the United Society of Believers Called Shakers.* Albany: Packard and Van Benthuysen, 1830.

————. *A Summary View of the Millennial Church, or United Society of Believers, (Commonly Called Shakers.) Comprising the Rise, Progress and Practical Order of the Society; Together with General Principles of Their Faith and Testimony. Published by Order of the Ministry, in Union with the Church.* Albany: Packard and Van Benthuysen, 1823, 1848.

Grosvenor, Roxalana (supposed author). *Incidents Related by Jemima Blanchard of Her Experience and Intercourse with Mother Ann and Our First Parents.* Unpublished manuscript, Sabbathday Lake, ME: Shaker Community, 1845?

———. *Sayings of Mother Ann and the First Elders.* Unpublished manuscript, Sabbathday Lake, ME: Shaker Community, 1845.

Haskell, Della. "What Is Shakerism?" *Shaker Quarterly* 1 (Spring 1961): 21-25.

Hollister, Alonzo G. *Christ the Harvester.* Mt. Lebanon, NY, 189? In *Manifesto* 29 (November 1899): 244-246.

———. *The Coming of Christ.* Mt. Lebanon, NY, 1890.

———. *Divine Motherhood.* Mt. Lebanon, NY, 1887.

———. *Mission of the Alethian Believers. Called Shakers: or, Alethianism or Shakerism: The Truth of Eternal Life, Lived Here and Now.* Mt. Lebanon, NY, 1892-1899.

Johnson, Theodore. "Life in the Christ-Spirit: Observations on Shaker Theology." Sabbathday Lake, ME: United Society, 1969.

———, ed. Calvin Green's *Biographical Account of the Life, Character, and Ministry of Father Joseph Meacham. Shaker Quarterly* 10:1, 10:2, 10:3 (1970).

Leonard, William. "Non-Resistance" *Manifesto* 14 (November 1884): 241-243.

Lomas, George Albert. *The Life of Christ Is the End of the World.* Albany: C. Van Benthuysen and Sons, 1869.

Manifesto, The. Published by the United Society. Volumes 1 through 29, January 1871 to December 1899. Title variations as follows:

The Shaker (1871-1872), G. A. Lomas, editor.

Shaker and Shakeress Monthly (1873-1875), F. W. Evans, editor; Antoinette Doolittle, editress.

The Shaker (1876-1877), G. A. Lomas, editor.

The Shaker Manifesto (1878-1882), G. A. Lomas, editor.

The Manifesto (1883-1899), H. C. Blinn, editor.

McNemar, Richard. *The Kentucky Revival, or, A Short History of the Late Extraordinary Out-Pouring of the Spirit of God, in the Western States of America, Agreeably to Scripture-Promises, and Prophecies Concerning the Latter Day: with a Brief Account of the Entrance and Progress of What the World call Shakerism, Among the Subjects of the Late Revival in Ohio and Kentucky. Presented to the True Zion-traveller, as a Memorial of the Wilderness Journey.* Cincinnati: John W. Browne Press, 1807.

————, comp. *A Review of the Most Important Events Relating to the Rise and Progress of the United Society of Believers in the West, with Sundry other Documents Connected with the History of the Society. Collected from Various Journals,* by E. Wright [pseud.]. Union Village, OH: Union Press, 1831.

Meacham, Joseph. *A Concise Statement of the Principles of the Only True Church, according to the Gospel of the Present Appearance of Christ. As Held to and Practiced upon by the True Followers of the Living Saviour, at New Lebanon, & Together with a Letter from James Whittaker, Minister of the Gospel in this Day of Christ's Second Appearing* — to *His Natural Relations in England. October 9, 1785.* Bennington, VT: Haswell and Russell, 1790.

————. *A Concise Statement of the Principles of the Only True Church.* Mt. Lebanon, NY, n.d. Reprinted 1900.

Millennial Praises, Containing a Collection of Gospel Hymns, in Four Parts; Adapted to the Day of Christ's Second Appearing, compiled by S. Y. Wells. Hancock, MA: J. Talcott, 1813.

Shaker Covenant of 1795. Mt. Lebanon, NY.

Stewart, Philemon. *A Holy, Sacred and Divine Roll and Book; From the Lord God of Heaven, to the Inhabitants of Earth: Revealed in the United Society at New Lebanon, County of Columbia, State of New-York...Read and Understand all Ye in Mortal Clay.* In Two Parts. Received by the Church of This Communion, and Published in Union with the Same. Canterbury, NH: United Society, 1843.

Wells, Seth Youngs, and Calvin Green, eds. *Testimonies Concerning the Character and Ministry of Mother Ann Lee and the First Witnesses of the Gospel of Christ's Second Appearing; Given by Some Aged Brethren and Sisters of the United Society, Including Sketches of Their Own Religious Experience: Approved by the Church.* Albany: Packard and Van Benthuysen, 1827.

White, Anna. *The Motherhood of God.* Canaan Four Corners, NY: Press of the Berkshire Industrial Farm, 1903.

———. *Present Day Shakerism.* Mount Lebanon, NY: North Family, 1906?

White, Anna, and Leila Sarah Taylor. *Shakerism: Its Meaning and Message; Embracing an Historical Account, Statement of Belief and Spiritual Experience of the Church from Its Rise to the Present Day.* Columbus, OH: Fred J. Heer, ca. 1904.

Youngs, Benjamin S. *The Testimony of Christ's Second Appearing Containing a General Statement of All Things Pertaining to the Faith and Practice of the Church of God in This Latter*

Day. Published in Union. By Order of the Ministry. Lebanon, OH: John M'Clean, Western Star, 1808, 1810, 1823, 1856.

WORKS ABOUT THE SHAKERS

Andrews, Edward Deming. *Community Industries of the Shakers*. Greenwich, CT: New York Graphic Society, 1974.

————. *The Gift to Be Simple: Songs, Dances and Rituals of the American Shakers*. New York: Dover Publishing, 1962.

————. *The People Called Shakers: A Search for the Perfect Society*. New York: Dover Publishing, 1953.

————. *Shaker Furniture*. New York: Dover Publishing, 1964.

————. *Visions of the Heavenly Sphere: A Study in Shaker Religious Art*. Charlottesville, VA: University Press, 1969.

————. *Work and Worship: The Economic Order of the Shakers*. Greenwich, CT: New York Graphic Society, 1974.

Andrews, Edward Deming, and Faith Andrews. *Fruits of the Shaker Tree of Life: Memoirs of Fifty Years of Collecting and Research*. Stockbridge, MA: Berkshire Traveller Press, 1975.

Brewer, Priscilla J. *Shaker Communities, Shaker Lives*. Hanover, NH: University Press of New England, 1986.

Campion, Nardi Reed. *Ann the Word: The Life of Mother Ann Lee, Founder of the Shakers*. Boston: Little, Brown, 1976.

Chandler, John. "The Communitarian Quest for Perfection." In *A Miscellany of American Christianity*, edited by Stuart C. Henry, 68-79. Durham, NC: Duke University Press, 1963.

Chase, Daryl. "The Early Shakers: An Experiment in Religious Communism." Ph.D. dissertation, University of Chicago, 1938.

Clark, Thomas. *The Kentucky*. New York: Farrar and Rinehart, 1942.

————. *Pleasant Hill and Its Shakers*. Pleasant Hill, KY: Shakertown Press, 1968.

Desroche, Henri. *The American Shakers: From Neo-Christianity to Presocialism*, translated and edited by John K. Savacool. Amherst: University of Massachusetts Press, 1971.

Dixon, William. *Spiritual Wives*. 2 vols. 4th ed. London: Hurst and Blackett, 1868.

Dyer, Mary M. *A Portraiture of Shakerism Exhibiting a General View of Their Character and Conduct, from the First Appearance of Ann Lee in New-England, Down to the Present Time*. Haverhill, NH: Printed for the author, by Sylvester T. Gross, 1822.

Faber, Doris. *The Perfect Life: The Shakers in America*. New York: Farrar, Straus and Giroux, 1974.

Foster, Lawrence. *Religion and Sexuality: Three American Communal Experiments of the Nineteenth Century*. New York: Oxford University Press, 1981.

Garrett, Clarke. *Spirit Possession and Popular Religion from the Camisards to the Shakers*. Baltimore, MD: Johns Hopkins University Press, 1987.

Guimond, James. "The Leadership of Three Experimental Communities." *Shaker Quarterly* 11 (Fall 1971): 95-113.

_____. "Nineteenth-Century American Millennial Experience," *Shaker Quarterly* 13 (Spring 1973): 3-15; 13 (Summer 1973): 27-37.

Hinds, William. *American Communities: Brief Sketches of Economy, Zoar...The Shakers.* New York: Corinth Books, 1961.

Hodgson, Stuart. "An American Communist Experiment." *Contemporary Review* 144 (September 1933): 320-328.

Holloway, Mark. *Heavens on Earth: Utopian Communities in America, 1680-1880.* London: Turnstile Press, 1951.

Horgan, Edward R. *The Shaker Holy Land: A Community Portrait.* Harvard: Harvard Common Press, 1982.

Humez, Jean M., ed. *Gifts of Power: The Writings of Rebecca Jackson, Black Visionary, Shaker Eldress.* Amherst: University of Massachusetts Press, 1981.

Kern, Louis. *An Ordered Love: Sex Roles and Sexuality in Victorian Utopias — The Shakers, The Mormons, and the Oneida Community.* Chapel Hill: University of North Carolina Press, 1982.

Lahutsky, Nadia M. "'So God Created Man in His Own Image, in the Image of God He Created Him: Male and Female He Created Them': Shaker Reflections on the Nature of God." *Encounter* 49:1 (Winter 1988): 1-18.

Lauer, Robert H., and Jeanette C. Lauer. *The Spirit and the Flesh: Sex in Utopian Communities.* Metuchen, NJ: Scarecrow Press, 1983.

Marini, Stephen. "Charisma, Gender, and Tradition in Mother Ann's Ministry." Paper presented at the Institute for Shaker Studies, Sabbathday Lake, Maine, July 1984.

————. *Radical Sects of Revolutionary New England*. Cambridge, MA: Harvard University Press, 1982.

Marshall, Mary. *A Portraiture of Shakerism*. New York: AMS Press, 1972.

Melcher, Marguerite Fellows. *The Shaker Adventure*. Princeton: Princeton University Press, 1941.

Merton, Thomas. "Pleasant Hill: A Shaker Village in Kentucky." In *Mystics and Zen Masters*, 193-202. New York: Farrar, Straus and Giroux, 1967.

————. "The Shakers: American Celibates and Craftsmen Who Danced in the Glory of God." *Jubilee* 11 (January 1964): 36-41.

Morgan, John Henry. "The Baptist — Shaker Encounter in New England." *Shaker Quarterly* 12 (Fall 1972): 83-94; 12 (Winter 1972): 152-163; 14 (Spring 1974): 27-32.

————. "Christology as a Communitarian Experience in the Theology of Shaker Christianity." M.A. thesis, Hartford Seminary Foundation, 1970.

————. "Communitarian Communism as a Religious Experience: Exemplified in the Development of Shaker Theology." Ph.D. dissertation, Hartford Seminary Foundation, 1972.

————. "Experience as Knowledge: A Study in Shaker Theology." *Shaker Quarterly* 14 (Spring 1974): 43-55.

————. "Radical Christianity: On Taking the Christ-Presence Seriously." *Shaker Quarterly* 14 (Fall 1974): 75-83.

————. "Religious Communism: The Shaker Experiment in Christian Community." *Shaker Quarterly* 14 (Winter 1974): 119-131.

Morse, Flo. *The Shakers and the World's People.* New York: Dodd, Mead, 1980.

Newman, Cathy. "The Shakers' Brief Eternity." *National Geographic* (September 1989): 302-325.

Nordhoff, Charles. *The Communistic Societies of the United States, from Personal Visits and Observation: Including Detailed Accounts of the Economists, Zoarites, Shakers, the Amana, Oneida, Bethel, Aurora, Icarian and Other Existing Societies.* New York: Schocken Books, 1965. (Originally published by Harper and Brothers, 1875.)

Noyes, John Humphrey. *History of American Socialisms.* New York: Hillary House Publishers, 1961. (Originally published 1870; reprinted as *Strange Cults and Utopias of Nineteenth Century America.* New York: Dover Publications, 1966.)

Patterson, Daniel W. "The Influence of Inspiration and Discipline upon the Development of the Shaker Spiritual." *Shaker Quarterly* 6 (Fall 1966): 77-87.

_____. *The Shaker Spiritual.* Princeton: Princeton University Press, 1979.

Proctor-Smith, Marjorie. *Women in Shaker Community Worship: A Feminist Analysis of the Uses of Religious Symbolism.* Lewiston, NY: Edwin Mellon Press, 1985.

Rank, Henry. "Establishment, Evangelicals, and Enthusiasts in Eighteenth-Century Manchester." Paper presented at the Institute for Shaker Studies, Sabbathday Lake, Maine, July 1984.

Richmond, Mary L., compiler and annotator. *Shaker Literature: A Bibliography.* 2 vols. Hancock, MA: Shaker Community; Hanover, NH: distributed by University Press of New England, 1977.

Richter, Fritz K. "Ludwig Tieck's Novel About the Camisard Revolt in the Cévennes Mountains." *Shaker Quarterly* 14 (Spring 1974): 3-11.

Sasson, Sarah Diane. *The Shaker Spiritual Narrative.* Knoxville, TN: University of Tennessee Press, 1983.

Setta, Susan. "From Ann the Christ to Holy Mother Wisdom: Changing Goddess Imagery in the Shaker Tradition." *Anima* 7 (Fall 1980): 5-13.

Sill, John Stewart. "The Impossible Dream: Tensions in the Utopian Ideal." *Free Inquiry in Creative Sociology* 16 (May 1988) 15-22.

Stein, Stephen J. *Letters from a Young Shaker: William S. Byrd at Pleasant Hill.* Lexington: University Press of Kentucky, 1985.

Swain, Thomas. "The Evolving Expressions of the Religious and Theological Experiences of a Community: A Comparative Study of the Shaker *Testimonies*." *Shaker Quarterly* 12 (Spring 1972): 3-31; 12 (Summer 1972): 43-60.

Symond, John. *Thomas Brown and the Angels.* London: Hutchinson, 1961.

Taylor, Michael Brooks. "Developments in Early Shaker Ethical Thought." Ph.D. dissertation, Harvard University, 1976.

Thompson, Rhodes. *Voices from Cane Ridge.* Bethany, WV: Bethany Press, 1954.

Upton, James M. "The Shakers as Pacifists in the Period Between 1812 and the Civil War." *Filson Club History Quarterly* 47 (July 1973): 267-283.

Weis, Virginia. "A Travel into Warfare: A Consideration of the Figures of the Heavenly Journey and the Internal

Combat with Evil in the Shaker Experience." *Shaker Quarterly* 11 (Summer 1971): 47-80.

Wertkin, Gerard C. *The Four Seasons of Shaker Life: An Intimate Portrait of the Community at Sabbathday Lake, Maine.* New York: Simon and Schuster, 1986.

Whitaker, Thomas. "A Benedictine Link with the Shakers." *Kentucky Historical Society Register* 67 (October 1969): 360-369.

Whitson, Robley. "The Renewal of the Shaker Tradition." *Shaker Quarterly* 7 (Winter 1967): 139-152.

_____, ed. *Shaker Theological Sources: An Introductory Selection.* Bethlehem, CT: United Institute, 1969.

_____. *The Shaker Way: Two Centuries of Spiritual Reflection.* New York: Paulist Press, 1983.

_____. "The Spirit of Shaker Christianity." *Shaker Quarterly* 5 (Fall 1965): 83-101.

Whitworth, John McKelvie. *God's Blueprints: A Sociological Study of Three Utopian Sects.* Boston: Routledge and Kegan Paul, 1975.

Williams, Emily. "Spirituality as Expressed in Song." *Connecticut Magazine* 9 (Autumn 1905): 745-751.

Williams, Richard E. *Called and Chosen: The Story of Mother Rebecca Jackson and the Philadelphia Shakers.* Metuchen, NJ: Scarecrow Press, 1981.

GENERAL

Ahlstrom, Sidney. *A Religious History of the American People*. New Haven: Yale University Press, 1972.

Bacon, Margaret H. *The Quiet Rebels: The Story of the Quakers in America*. New York: Basic Books, Inc., 1969.

Bailyn, Bernard, et al., eds. *The Great Republic: A History of the American People*. 2nd ed. Lexington, MA: D. C. Heath, 1981.

Ballou, Hosea. *A Treatise on the Atonement*. Randolph [VT]: Sereno Wright, 1805.

Baltazar, Eulalio. "A Processive View of the Eschaton as a Community of Love." In *The Eschaton: A Community of Love*, 5: 145-172. Joseph Papin, ed. Villanova, PA: Villanova University Press, 1971.

Barbour, Hugh, and Arthur Roberts, eds. *Early Quaker Writings, 1650-1700*. Grand Rapids: William B. Eerdmans Publishing Company, 1973.

Barbour, Hugh, and J. William Frost. *The Quakers*. Westport, CT: Greenwood Press, 1988.

Barkun, Michael. *Disaster and the Millennium*. New Haven: Yale University Press, 1974.

Baum, Gregory. *Religion and Alienation*. New York: Paulist Press, 1975.

Beardslee, William. "New Testament Apocalyptic in Recent Interpretation." *Interpretation* 25 (October 1971): 419-435.

Benoit, Pierre, and Roland Murphy, eds. *Immortality and Resurrection. Concilium 60*. New York: Herder and Herder, 1970.

Bentov, Itzhak. *Stalking the Wild Pendulum*. New York: E. P. Dutton, 1977.

Bestor, Arthur Eugene. *Backwoods Utopias: The Sectarian Origins and the Owenite Phase of Communitarian Socialisms in America, 1663-1829*. Philadelphia: University of Pennsylvania Press, 1950.

Bonaventure. *The Works of Bonaventure*. Vol 5: *Collations on the Six Days*, ed. Jose de Vinck. Paramus, NJ: St. Anthony Guild Press, 1970.

Braaten, Carl. *The Future of God: Revolutionary Dynamics of Hope*. New York: Harper and Row, 1969.

————. "The Significance of Apocalypticism for Systematic Theology." *Interpretation* 25 (October 1971): 480-499.

Brown, Raymond E. *The Virginal Conception and the Bodily Resurrection of Jesus*. New York: Paulist Press, 1973.

Bruggemann, Walter. *The Prophetic Imagination*. Philadelphia: Fortress Press, 1978.

Bultmann, Rudolf. *History and Eschatology*. New York: Harper and Row, 1957.

————. *The Presence of Eternity*. Westport, CT: Greenwood Press, 1975.

Capp, Bernard S. *Fifth Monarchy Men: A Study in Seventeenth-Century English Millennialism*. Totowa, NJ: Bowman and Littlefield, 1972.

Carwardine, Richard. *Transatlantic Revivalism: Popular Evangelicalism in Britain and America*. New York: Dial Press, 1970.

Catholic Biblical Quarterly. Special issue on Apocalyptic, 39:3 (July 1977).

Chamberlin, Eric Russell. *Anti-Christ and the Millennium*. New York: Saturday Review Press, 1975.

Charles, R. H., ed. *Apocrypha and Pseudepigrapha*. Vol. 2. London: Oxford University Press, 1913-1976.

————. *Eschatology: The Doctrine of a Future Life—A Critical History*. New York: Schocken Books, 1963.

Christianson, Paul. *Reformers in Babylon: English Apocalyptic Visions from the Reformation to the Eve of the Civil War*. Toronto: University of Toronto Press, 1978.

Cleveland, Catherine. *The Great Revival in the West*. Gloucester, MA: Peter Smith, 1959.

Cohn, Norman. *The Pursuit of the Millennium*. Oxford: Oxford University Press, 1970.

Collins, John J. *The Apocalyptic Imagination: An Introduction to the Jewish Matrix of Christianity*. New York: Crossroad, 1984.

————. "Pseudonymity, Historical Reviews and the Genre of the Revelation of John." *Catholic Biblical Quarterly* 39:3 (July 1977): 329-343.

Congar, Yves. "Pour une christologie pneumatologique," *Revue des sciences philosophiques et théologiques*. 63 (July 1979): 435-442.

Cousins, Ewert. *Bonaventure: The Soul's Journey into God; The Tree of Life: The Life of St. Francis*. Classics of Western Spirituality. New York: Paulist Press, 1978.

————, ed. *Hope and the Future of Man*. Philadelphia: Fortress Press, 1972.

Cross, Whitney. *The Burned Over District: The Social and Intellectual History of Enthusiastic Religion in Western New York, 1800-1850*. New York: Harper and Row, 1950.

Cullmann, Oscar. *Christ and Time: The Primitive Christian Conception of Time and History*. Philadelphia: Westminster Press, 1950.

Daniel, E. Randolph. "St. Bonaventure: Defender of Franciscan Eschatology," in *S. Bonaventura* 4 (Gottaferrata: Collegio S. Bonaventura, 1974): 793-806.

Daniélou. Jean. *The Theology of Jewish Christianity*. Vol. 1: *The Development of Doctrine Before the Council of Nicaea*. London: Darton, Longman and Todd, 1964.

Davidson, James West. *The Logic of Millennial Thought: Eighteenth-Century New England*. New Haven: Yale University Press, 1977.

Deen, Edith. *Great Women of Christian Faith*. New York: Harper, 1959.

Ditmanson, Harold H. "The Significance of the Doctrine of the Holy Spirit for Contemporary Theology." In *The Holy Spirit in the Life of the Church*, edited by Paul D. Opsahl, 204-218. Minneapolis: Augsburg, 1978.

Dodd, C. H. *The Founder of Christianity*. New York: Macmillan, 1970.

Dollard, Jerome R. "Eschatology: A Roman Catholic Perspective." *Review and Expositor* 79 (Spring 1982): 367-380.

Dunn, James D. G. "Rediscovering the Spirit." *Expository Times* 84 (October/November 1972): 7-12; 40-44.

Duquoc, Christian, and Flouristan Casiano, eds. *Spiritual Revivals. Concilium*, N.S. 9. New York: Herder and Herder, 1973.

Elder, Roxanne, ed. *The Spirituality of Western Christendom*. Kalamazoo, MI: Cistercian Publications, 1976.

Eliade, Mircea. *Cosmos and History: The Myth of the Eternal Return*. New York: Harper, 1957.

"Facing Apocalypse": Conference on the Apocalyptic Aspects of the Nuclear Age. Salve Regina College, Newport, RI, August 1983.

Ferm, Robert, comp. Issues in American Protestantism. Garden City, NY: Anchor Books, 1969.

Firth, Catherine. The Apocalyptic Tradition in Reformation Britain, 1530-1645. New York: Oxford University Press, 1979.

Fortman, Edmund. The Triune God. Philadelphia: Westminster Press, 1972.

Goen, C. C. Revivalism and Separatism in New England, 1740-1800. New Haven: Yale University Press, 1962.

Greven, Philip. The Protestant Temperament: Patterns of Child-rearing, Religious Experience, and the Self in Early America. New York: Knopf, 1977.

Grimm, Harold. The Reformation Era. New York: Macmillan, 1954.

Guardini, Romano. The Last Things. Notre Dame: University of Notre Dame Press, 1954.

Habig, Marion, ed. St. Francis of Assisi: Writings and Early Biographies — English Omnibus of Sources of the Life of St. Francis. Chicago: Franciscan Herald Press, 1973.

Hall, Thomas C. The Religious Background of American Culture. New York: Frederick Ungar, 1959.

Haller, William, and Godfrey Davies, eds. The Leveller Tracts, 1647-1653. New York: Columbia University Press, 1944.

Hamilton, Neill O. "The Holy Spirit and Eschatology." Scottish Journal of Theology. Occasional Papers, 6. Edinburgh: Oliver and Boyd, 1957.

Hanson, Paul. *The Dawn of Apocalyptic*. Philadelphia: Fortress Press, 1975.

Harrison, J. F. C. *The Second Coming: Popular Millenarianism, 1780-1850*. New Brunswick, NJ: Rutgers University Press, 1979.

Haughey, John. *The Conspiracy of God*. Garden City, NY: Doubleday, 1973.

Hick, John H. *Death and Eternal Life*. New York: Harper and Row, 1976.

Hiers, Richard H. *Jesus and the Future: Unresolved Questions of Eschatology*. Atlanta: John Knox Press, 1981.

Hill, John E. C. *The World Turned Upside Down*. London: Temple Smith, 1972.

Hong, Christopher. *A History of the Future: A Study of the Four Major Eschatologies*. Washington, DC: University Press of America, 1981.

Hudson, Winthrop S. *Religion in America*. 3rd ed. New York: Charles Scribner's Sons, 1981.

Huizing, Peter, and William Bassett. *Experience of the Spirit. Concilium*, N.S. 9, 10. New York: Seabury Press, 1974.

Interpretation. Special issue on Apocalyptic, 25 (1971).

Jedin, Hubert, and John Dolan, eds. *Handbook of Church History*. Vol. 4: *From the High Middle Ages to the Eve of the Reformation*. New York: Herder and Herder, 1970.

Jeremias, Joachim. *New Testament Theology: The Proclamation of Jesus*. New York: Charles Scribner's Sons, 1971.

Jonas, Gerald. *On Doing Good: The Quaker Experiment*. New York: Charles Scribner's Sons, 1971.

Journal for Theology and the Church. Special issue on Apocalyptic, 6 (1969).

Jurgens, W. A. *The Faith of the Early Fathers*. Collegeville, MN: Liturgical Press, 1970.

Kantor, Elizabeth Moss. *Communes and Utopias in Sociological Perspective*. Cambridge: Harvard University Press, 1972.

Kasper, Walter. *Jesus the Christ*. New York: Paulist Press, 1976.

Kilian, Sabbas. "The Holy Spirit in Christ and in Christians." *American Benedictine Review* 20 (March 1969): 99-121.

Kitch, Sally L. *Chaste Liberation: Celibacy and Female Cultural Status*. Chicago: University of Illinois Press, 1989.

Koch, Klaus. *The Rediscovery of Apocalyptic: A Polemical Work on a Neglected Area of Biblical Studies and Its Damaging Effect on Theology and Philosophy*. New York: Alec R. Allenson, 1970.

Ladd, George Eldon. *The Presence of the Future*. Grand Rapids: W. B. Eerdmans, 1974.

Lewis, R. W. B. *The American Adam*. Chicago: University of Chicago Press, 1955.

Longenecker, Richard N. *The Christology of Early Jewish Christianity*. London: SCM Press, 1970.

Malatesta, Edward, ed. *The Spirit of God in Christian Life*. New York: Paulist Press, 1977.

Marty, Martin E. *Righteous Empire: The Protestant Experience in America*. New York: Dial Press, 1970.

McDermott, Brian O. "Roman Catholic Christology: Two Recurring Themes." *Theological Studies* 41 (June 1980): 339-367.

McDonald, Killian. "The Determinative Doctrine of the Holy Spirit." *Theology Today* 39 (July 1982): 142-161.

McGinn, Bernard, ed. *Apocalyptic Spirituality*. Classics of Western Spirituality. New York: Paulist Press, 1979.

————. *Visions of the End*. New York: Columbia University Press, 1979.

McLoughlin, William G. *Revivals, Awakenings and Reform: An Essay on Religion and Social Change in America, 1607-1977*. Chicago: University of Chicago Press, 1978.

Moltmann, Jürgen. *The Church in the Power of the Holy Spirit*. London: SCM Press, 1977.

————. *Theology of Hope: On the Ground and Implications of a Christian Eschatology*. New York: Harper and Row, 1967.

Moltmann, Jürgen and Frederick Herzog, eds. *The Future of Hope: Theology as Eschatology*. New York: Herder and Herder, 1970.

Montague, George T. *The Holy Spirit: Growth of a Biblical Tradition*. New York: Paulist Press, 1976.

————. "The New Testament and the Future." *Bible Today* 57 (December 1971): 554-563.

Morris, Leon. *Apocalyptic*. Grand Rapids: W. B. Eerdmans, 1972.

Muckenhirn, Maryellen, ed. *The Future as the Presence of Shared Hope*. New York: Sheed and Ward, 1968.

Muller-Goldkuhle, Peter. "Post-Biblical Developments in Eschatological Thought." *The Problem of Eschatology*. *Concilium* 41, edited by Edward Schillebeeckx, 24-41. New York: Paulist Press, 1969.

Mussner, Franz. *Christ and the End of the World.* Notre Dame: University of Notre Dame Press, 1965.

Navone, John J. "The Apocalyptic Theology of History." *Bible Today* 59 (March 1972): 676-683.

Neumann, Eric. *The Great Mother.* Princeton: Princeton University Press, 1972.

New Catholic Encyclopedia, 1967-1974. S.v. "Eschatology," by F. Martin and M. E. Williams; "Millennialism and Eschatology," by J. P. Dolan.

Niebuhr, H. Richard. *The Kingdom of God in America.* New York: Harper and Row, 1937.

Numbers, Ronald L., and Jonathan M. Butler, eds. *The Disappointed: Millerism and Millenarianism in the Nineteenth Century.* Bloomington: Indiana University Press, 1987.

Pannenberg, Wolfhart. *Basic Questions in Theology.* Philadelphia: Fortress Press, 1970.

————. "The Doctrine of the Spirit and the Task of a Theology of Nature." *Theology* 75 (January 1972): 8-21.

————. *Jesus: God and Man.* Philadelphia: Westminster Press, 1968.

————. *Revelation as History.* New York: Macmillan, 1968.

————. *Theology and the Kingdom of God.* Philadelphia: Westminster Press, 1969.

————. *What Is Man?* Philadelphia: Fortress Press, 1970.

Pannenberg, Wolfhart, Avery Dulles, and Carl Bratten, eds. *Spirit, Faith and Church.* Philadelphia: Westminster Press, 1969.

Papin, Joseph, ed. *Eschaton: A Community of Love.* Villanova, PA: Villanova University Press, 1971.

Perrin, Norman. "Eschatology and Hermeneutics." *Theology Digest* 23 (Summer 1975): 149-156.

―――. *The Kingdom of God in the Teaching of Jesus.* Philadelphia: Westminster Press, 1963.

Prigent, Pierre. "The Apocalypse of John and Apocalyptic Literature." *Theology Digest* 23 (Spring 1975): 53-59.

Rahner, Karl. *Foundations of Christianity.* New York: Seabury Press, 1978.

Reeves, Marjorie. "History and Eschatology: Medieval and Early Protestant Thought in Some English and Scottish Writings." *Medievalia et Humanistica*, no. 4 (1973): 99-123.

―――. *The Influence of Prophecy in the Later Middle Ages.* New York: Oxford University Press, 1969.

―――. "The Originality and Influence of Joachim of Fiore." *Traditio* 36 (1980): 269-316.

Reeves, Marjorie, and Beatrice Hirsch-Reich. *The Figurae of Joachim of Fiore.* Oxford: Clarendon Press, 1972.

Regan, Patrick, "Pneumatological and Eschatological Aspects of Liturgical Celebration." *Worship* 57 (1977): 332-350.

Richter, Peyton. *Utopias: Social Ideals and Communal Experiments.* New York: Hollbrook Press, 1971.

Rodman, William J. "The Holy Spirit and Eschatology." *Pneuma* 3 (Fall 1981): 54-58.

Rosato, Philip. "Spirit Christology: Ambiguity and Promise." *Theological Studies* 38 (Spring 1977): 423-449.

Rourke, Constance. *Roots of American Culture and Other Essays.* New York: Harcourt, Brace, 1942.

Ruether, Rosemary, and Eleanor McLaughlin, eds. *Women of Spirit: Female Leadership in the Jewish/Christian Traditions.* New York: Simon and Schuster, 1979.

Russell, D. S. *Apocalyptic: Ancient and Modern.* Philadelphia: Fortress Press, 1978.

————. *The Method and Message of Jewish Apocalyptic.* Philadelphia: Westminster Press, 1964.

Sacramentum Mundi, 1968. S.v. "Eschatology," by Karl Rahner; "Millenarianism," by Estevao Bettencourt.

Sacramentum Verbi, 1970. S.v. "Parousia," by Epidius Pax: "Spirit," by Robert Koch.

Schillebeeckx, Edward, ed. *The Problem of Eschatology.* *Concilium* 41. New York: Paulist Press, 1969.

Schmithals, Walter. *The Apocalyptic Movement.* New York: Abingdon Press, 1975.

Scholem, Gershom. *The Messianic Idea in Judaism.* New York: Schocken Books, 1971.

Schwartz, Hans. *On the Way to the Future: A Current View of Eschatology in Light of Current Trends in Religion, Philosophy and Science.* Minneapolis: Augsburg Publishing House, 1972.

Schwartz, Hillel. *The French Prophets.* Berkeley: University of California Press, 1980.

Schweitzer, Eduard. *The Holy Spirit.* Philadelphia: Fortress Press, 1980.

Sears, Robert T. "Spirit: Divine and Human — The Theology of Heribert Mühlen and Its Relevance for Evaluating the Data of Psychotherapy." Ph.D. dissertation, Fordham University, 1974.

Sill, John Stewart. "Impossible Dream: Tensions in the Utopian Ideal." *Free Inquiry in Creative Sociology* 16:1 (May 1988): 15-22.

Smalley, Beryl, ed. *Trends in Medieval Political Thought.* New York: Barnes and Noble, 1965.

Smith, Timothy. *Revivalism and Social Reform in Mid-Nineteenth Century America.* New York: Abingdon Press, 1957.

Steere, Douglas, ed. *Quaker Spirituality: Selected Writings.* New York: Paulist Press, 1984.

Stock, Augustine. *Kingdom of Heaven.* New York: Herder and Herder, 1964.

Sweet, William W. *Revivalism in America: Its Origin, Growth and Decline.* New York: Charles Scribner's Sons, 1944.

Tannehill, Robert C. *Dying and Rising with Christ: A Study in Pauline Theology.* Berlin: Verlag Alfred Topelmann, 1967.

Tavard, George. *Women in Christian Tradition.* Notre Dame: University of Notre Dame Press, 1973.

Thrupp, Sylvia. *Millennial Dreams in Action: Studies in Revolutionary Religious Movements.* New York: Schocken Books, 1970.

Tillich, Paul. *Systematic Theology.* Vol. 3: *Life and the Spirit: History and the Kingdom of God.* Chicago: University of Chicago Press, 1963.

Tracy, David. *The Analogical Imagination: Christian Theology and the Culture of Pluralism.* New York: Crossroad, 1981.

Tuveson, Ernst. *Millennium and Utopia: A Study in the Background of the Idea of Progress.* New York: Harper and Row, 1964.

Vahanian, Gabriel. *God and Utopia: The Church in a Technological Civilization.* New York: Seabury Press, 1977.

Wainwright, Geoffrey. *Eucharist and Eschatology.* New York: Oxford University Press, 1981.

Walker, Williston, Richard A. Norris, David W. Lotz, and Robert T. Handy. *History of the Christian Church,* 4th ed. New York: Charles Scribner's Sons, 1985.

Weinstein, Donald. *Savanarola and Florence: Prophecy and Patriotism in the Renaissance.* Princeton: Princeton University Press, 1970.

Weisberger, Bernard. *They Gathered at the River: The Story of the Great Revivalists and Their Impact on Religion in America.* Boston: Little, Brown, 1958.

Wilder, Amos. "The Rhetoric of Ancient and Modern Apocalyptic." *Interpretation* 25 (October 1971): 436-453.

Williams, George H. *The Radical Reformation.* Philadelphia: Westminster Press, 1957.

Willis, John R., ed. *The Teachings of the Church Fathers.* New York: Herder and Herder, 1966.

Winklhofer, Alois. *The Coming of His Kingdom: A Theology of the Last Things.* New York: Herder and Herder, 1963.

Winthrop, Hudson. *American Protestantism.* Chicago: University of Chicago Press, 1961.

Zamora, Lois Parkinson, ed. *The Apocalyptic Vision in America: Interdisciplinary Essays on Myth and Culture.* Bowling Green, OH: Bowling Green University Popular Press, 1982.

Index

Abolitionism, xii, 167, 212

Abraham, 79, 87, 102

Acts of the Apostles, x

Adam, primordial, 97, 102, 104-109, 116, 117, 123, 135, 150, 152

Adam, Second, *see under* Christ; Jesus

Adam of Whitehorn, 17

Adventism, 206

Age of the Father, 19

Age of the Son, 19

Age of the Spirit, 15, 18, 19, 227

Alaric, 16

Albany, NY, 37, 130

Albigensians, 18

Alethian Shakers, 216-229, 240

Alethianism or Shakerism: The Truth of Eternal Life Lived Here and Now (1892-1899), 232

Allen, Catherine, 194, 220

Amana Society, 128

American Revolution, ix

Anabaptists, 20, 128

Andrews, Edward Deming, 31

Andrews, Stephen P., 224

Angelic Pope, 20

Anglicanism, 22, 30, 32

Anselm of Havelberg, 17

Anselm of Laon, 17

Anthropology, 98-99, 133-135

Antichrist, 36, 83, 86

Apocalyptic: Augustinian revision, 16-17; Christian, 10-12, 15; as end of history, 15; Jewish, 7; medieval, 17-20; Reformation, 20-22; *see also under* Chiliasm

Apostolic Brethren, 18

Atonement, 138; exemplaristic xi, 207-208

Augustine of Hippo, 16-17, 19

Aurora and Bethel Communes, 128

Avery, Giles B., 194, 222, 223, 224, 225, 226, 229, 231, 232, 233

Ballou, Hosea, 207

Baptists, 31, 90

Bates, Issachar, 90, 91, 92

Bede, 17

Beghards, 18

Beguines, 18

Bible, Shaker attitude toward, 243

Biographical Account (1827) of Joseph Meacham, 157

Biographic Memoir (1861) of Calvin Green, 157

Bishop, Job, 71

Bishop, Rufus, 40

Bishop, Talmadge, 69

Black Death, 20

Blacks, 162

Blanchard, Jemima, 41

Blinn, Henry C., 194, 198, 210-211

Body, the: and celibacy, 181; as communitarian term, 73-74; as ecclesiological term, 9, 81-82, 103-105, 107, 113, 117-118, 142, 145, 165-66, 171; as ecumenical term, 221; as ground of salvation, 79; as Millennial Church, 124; and resurrection, 153-154, 182; as sin, 78; and the soul, 98

Body of Christ: as ecclesiological term, 103-105, 131, 140; as ecumenical term, 221; as Millennial Church, 81-82, 124; as pneumatological term, 82; *see also under* Christ

Boehme, Jacob, 31
Bonaventure, 18
Brethren of the Free Spirit, 18
Brief Exposition of the Established Principles and Regulations of the United Society Called Shakers (1830), 157
Bruno of Segni, 17
Buckley, Sir Richard, 24
Buddha, 223, 224
Buddhism, 223
"Burned Over District," 206
Bushnell, Richard, 228
Bushness, William, 212

Calvinism, 32, 66, 126
Calvinists, 24, 125, 133, 138
Camisards, *see* French Prophets
Cane Ridge, 90, 91, 125
Canterbury, NH, 197
Catholic Mystics, 31
Catholicism, 21, 83
Cavalier, Jean, 24
Cedar Vale Commune, 128
Celibacy, x, 70, 73, 77, 85; and Ann Lee, 35, 42, 111; cross of, 81, 83, 89, 105, 106, 152; eschatological, 43, 45-46, 79, 145, 231, 232; and following Christ, 139; and new birth, 174-175; and redemption, 145, 242; Shaker Gospel of, 38, 237; as sign of true church, 155; as social ethic, 213; and union, 147-151, 239; and virgin life, 180-181; *see also under* Shaker Gospel
Cerinthus, 15
Cévennole Prophets, *see* French Prophets
Charismatic exercises, 34, 68, 69, 71, 84, 91, 202, 203; and Shaker dance, 75
Charismatics, 68
Chiliasm, 15, 20; apocalyptic, 32
Christ: as anointing spirit, 82, 103, 106, 108, 164-166; bipolar nature of, 97, 107-124, 170-172, 175, 239, 243; body of, xi,

103, 186; as bridge of natural and divine, 121; as eschatological spirit, 153-154; in the female, xi, 43, 44, 48, 50-53, 57-58, 97, 108-115, 117-119, 168-174, 186, 238, 239, 243; imminent return of, 32, 34; Jesus, 6, 8-10, 82; as male and female, 108-111; as messiah, 6-9; as Second Adam, 108; and spiritual empowerment, 102; *see also* Christ Spirit; Christ's First Appearing; Christ's Second Appearing

Christ Spirit, x, 3, 4, 70, 77, 84, 114, 136, 159; and celibacy, 231; and eschatology, 155, 201, 230, 241; in Millennial Church, 177; in non-Christian religions, 223; and pneumatology, 3, 4; progressive unfolding of, 162; rebirth in, 161; role in salvation, 165; and social order, 240; transforming power of, 161, 181; and union, 76, 154, 220, 221, 233, 239, 241; universal, 223, 227

Christian Science, 208

Christic Adam, 105

Christic parents, 47, 115-124

Christological couple, 115, 116, 117

Christology, xi, 4; Alethian development of, 217-219; of Ann Lee, 111-115; in Dunlavy, 137-140, 141, 142; early controversies, 13; eschatological, 66; as eschatological ecclesiology, 186; as eschatological spirit, 165, 185; exemplaristic, 81, 109, 138, 139, 140; feminine basis of, 49, 173; of the First Appearing, 97; in Green, 179; and Jesus and Ann Lee, 111; and pneumatology, 138, 139, 200; of the Second Appearing, 97, 107-115, 217; in Youngs, 95, 104

Christ's First Appearing, 103-111, 122-123, 153, 165-166

Christ's Second Appearing, x, xiii, xv, xvi, 2-4, 6, 161; in Ann Lee, 29-59 *passim*, 124, 237; christology of, 97; as climax of mother metaphor, 57; in Dunlavy, 65, 125-156; in early Shaker understanding, 29, 32-34, 36, 40-59 *passim*; ecclesiological understanding of, 84-85, 98, 185-187; and eschatological spirit, 165, 185; in the female, 168-172, 176; and feminine pole of deity, 121-122, 170; in Green, 65, 163-164; known by experience, 87; late 19th c.

understanding of, 194-195; in Meacham, 65, 81, 82, 83, 84; as Millennial Church, 65-187 *passim*, 115, 124; and Millerite Adventism, 206-207; in new birth, 172-176; as pneumatology, 3, 164-165, 200, 217-219, 227; progressive, 88, 165-168, 210, 240; and revelation of Mother, 123; summary of Shaker understanding of, 237-244 *passim*; in *Testimonies* tradition, 42-59 *passim*; theology of, 98; in Youngs, 65, 95, 119-124

Church: Augustinian 16-17; as body of Christ's First Appearing, 106; born of woman, 124; and christic parents, 115-117; as corporate organism, 118; in Dunlavy, 140-142; early, 6-11; patristic, 11-16; *see also* Gathered Church; Millennial Church; Shaker Church

Church Fathers, 13

Civil War, ix, 196

Collegial Episcopate, *see* Ministry, the

Commodian, 15

Communism, 132

Communitarianism, 45, 72, 127-132, 202, 239

Community of goods, *see* Joint interest

Community of the Publik Universal Friend, 128

Concise Statement of the Principles of the Only True Church (1790), 67, 76-77, 126, 238

Confession, 73

Confucius, 223

Conservatives, Shaker, 197

Cooley, Ebenezer, 91

Cotton, Thomas, 24

Covenants, Shaker, 74

Creation, Shaker understanding of, xi, 8, 11, 76, 89, 133, 134, 150, 177, 183, 232; spiritual, 51-53, 154, 169, 170, 171; *see also* First creation; New creation

Cross, *see under* Celibacy

Cyril of Jerusalem, 15

Daniel, Book of, 77
David, 8
Deacons/Deaconesses, 74
Deborah, 169
Declaration of the Doctrine and Practice of the Church of Christ, see Manifesto
Deity, feminine pole, 121-122, 170
Depravity, in Shakerism, 134, 137
Diggers, 22
Dispensationalism: and Christ's Second Appearing, 84; in *Concise Statement*, 76-87; in Dunlavy, 142; in 19th c., 208
Domitian, 11
Doolittle, Antoinette, 194, 210
Dowe, Arthur W., 198
Dunlavy, John, xvii, 91, 93, 185, 239; alternate view of Shakerism, 126; compared to Green, 158; and ecclesiology, 160; and the *Manifesto*, 65, 125-156

Eads, Harvey, 194, 197
Eagle Creek, Ohio, 125
Eastern wisdom, 208
Eberwin of Steinfeld, 17
Ebionites, 15
Ecclesiology, xi, 4, 65, 115; Alethian pneumatic development, 219-225; in Dunlavy, 140-156; eschatological, 66; exemplaristic, 159, 161, 162, 185, 215; as form of Christ's Second Appearing, 81-85, 115-118, 185-187, 217; in Green, 179; in Meacham, 72-76; pneumatological, 155, 165; in Youngs, 94-95, 124
Ecumenism, xii, 221
Edict of Nantes, 23
Edwards, Jonathan, 67, 76, 77
Elders/Eldresses, 74, 75
Election, 137
End of the world, 1, 6

Equality, gender and racial, xii, 162; *see also* Race relations;
    Sexual equality
Eschatological consciousness, 43
Eschatological creation: and Jesus and Ann, 123-124
Eschatological Gospel, 37
Eschatology, 1; apocalyptic, 7, 10, 11, 15, 16, 18, 20, 24;
    Augustinian revision, 16-17; chiliastic, 15, 20; in Christian
    movements, 14-16; in Christian scripture, 8-12; defined, 3;
    in early church, 12-14; English Protestantism, 22-25; and
    French Prophets, 23-25; in Jewish scripture, 6-7; in
    Joachism, 18-19; in Middle Ages, 17-20; as millennialism,
    14; as pneumatology, xvii, 3, 4; Quaker, 22-23; realized, x,
    2, 66, 237, 241, 242; in Reformation, 20-22; and Shaker
    faith, 6, 243; *see also* Eschatology, Shaker; Millennialism
Eschatology, Shaker, ix, x, xv, xvi; and Alethian pneumatic
    development, 225-229; in Dunlavy, 126, 133, 155; early,
    29-59 *passim;* and ecclesiological metaphor, 65, 66, 238;
    evolutionary, 229; feminine basis of, 49; in Green, 159;
    growth of, 66; maturity of, 193-244; and membership
    decline, 197; and new birth metaphor, 65; and
    pneumatology in Green, 160, 239-240; and
    pneumatology in Youngs, 122-124; progressive, 77-89
    passim; and progressivism, 215; relation to pneumatology,
    185-187, 200, 204-205, 217, 233, 240-241; and
    resurrection and judgment, 181-185 *passim;* revision of,
    199, 216-229; and spiritualism, 201; and *Testimonies*
    tradition, 42-59 *passim;* and universalism, 209; of woman,
    107-111; in Youngs, 94-111
Eschaton, 38, 43, 89, 149, 155; Christ as minister of, 155;
    emerging, 227; as end of fleshly life, 149; and Holy Spirit,
    172; revision of, 219, 225, 241; Shakerism as, 197
Esther, 169
Eternal progression, 215, 225-226, 228
Eucharist, Shaker rejection of, 55
Eusebius of Caesarea, 13

Evangelical Liberalism, 208
Evangelical Rationalists, 20
Evans, Frederick, 194, 195, 197, 205, 211, 214-215
Evans, Jessie, 217, 218
Eve, 100, 124
Exile, 8
Ezekiel, 77, 78

Fage, Durand, 24
Fall and redemption, 100-124, 135
Family, Shaker: structure of, 74
Farley, Martha, 89
Fathers of the Church, 12-17
Female, *see* Christ: in the female; Mother,Divine; Wisdom,
    Holy Mother; Woman
Female charismatics, *see* Lee, Ann; Maximilla; Priscilla;
    Wardley, Jane; Wharton, Hannah
Feminism, xii; and Shakerism, 173
Fifth Monarchy, 21, 22
Finney, Charles, 210
First creation, 95; fall of, 99-102; redemption of, 102;
    theological anthropology of, 97-99
Fitch, Samuel, 56
Fleshly existence: destruction of, 151-154; relation to soul, 181-182
Fourierist groups, 128
Fox, George, 22
Fox, Kate, 201
Fox, Margaret, 201
Francis of Assisi, 19
Franciscans, 18; *see also* Spirituals, medieval
Fraser, Daniel, 194
Fraticelli, 18
Free Church, 128
French Prophets, xvii, 23-25, 32
Friends, Society of, *see* Quakers

Gathered Church, 68, 75, 118, 127

Genesis, 108

Gerard of Borgo San Donnino, 17

Gerhoh of Reichersberg, 17

God: city of, 11, 16; people of, 77-80; reign of, 1, 3, 4, 6; revelation to Ann Lee, 36, 42-43, 48, 50, 51; spirit of, 7, 8, 9, 10, 12, 13; victory of, 7, 11, 12, 13; *see also* Christ Spirit; God in Shakerism; Holy Spirit; Mother, Divine; Spirit in Shakerism

God in Shakerism: Alethian revision of, 217, 218, 220, 223, 224, 226, 227, 243; in Dunlavy, 127, 134, 155-156; in Green, 159, 163-185 *passim;* in Meacham, 76-89; in Youngs, 95-124

Gospel, theme in Dunlavy, 133, 136-144

Gospel Order, 72, 73, 74

Great Awakening, 67, 68,

Greeley, Horace, 201

Green, Calvin, xvii, 65, 67, 86, 88, 129, 185, 199, 239; and *Millennial Church,* 157-185

Guglielmiti, 18

Guilford, NH, 90

Hammond, Amos, 91

Hampton, Oliver, 194, 226, 227

Harlow, Calvin, 70, 71, 157

Harmonists at Economy, 128

Harvard Township, 38, 39

Harvest, as eschatological metaphor, 229-233 *passim*

Hellenism, 12

Hildegard of Bingen, 17

Hocknell, John, 130

Hoffman, Melchior, 21

Hollister, Alonzo, 194, 216, 224, 229, 232

Holy Mother Wisdom, *see* Wisdom, Holy Mother

Holy Spirit, x, xi, 3, 6; in Augustine, 16-17; and Christian movements, 14-16; in Christian scripture, 8-9; in the

Church, 10, 12-13; in English Protestantism, 22-25; eschatological, 12; as eschatological person of Trinity, 19; in French Prophets, 23-25; in Jesus, 9; in Jewish scripture, 7; in Joachim of Fiore, 17-19; in Middle Ages, 17-20; and new birth, 31, 32; in Quakerism, 22-24; in Radical Reformation, 20-22; *see also* Christ Spirit, Spirit in Shakerism
Honorius of Autun, 17
Hugh of St. Victor, 17
Human couple paradigm: and Adam and Eve, 97; and Christ's feminine analogue, 107; and Jesus and Ann, 115-117; and renovated relations of sexes, 114; and Youngs' christology, 103-107
Humanitarian movements, 161
Hussites, 20
Hut, John, 21

Icarians, 128
Image of God, 134-135
Incarnation, 2
Inner light, experience of, 32
Introversionists, *see* Conservatives, Shaker
Irenaeus, 15
Isaiah, 8
Islam, 18
Israelites, 8

Jacquerie, 20
Jesus, 2, 55, 87; and celibacy, 81, 105; as christic Adam, 105; as father of new creation, 103; as messiah, 8; as model of salvation, 138-139; as new spiritual man, 109; redemptive labor of, 104; and the Spirit, 8-9, 139; *see also under* Christ
Jews, 30, 162
Joachim of Fiore, 17, 18, 19
Joachism, 19, 20, 21
Joachites, x

Joel, 9
John, 9
John of Parma, 17
Joint interest, x, 73, 75, 145-147, 150, 155, 179, 238, 239
Joint parents, *see* Christic parents
Judaism, 12
Judgment, last, 1, 11, 16; Shaker redefinition of, 181-185 *passim*
Justin Martyr, 15

Kentucky Revival, 90, 91, 125, 129
Kentucky Synod, 91
Kenworthy, John, 232

Lactantius, 15
Lacy, John, 24
Last World Emperor, 18
Lee, Ann, 25, 93, 237; biographical sketch of, 30-39; and birth
    of Millennial Church, 124; and celibacy, 35, 42, 111;
    christology of, 97, 111-115, 170, 239; in *Concise Statement*,
    87; as eschatological bride of Christ, xi, 112; leader of
    English Shakers, 35-36; and *Manifesto*, 126-127, 138; and
    membership decline, 196; as messianic mother, xvii; and
    the new birth, 36, 41-44; religious experience of, 29, 35,
    41-44; spiritual maternity, 29, 43, 117; as theological
    founder of Shakerism, 29-59 *passim; see also* Mother Ann
Lee, William, 39, 51, 130
Lees, John, 30
Levelers, 22
Literature, Shaker: differences in, 194
Lomas, George, 194, 218, 219, 221
Louis XIV, 23

Mace, Aurelia, 194, 216
McNemar, Richard, 91, 92, 93
Maine, 38

Male, as referent to divine power, 120

Manchester, England, x, 25, 30, 41, 44

Manifesto; or, A Declaration of the Doctrines and Practice of the Church of Christ, 125-156, 223, 226, 227, 239

Manifesto, The, see Shaker journals

Marion, Elie, 24

Marriage, in Shakerism, x, 149-150, 175, 243

Massachusetts, 37, 38

Maximilla, 15

Meacham, David, 57, 71, 91

Meacham, John, 91, 92

Meacham, Joseph, xvii, 39, 51, 65, 67, 68, 69-72, 74, 76, 78, 79, 93, 185, 194, 238

Membership: decline, 196-201, 205, 231; early growth, 71, 90; and Millerism, 206; and "Mother Ann's Work," 205; statistics, ix, 197

Merton, Daniel, 200

Methodists: and revivalism, 90; English, 31, 32

Millennial Age, xii

Millennial Church: in Dunlavy, 127, 155; founding of, 29, 39, 47, 56, 58, 72; as gathered community, 72, 73, 132; and Gospel Order, 72-76; in Green, 157-185; joint parentage of, 74, 115; late Shaker attitude toward, 220; Lee's leadership of, x, xi, 51-53; as offspring of eschatological woman, 117-119; progressive work of, 176, 212; and Second Appearing of Christ, 65, 85, 87, 181, 186, 200; structure and polity of, 74-76; in Youngs, 95

Millennial Laws, as perfectionist code, 75

Millennialism: in Augustinian revision, 16-17; in Christian movements, 14-16; defined, 14; and French Prophets, 23-25; in Middle Ages, 17-20; and New Light Stir, 68; in 19th c. America, 128, 210; and Quakers, 23; and reform movements, 20; Shaker revision of, 194; *see also* Millennial Church

Millennium, in Shakerism, x, xii, 237; and Christ's Second Appearing, 86, 87, 88, 164, 167, 240; progressive, 88-89,

211; and resurrection, 181-185; seven principles of, 177-181; *see also* Millennial Church
Miller, William, 206
Millerite Adventism, 202, 206-207
Millerites, 206, 207
Ministry, the: a collegial episcopate, 75
Miriam, 169
Moltmann, Jürgen, 13
Montanism, 15-16
Montanists, x
Montanus, 15
Moravians, 31
Moses, 79, 87, 102
Mother, Divine, 97, 111, 114, 119-124, 170, 223, 239, 243
Mother Ann: and Christ's Second Appearing, 29-59 *passim*; and communitarianism, 129; in *Concise Statement*, 84, 87; death of, 39, 130, 238; eschatological character of, 45, 59, 97, 186, 238; and Joseph Meacham, 71; revelation of, 41-44; of Shaker faith, 36, 38, 39, 40-59; spiritual maternity and new birth, xvii, 35-36, 38, 40-59, 238; in *Testimonies* tradition, 40-59 *passim*; *see also* Lee, Ann; Mother, Divine; "Mother Ann's Work"; Mother Spirit
"Mother Ann's Second Appearing," *see* "Mother Ann's Work"
"Mother Ann's Work," 94, 202-205
Mother Spirit, 170-173
Motherhood of God (1903), 195
Müntzer, Thomas, 21
Murray, John, 207

New age, eschatological, 2, 149, 153, 162, 167
New birth, 31, 35, 38, 41-42, 48, 68, 80, 92, 172-175
New creation, 43, 44, 46, 54, 71, 165, 174, 210, 218; as the Millennium, 176; in Youngs, 97-100, 103-110, 114-118, 119, 120, 124, 126
New Era, the, *see* "Mother Ann's Work"
New Hampshire, 38, 90

New Lebanon, NY, 39, 40, 67, 68, 71, 129, 131
New Lebanon Society, 74
New Light Stir, 68-69
New Lights, 67, 91, 125
New Philadelphia, 128
New Prophecy, 15
New Testament, xvii
New York Tribune, 201
Nicene Creed, 3
Niskeyuna, NY, 37, 38, 69, 70, 130, 202
Noyes, John Humphrey, 131, 203

Oneida Community, 128, 131
Order of correspondences, in Youngs' *Testimony*, 96-98, 99, 100,
    108, 110, 112, 116, 239
Otsego, NY, 90
Owenites, 128

Pacifism, xii, 37, 212; *see also* Peace, practical
Papias of Heiropolis, 15
Parousia, 1, 2, 3, 11, 16, 17, 238; and Millerites, 206; as social
    event, 165; *see also* Second Coming of Christ
Passion, 2, 48
Paul, Saint, 70, 80; objection to female leadership, 50, 51
Peace, practical, xii, 178, 214
Peace movement and societies, 212
Peasant Revolt, 20
Peekskill, NY, 91
Penn, William, 23
Pentecost, 9
People of God, as ecclesiological motif, 77, 78
Perfectionism, xii, 66, 68, 70, 77, 128, 196, 205, 206, 215
Perkins, Abraham, 214
Phillips, Sir John, 24
Pietists, 128

Pittsfield, Vermont, 90
Plato, 224
Pleasant Hill, Kentucky, 125
Pneumatology: in Augustinian revision, 16-17; in Christian
    movements, 14-16; defined, 3; in Dunlavy, 126, 140, 154, 156;
    in early church, 6-12; and female character of Christ's Second
    Appearing, 164-165, 169, 194, 217-219; and French Prophets,
    23-25; in Green, 161, 162, 171-172, 185; Joachite, 18-19; and
    late 19th c. revision of, 193, 199, 204, 207, 228, 229, 233, 240,
    241, 243; in Middle Ages, 17-20; in patristic church, 12-14;
    Quaker, 22, 23; in Radical Reformation, 21; relation to
    eschatology, xi, xvii, 4, 6, 185-187; in Youngs, 122-124; *see also*
    Christ Spirit; Holy Spirit
Polity, Shaker, 75
Postmillennialists, 161
Prairie Home, 128
Predestination, 137
Presbyterianism, 30, 90, 125
Present Day Shakerism (1906?), 195, 223, 231
Priscilla, 15
Private property, *see* Joint interest
Progressives, Shaker revisionists, 193, 194-195, 197, 209, 210,
    212, 213, 222, 240; *see also* Alethian Shakers
Progressivism, 193-194; and later Shaker eschatology, 209-217
Protestantism, 20-22, 208
Puritanism, x, 22

Quakers, x, 22, 30, 32; *see also* Shaking Quakers

Race relations, 212
Rahner, Karl, 3
Ranters, 22
Rebirth, *see* New birth
Redemption: history of, 76, 77; progressive, xi; role of women
    in, 101; *see also* Dispensationalism; Fall and redemption

Reeves, Marjorie, 19

Reformation, the, 20, 21, 34, 128

Reformism, of Shakers, 210

Regeneration, 77, 174, 176, 232

Reign of God, *see under* God

Relly, James, 207

Resurrection, 1, 2, 7, 8, 77, 82; as consequence of union, 151-156; and eschatological spirit, 151; of Jesus, 9; as pneumatological term, 154; progressive nature of, 70, 154; as regeneration, 85; Shaker redefinition, 181-185 *passim*

Revelation, Book of, 10-12, 112

Revelation, progressive, xi, 1, 85, 95, 226

Revisionists, Shaker, 193, 197, 214; *see also* Alethian Shakers

Revivalism: evangelical, 31, 37-38; and millennialism, 68, 90; and "Mother Ann's Work," 203; New Light Stir, 68; and Shakerism, 66, 128, 196; *see also* Cane Ridge; Kentucky Revival; Millerite Adventism; New Light Stir

Roach, Richard, 24

Roman Catholics, 30

Roman Church, 45

Roman Empire, 13

Rupert of Deutz, 17

Sabbath-breaking, 35

Sabbathday Lake, Maine, 157, 197

Sacraments, 3

Sacred dance, as Shaker worship, 75

Salvation: and celibacy, 148, 149; progressive, 77, 85, 99; Shaker, 101-102; social nature of, 119; through union, 145; universal, 66, 208; through the woman, 109-111

Satan, 11

Savanarola, 20

Schenectady, NY, 89

Schismatics, 91; *see also* New Lights

Scripture, Shaker approach to, 32

Second Advent of Christ, *see* Second Coming of Christ

Second Appearing of Christ, *see* Christ's Second Appearing

Second Coming of Christ, xv, xvii, 1-4; in Augustinianism, 16-17; in Book of Revelation, 10-12; at Cane Ridge, 91; in Christian movements, 14-16; in English Protestantism, 22-25; in French Prophets, 23-25; in Middle Ages, 17-20; in New Testament, 6-10; in patristic church, 12-14; in Reformation, 20-22

Second Creation, 95, *see also* New creation

Second Great Awakening, 161

Seekers and Finders, 22

Servetus, Michael, 21

Seven Moral Principles of Millennial Church, 164, 177-181

Sex: and the fall, 101; renunciation of, xii; as sin, 79, 169, 242; *see also* Celibacy

Sexual equality, x, xii, 212; in leadership, 73, 162; as sign of eschatological age, 73; as theological motif, 97, 121

Sexuality: and spiritual analogue, 102

Shaker Bible, 93, 95; *see also Testimony of Christ's Second Appearing*

Shaker Church: proclaimer of Millennium, 87-88; *see also* Millennial Church

Shaker Gospel: of celibacy, 42-59 *passim;* closing of, 71; of fall and redemption, 42; and mother kerygma, 29, 41-59 *passim;* opening of, 38, 71, 90; re-opening of, 75; of sin as disordered sex, 42

Shaker journals: as sources for later 19th c. theology, 195-233 *passim;* titles of, 194-195

Shakerism: Its Meaning and Message (1904), 195; *see also* White, Anna; Taylor, Leila

Shakerism: charismatic nature of, 76; and communitarianism, 131; and ecclesiological eschatology, 155; and Millerism, 206-207; relation to world, 160; religious values of, 73; and revivalism, 90, 91; westward expansion of, 90, 91

Shakers, ix; early history, 32-39; *see also* Communitarianism; Membership; Millennial Church; Revivalism; United Society of Believers in Christ's Second Appearing

Shaking Quakers, in England, 32, 33, 34, 35-36

Shepherd, Walter, 221

Sin: defined in Youngs, 99; sex as, 79, 169, 242

Smith, Colonel, 50, 51

Social Freedom Community, 128

Social Gospel, 210

Social progress, issues in, 212

Social reform movements, xii, 210

Socialism, 131, 212

Society of Friends, *see* Quakers

Soteriology: in Dunlavy, 133, 155; eschatological, 66; evangelical, 135; feminine basis of, 49

Soul, human, 174-175

Spirit in Shakerism: appearance in Son and Daughter, 121-122; as christic anointing, 50, 103, 106; in Dunlavy, 153; embodied in Christ, 82, 123; emphasis on, 141, 242-243; eschatological, 69, 146-147, 151, 172; in Green, 164-172, 181; as Mother in God, 121-124, 170-173; as power in social order, 212; revealed in woman, 110-112, 115, 168-172; Second Appearing of Christ, 164-167, 185-187, *and passim;* as source of union, 145, 242; subordination of Christ to, 218; in Youngs, 123-124; *see also* Christ Spirit; Holy Spirit; Pneumatology; Spiritualism; Wisdom, Holy Mother

Spirit of God, *see* God

Spiritual Life: renunciation of the flesh, 148, 149; *see also* Celibacy

Spiritual World, and men and women, 170

Spiritualism, and later Shaker eschatology, 193-194, 196, 201-207, 215, 217, 225, 228

Spirituals, medieval, x, 18, 19, 29

Springfield Presbytery, 91, 125

Standerin, Abraham, 34

Standerin, Elizabeth, 35
Stone, Barton, 91, 93, 126, 129
Summary View of the Millennial Church, A (1823, 1848), 157-185, 239
Swedenborgians, 31, 202

Taborites, 20
Taylor, Leila, 200
Tertullian, 15, 16
Testimonies of the Life, Character, Revelations and Doctrines of Our Ever Blessed Mother Ann Lee, and the Elders with Her (1816), 41, *see also Testimonies* tradition
Testimonies tradition, xvii, 29, 35, 40-41, 44, 45, 47, 58, 238
Testimony of Christ's Second Appearing, The (1808, 1810, 1823, 1856), 89, 94, 95-124, 126, 157, 239; *see also* Youngs, Benjamin Seth
Theology, Shaker, xvi; developments in, 194; major theologians of, 65-185; progressive, 77-89 *passim; see also* Alethian Shakers; Dunlavy, John; Green, Calvin; Meacham, Joseph; Youngs, Benjamin Seth
Theosophy, 208
Transcendentalists, 128
Treatise on the Atonement (1805), 207
Trinity, 3, 4, 191n; eschatological person of, 3, 4, 19; *see also* Holy Spirit
Tufts College, 208
Turtle Creek, Ohio, 92, 94, 125
Tyringham, Massachusetts, 197

Union: of Believers, 125, 145-147; as Christ's Second Appearing, 155-156; and Christ Spirit, 225, 233; of churches and religions, 221, 223-225; and communitarianism, 128-132; degrees of, 154; as Dunlavy theme, 127-128, 144-156; in language, 179; and late

Shakerism, 220, 222; of sexes as spiritual, 73, 170-171, 242-243; as sign of true church 144-145
United Society of Alethians, *see* Alethian Shakers
United Society of Believers in Christ's Second Appearing, ix, 2, 29, 124, 126, 160; as corporate form of Second Appearing, 73; founded by Joseph Meacham, 72; and millennialism, 207; as model to world, 161; *see also* Shakers
Universalism, xii, 85, 193-194, 201, 215, 217; in *Concise Statement*, 77; and ecclesiology, 228; and later Shaker eschatology, 207-209; and Shaker openness to world, 220
Universalist Church, 207, 208
Universalists, 202
Universality, 225
Utopianism, Shaker, 72, 128

Victorinus, 15

Walafrid, 17
Waldensians, 18
Wardley, James, 32, 33, 35
Wardley, Jane, 32, 33, 35
Wardley Sect, 32-33, 34, 35, 84
Watervliet, NY, 40, 47, 89, 130
Wells, Seth Youngs, 40, 157, 158
Wesley, Charles, 31, 207
Wesley, John, 31, 207
Wharton, Hannah, 25
White, Anna, 195, 200, 210, 213, 216, 223, 231
White, Reuben, 69
Whitefield, George, 31, 32, 37, 68
Whittaker, James, 39, 56, 57, 71, 75, 93, 130
Will, human, 66, 134, 137
Wisdom, Holy Mother, xi, 97, 111, 114-115, 119, 170, 203; *see also* Mother, Divine

Woman: eschatological significance of, 117-124, 242, 243; as
        head of Church, 70; leadership in Second Creation, 99;
        role in fall and redemption, 101-124; Second Appearing of
        Christ in, 170; Shaker openness to, 172-173; theological
        significance of, 97
Women, as religious leaders, 32-33; French Prophets, 25; New
        Prophecy, 15; *see also* Lee, Ann; Wardley, Jane; Wright,
        Lucy
Worley, Malcolm, 91, 92
Worship, Shaker, 69, 75
Wright, Lucy, 39, 74, 93

Youngs, Benjamin Seth, xvii, 65, 89-124, 129, 155, 157-158,
        160, 185, 239

Zephyrinus, 16
Zoroaster, 223

About the Author

KATHLEEN DEIGNAN is a graduate of Sacred Heart University in Fairfield, Connecticut. She earned her M.A. in Spirituality and Ph.D. in Historical Theology from Fordham University, New York. Dr. Deignan is an associate professor of Religious Studies at Iona College, New Rochelle, New York, where she formerly coordinated Peace and Justice Studies and is currently the director of the Iona Spirituality Institute. She is a liturgical musician, singer and composer with five published albums to date. Her interest in spirituality, community, feminist theology and peacemaking drew her to Shaker studies. She has presented papers on Shakerism at professional conferences and has published articles in other areas of spirituality. She is a member of the Congregation de Notre Dame.